LIKE A WAVE WE BREAK

LIKE A WAVE WE BREAK

A memoir of falling apart

and finding myself

JANE MARIE CHEN

HARMONY

NEW YORK

Harmony Books
An imprint of Random House
A division of Penguin Random House LLC
1745 Broadway, New York, NY 10019
harmonybooks.com | randomhousebooks.com
penguinrandomhouse.com

ISBN 978-0-593-58234-3
Ebook ISBN 978-0-593-58235-0

Printed in the United States of America on acid-free paper

1st Printing

First Edition

BOOK TEAM: Production editor: Andy Lefkowitz • Managing editor: Allison Fox • Production manager: Sandra Sjursen • Copy editor: Rachelle Mandik • Proofreaders: Rebecca Maines, Lori Newhouse, Robin Slutzky, and Barbara Stussy

Book design by Betty Lew

The authorized representative in the EU for product safety and compliance is Penguin Random House Ireland, Morrison Chambers, 32 Nassau Street, Dublin D02 YH68, Ireland. https://eu-contact.penguin.ie

*For the little one in each of us
who ever felt they weren't enough:
you are enough, exactly as you are.*

Contents

CONTENTS

Prologue

This is the story of a wipeout.

The monster wave came out of nowhere. It rose on the horizon and surged toward me, looking hungry. Furious. My heart hammered in my chest. Adrenaline shot through my veins like electricity.

Paddle! Paddle as fast as you fucking can.

I dropped to my stomach, paddling frantically to get past the crest of the wave. A solid wall of blue towered in front of me, rising higher and higher. My arms sliced through the water with desperation. My shoulders and triceps burned as I tried to outpace a force so much bigger and stronger than I was. I was no match for the power of this wave.

The top of the wave began to curl, frothing with white foam. *Just one more stroke, and you'll be over the crest. Push, Jane. PUSH!* My right arm exploded forward, as I threw everything I had into a final stroke. But it wasn't enough. With a great thundering crash, the wave detonated, slamming into me with brutal force. I somersaulted backward and plunged violently underwater, hurtling toward the sharp rocks. The sea churned, spinning me, flinging my arms and legs like strands of kelp.

Everything went dark. I lost all sense of left and right, up and down.

This is the end. This is it.

Time slowed to a crawl, every second stretching out into an eternity. For a moment, I stopped struggling, and my body went limp. It would have been so easy to give up, to give in. But I gave one last push until finally, my head broke the surface. I gasped for air, coughing as I spat out seawater, my throat and nose burning. The horizon was spinning, the earth tilting and seesawing. I felt nauseous as I climbed back on my board and paddled toward what I thought was the shore. When I reached the sand, I collapsed.

You're okay, I whispered to myself, trying to soothe my trembling body. *It's over. You're fine now.* But that was a lie.

I wasn't fine—not here, not anywhere.

At its core, a wave is pure energy moving through water. A wave breaks when that energy collides with something—a sandbar, the shore, the reef.

A wave breaking is energy reaching its end.

Just as I had reached my end.

When I was a kid, I would climb in bed to snuggle with my dad on weekend mornings. My feet were always cold, so he'd tuck them under his, warming my icy toes. As the warmth flooded back into my feet, he'd drill me on my times tables, barking out numbers rapid-fire:

"Seven times seven!"

"Three times nine!"

"Two times ten!"

With each right answer, his eyes lit up. Thanks to those drills, I won all the math competitions in second grade. When I reported my wins, Dad would smile proudly. "Goody-goody!" he'd say, and I could feel the golden beam of his approval shining down upon me.

The flipside was that when I fell short of his demands, he made sure I knew it—with a belt, his hands, a nearby stick. I quickly learned that mistakes were not permissible.

That what I achieved was more important than who I was.

And who I was depended on what I achieved.

I didn't realize how deeply these beliefs shaped me—until everything fell apart.

In graduate school, I was part of a team that invented a groundbreaking infant incubator for the world's most vulnerable communities. We launched a company that helped save hundreds of thousands of premature babies. There were some incredible highs along the way. I presented our technology to President Obama at the White House. Beyoncé personally handed me a check to support our work. My job was more than a job. It was my purpose. My identity. The sole focus of my life. For a decade, I had sacrificed everything in my life to keep the company afloat—my time, my relationships, my sanity. But ultimately, it had failed. I had failed.

So yes, this is the story of a wipeout. Not just the one that left me shaking on the shore that day, but the collapse of the dream I'd poured my soul into. When it all came crashing down, I didn't just lose a dream. I lost myself.

My wipeout was the beginning of a multiyear quest, in which I traded my dedication to my career for a different obsession: piecing myself back together. I became *that* woman. The one who saw signs in her morning tea leaves and planned her life based on vision boards and manifestations. I chased answers in the world's most iconic waves. I sat in days of silent meditation in the Indonesian jungle, went on psychedelic journeys, and searched for my inner child in all the wrong places. I burned holes in my legs for an Amazonian frog-poison ceremony to cleanse my soul. I went to every self-help seminar I could find. I even talked one of the world's foremost trauma researchers into becoming my therapist.

If every journey begins with a call, mine came from within.

Fix me, it cried.

Save me, it pleaded.

LIKE A WAVE WE BREAK

CHAPTER 1

GENESIS

The dining room was dim, the blinds half-drawn. My mother was dishing up a traditional Taiwanese dinner: a whole pan-fried fish, chicken with stir-fried vegetables, sauteed spinach, and egg-drop soup. She cooked like this every night. She placed the dishes on the table, then handed a plate of spaghetti and meatballs to Joyce. With a fork. Joyce grinned, pleased at her special treatment.

"Why does she get a fork?" I asked.

"Too little," Mom said. Though what she really meant was *too American*. My older sister, Nancy, was eleven, and I was seven. We all used chopsticks, but Joyce, who was four, still hadn't learned. I sat in my chair, one knee drawn to my chest, and started digging into my bowl of rice.

"Xiao Yu, don't squat like that," Mom scolded, calling me by my Taiwanese name. "You look like you sell vegetables at the outdoor market in Taiwan! What if you have dinner with a princess one day? You need to have good manners."

After we finished eating, Mom stood to clear the dishes. Dad lit a cigarette and settled into his rust-colored La-Z-Boy in the living room. The familiar theme music of *Wheel of Fortune* played in the background as he grabbed the remote, turning the volume up.

"Our final puzzle is a person," said Pat Sajak. "Lorraine, spin the wheel."

Dad's eyes glittered as the wheel slowed near $5,000. He loved the spin, the gamble, the moment that it might hit big. It clicked past, landing on $500.

"Agggghh!" Dad groaned.

"I'd like to buy a vowel, Pat," said the contestant. "*E*."

"Vanna, show us E."

Vanna White floated across the screen in a sequined dress and flipped over a giant letter *E*.

Pat Sajak narrated the show, but my eyes were on Vanna, a live-action Barbie with perfectly coiffed golden hair, blue eyes, and what seemed like a permanent smile. If Vanna White was America, then I, with my black hair, brown eyes, and olive skin, most definitely was not.

Dad stared at the puzzle on the screen, brow furrowed.

"*L*," said the contestant.

"*L*," echoed Pat Sajak as Vanna began her strut. "There are four *L*'s."

As Vanna flipped letters, Dad's eyes flashed. Scanning back and forth over the puzzle, I could see him trying to spell the word, to piece it together. But with his limited English, he never could.

"You have $2,550," Pat Sajak told the contestant. "Will you spin again?"

"No," she said confidently. "I'm going to solve the puzzle."

Dad pitched his body toward the screen, his eyes wide.

"Jolly good fellow!" said the woman.

"She's got it!" Pat cried. Canned applause flooded the living room as Vanna revealed the rest of the puzzle. Watching the letters click into place, Dad's face lit up, its soft wrinkles going taut.

"Zo Gao!" he exclaimed in Taiwanese, taking a deep, satisfied drag of his cigarette. *Very good. So talented.* I don't think he knew what the phrase actually meant, but he was impressed when anyone solved the puzzle quickly. We passed most nights after dinner like this: Dad watching Vanna flip letters, while I added game-show phrases to my quickly growing vocabulary.

I was four years old when we immigrated to Southern California from Kaohsiung, a bustling port city on the southwestern tip of Taiwan. It was 1982, and Taiwan was still under one of the longest periods of martial law in history—and more than a decade away from its first open presidential election. Post-World War II, after fifty years of Japanese colonial rule, Taiwan was handed back to the Republic of China. A year later, civil war erupted on Mainland China between Mao Zedong's Communist Party and the Nationalist Party, the Kuomintang (KMT). In 1949, the KMT lost the war and retreated to Taiwan, where it imposed a brutal one-party regime and placed the island under martial law for the next thirty-eight years.

The KMT ideology was to maintain power and crush dissent at all costs. As part of its anti-communist measures, free speech was curtailed and expression of Taiwanese national identity was restricted. Even publications in Taiwanese Hokkien—our native language—were banned. In what came to be known as "the White Terror," the KMT imprisoned and murdered many of Taiwan's intellectuals, artists, and social leaders in fear that they might resist the new rule. It's estimated that more than 140,000 people were imprisoned during this time, and countless others were executed or disappeared. It was a surveillance state, an environment crackling with fear and paranoia.

A risk-taker with a restless spirit, my father sought autonomy in a place where autonomy could cost your life. A few years before

I was born, he took a trip to the United States with his brother-in-law and came back electric with vision: we were going to immigrate to the Land of the Free. America represented modernity, opportunity, and freedom of thought. People in Taiwan coveted anything American, from soap to refrigerators. All the best cinema and music came from America. Mom's favorite actress was Elizabeth Taylor. She loved listening to the Carpenters and watching movies like *Roman Holiday* and *Giant*. Plus, two of Mom's sisters were already living in California. One of Dad's was there as well. America was going to be Dad's fresh start.

Mom was amenable to the plan, though really she had no concept of how far away America was—geographically or culturally. Or what she'd do when we got there. She didn't ask those sorts of questions. My mother had been raised to believe that the best thing that could happen to her was to find a good husband. So, when Dad said they were moving, she trusted him implicitly. Not because he'd earned it, but because he was the man.

Like most couples in Taiwan in the 1970s, my parents had an arranged marriage. Matches were mostly based on socioeconomic status, and the fact that my grandfathers on both sides were respected doctors made my parents an appropriate pairing. Dad was working as an engineer at a plastics company. He had a good job and a pleasant demeanor, and after asking around town, Mom's family found no evidence that he was either of the two things they believed a husband should never be—a drinker or a gambler.

My parents met only twice before their engagement. Once with all four parents, and once, alone, for dinner. Three months passed between the dinner and the engagement, which my grandfather agreed to on my mother's behalf.

"Why didn't you ask me?" she demanded when she found out.

"You didn't say you disliked him," her father replied.

Her silence was consent enough. After their wedding, Dad was promoted to a managerial role at the plastics company and they moved to Taipei, where Mom got pregnant with Nancy, my older sister. Dad's father passed away soon after, so my dad quit his job and my parents moved back to Kaohsiung. Dad decided to dabble in something new and started a construction company. It kept him busy for a while, but his sights were already set on something bigger.

Dad started the green card application process shortly before I was born in 1978. Ten days after my birthday, Jimmy Carter announced that the United States would sever diplomatic relations with Taiwan and establish official relations with the People's Republic of China. "There is but one China and Taiwan is a part of China," he said, echoing the position that more than fifty other countries had already adopted. Carter's announcement was a huge blow to Taiwan's international standing and hope for independence. In the wake of this policy, immigration processing in the United States for Taiwanese nationals slowed significantly. The fear of a full communist takeover loomed.

By the time our green cards finally came through, Nancy was eight, I was four, and our baby sister, Joyce, was one. Dad really wanted a boy, but as luck would have it, he had three girls. He didn't tell anyone we were leaving Taiwan until the week before our departure. Even though emigration was legal, the political situation was volatile, and he was paranoid about being detained or questioned. Mom set out packing, trying to shrink our entire lives into two massive army duffels. There was room for only the essentials, Dad said, which included an entire set of dishware and the rice cooker. On his first trip to America, he'd confirmed that there was rice, so he was more comfortable about the move. *No rice, no life!* Mom was relieved she wouldn't have to pack that too.

The day we left, Mom was dressed to the nines in a full-skirted purple lace dress and black heels. Afraid her jewelry might be stolen, she wore everything of value she had on the plane, draping half a dozen gold necklaces around her neck. When she ran out of room, she piled the rest around ours, looping the longest around twice. Decked out like Liberace and a band of glittering groupies, we faithfully followed my father through the airport to set off on our new lives. Nancy marched behind Mom, who bounced a sick baby Joyce on her hip. I held up the rear, wondering what America even was. My grandparents had come to see us off, and as we walked down the long corridor to board the plane, I looked back one last time and thought I could still make them out, crying and waving goodbye.

So, our family of five left Taiwan to pursue the American dream. We had family waiting for us when we landed, and my father's dreams for the future as we flew away from our past. My father was chasing freedom halfway around the world—only to soon realize that he couldn't shake his history so easily. There was nothing we could have packed that would have been enough to feel at home in our new country.

TWO BY TWO

We started out in Camarillo, a town in Ventura County about an hour northwest of Los Angeles where my father's sister lived. Compared to Taiwan, Camarillo felt huge and cartoonish, with wide avenues and big-box stores. Our new house was cavernous, the grass neon green and perfectly trimmed. Back in Kaohsiung, we'd gotten around on mopeds, or by bus and taxi. In California, Dad bought a white Oldsmobile station wagon. We piled in, sticking our heads out the window like happy dogs, letting the hot wind ripple our faces.

In massive, air-conditioned grocery stores, the food was lined up in neat rows—nothing like lively, chaotic open-air markets in Kaohsiung. We wandered wide-eyed through the aisles, setting waxy produce into our basket, our sneakers squeaking against the shiny linoleum. Everything was so bright and clean. We were fascinated by the bulk food bins, which we'd never seen before. "Maybe it's for sampling?" Dad said, scooping some nuts into his hand, and offering them to us. Two older white women walked by, glaring at us.

"*Barbarians,*" one muttered under her breath.

At home, we spoke mostly Taiwanese, given my parents' limited English. My parents believed strongly in Taiwan's independence, which is why we didn't speak Mandarin, the official language imposed after 1949. They wanted to make sure our language wasn't lost to the world, or to us. But they Americanized us in other ways. Our first Christmas, they went all out, setting up an enormous pine tree in the living room and decorating it with glittery ornaments. Tidy stacks of presents started to appear underneath it. No one bothered to explain the holiday to me and my sisters. One morning, my parents woke us up, saying, "Merry Christmas!" and led us to open presents. I gleefully tore the paper from mine, revealing a ceramic piggy bank. Dad handed me a coin to plop in, and the pig played a little song. Whatever this day was, I decided I loved it.

Later, a neighbor dropped off a holiday basket with cookies and knickknacks. We sat in a circle around the basket to examine its contents, and Nancy pulled out a waxy Santa Claus figurine with a wick at the top.

"What is it?" she asked. "A toy?"

"Maybe candy?" I guessed.

Everyone shrugged. I picked up the Santa and took a tiny bite from the side. It was greasy and perfumed and not like any candy I'd ever tasted. I immediately spat it out and wiped my tongue off on my shirt. My sisters fell over, cackling with laughter.

My parents enrolled me in a private Christian kindergarten. I was the only Asian kid and didn't speak any English. Every day, Mom packed my favorite lunch of rice balls with packets of seaweed. When the other kids made fun of me for eating weird food, I started to scarf down my rice balls in the corner of the room before anyone saw them and throw away my seaweed packets. Acutely aware of my differences, I watched the kids around me closely, taking note of anything that might help me fit in.

One day, Mom's dad came to visit from Taiwan and took me

and my sisters to the toy store. He told us we could get anything we wanted. I'd been watching *Smurfs* on TV, so I pointed to a family of small, plastic Smurfs figurines, and he bought them for me happily. The next day, when Mom wasn't looking, I tucked the Smurfs into my lunchbox. At lunchtime, I opened my box, and the toys tumbled out in a dramatic blue avalanche. My classmates shrieked and huddled around in excitement. There was a blond girl with blue eyes I'd been wanting to play with. I gathered the Smurf family and held them out as an offering.

"If you'll play with me," I told her in broken English, "you can have them."

She nodded, grinning as she grabbed her new treasures.

The next day at recess, I approached Blondie, excited to finally have a friend.

"No," she said, turning her back to me. "I don't *want* to play with you."

My heart sank. "Then give me my Smurfs back."

"I can't," she shrugged "They're at home."

I stood there, shocked. How could she go back on her word? I kept to myself after that. I wanted to disappear, to become invisible. If I could make it through the day without being noticed, it was a great day. If Mom tried to put me in a dress, I'd protest. I didn't want to stand out in any way. Not even to look pretty. Joyce sucked her thumb, which my parents were trying to get her to stop doing. During recess, I started to suck my thumb, too, just so the other kids wouldn't talk to me. No one could reject me if I made myself an outcast first. When Mom came to pick me up after school, she'd find me sitting alone on the curb. "Xiao Yu, where are your friends?" she'd ask in Taiwanese, encouraging me not to be shy. After a while, she stopped asking.

~~~~~~

One day, my teacher announced an annual poetry contest. Each student would memorize and recite a poem in front of the class. She let us choose from a big glossy book. After thumbing through the pages, I picked one about Noah's ark. I was captivated by the idea of the animals boarding a ship to leave home, thousands of them traveling across the sea, together, to a new land, just like we had. I felt kinship with the ravens and elephants, wolves, and monkeys. I loved that each animal was a pair—they had a perfect friend, their other half, so they would never be lonely in the new world. I wished I had one too.

My teacher was skeptical. It was the longest poem in the book.

"Are you sure?" she asked, squinting at the endless stanzas. "Why not try something a bit simpler?"

But my heart was set. And Mom encouraged me to go for it. Over the next few weeks, she helped me prepare for the performance. She ran me through daily rehearsals with the passion and commitment of a coach training a child for the Olympics. Every day, when I got home from school, she'd call me to center stage, aka the fireplace. I'd stand with my hands tucked behind my back and recite the poem.

"Again!" she'd cry after I'd finished, her eyes brightening as her cherry-shaped face sharpened with excitement. Mom's English was still basic—she'd been attending night classes to learn—but she'd memorized the poem, too, and mouthed all the words along with me as I said them.

"Remember, use your hands!" She'd hold up two fingers, pantomiming animals boarding the ark. "*Two by two*. You must perform it!"

At first, I refused. *Too embarrassing*. I kept my hands in my pockets. But her insistence and enthusiasm eventually wore me down. Her training worked. I won the contest. My teacher was floored. At the classroom awards ceremony, with all the parents in attendance, her eyes brimmed with tears as she announced my name.

"Just a year ago," she said, "this little girl didn't speak a word of English. And look at her now."

My parents, sitting in the front row, side by side, *two by two*, looked like they might explode with pride. The day after that, I won the class spelling bee and was advanced to the schoolwide bee. In the fourth round, I was given the word "chin," which I immediately heard as *Chen*—my last name. *Easy.*

"C-H-E-N," I said confidently into the microphone.

"I'm sorry, that's incorrect," said the moderator.

But it didn't matter. I'd broken a barrier.

And most important, I'd made my parents proud.

Those first few years in America, we moved around a lot. Dad and his sister had planned to open a printing shop, but they couldn't agree on the terms. So, we moved to a nearby town, where Mom's younger sister lived. The town had a large Asian population, but Dad decided that it was *too* Asian. He wanted us to assimilate quickly and thought it would be easier in a predominantly white neighborhood.

We settled in an arid, manicured middle-class suburb at the foot of the San Gabriel Mountains. Mom liked that it was halfway between her younger and older sister. Dad loved the endless rows of silk oaks and camphor trees. My sisters and I were the only Asian kids in our neighborhood, and there were just a handful in the whole school. There, in a tidy two-story house at the end of a cul-de-sac, we were going to become capital-A Americans.

Dad bought a fish-and-chips fast food restaurant called Old London. Back in Taiwan he'd been an executive, but at Old

London he seemed happy to fry frozen cod while Mom ran the register. She added her homemade egg rolls to the menu, which were a huge hit. They worked long hours, often not coming home until late in the evening. Some days, after school, when Nancy had piano lessons and Joyce was in daycare, Mom would take me with her to the restaurant. I'd sit on top of the deep freeze in the office and listen to the radio while pretending to do homework.

Later that year, Dad's mom came to visit from Taiwan for the first time. She was gentle and warm, and strikingly beautiful, with deep-set eyes, high cheekbones, and porcelain skin. My mom and aunts said our grandmother's beauty was known everywhere she went. She was surprisingly liberal for a woman of her generation, and let her kids explore their own interests without forcing them into set roles. She hadn't objected when my father wanted to move to America. But when she visited Old London, she looked visibly distraught. I think it was bad enough to lose her son to America, but to see him squander his education frying fish was too much.

Shortly after she went back to Taiwan, Dad sold the restaurant. He pivoted quickly, getting his stockbroker's license—no small feat with his limited English. I was going into fourth grade when he started day trading. For a while, it seemed like he'd found his thing. In trading, there was no time for boredom or discontent. Numbers needed no translation—they were either up or down. The gamble and pace of the work seemed to energize him. But he hated chasing clients. And he hated the idea of losing someone else's money even more. In the end, he decided the work wasn't for him. Dad pretty much stopped working altogether after that. The money he'd inherited from his father was enough to support our family if he was frugal and smart.

Fishing was the thing Dad loved most, other than playing mahjong with his friends. He'd spent much of his childhood fishing along the coast of Taiwan. On sunny weekends, he'd join a group of men on a small boat that launched from Huntington Harbor. Dad would bring his catch home and Mom would cook the fish in a fragrant ginger soup, including the head, which added the most flavor. Fish heads were considered a delicacy in Taiwanese culture and were reserved for the most honored guests. Joyce and I would fight over who got to eat the eyeballs.

One day, Dad noticed the other men tossing the fish heads back in the water after gutting and cleaning their catch. It was like watching someone dump caviar down the drain. He mustered the courage to ask if he could keep them. *Sure*, the captain said, agreeing to save them. After the boat docked, Dad went to collect his bounty. The captain locked eyes with him, then tossed the pile of heads into the sea.

"Why would you even want that?" He sneered. "It's trash."

In America, Dad's treasure, *our treasure*, was trash. Dad was so profoundly offended that he stopped going out on the boat. Eventually, he stopped fishing altogether.

Mom struggled too. At first, she tried to fit in and make friends with the neighbors by offering home-cooked food. In Taiwan, food *is* hospitality. "Gam jia bung, ah?" (*Have you eaten?*) is literally how people greet each other. Mom was an incredible chef. She made all our favorite staples—dumplings, fried noodles, spicy beef stew—and delivered them to the neighbors. Until one day, Mrs. Toms, who lived next door, stopped by. She didn't thank Mom. Instead, she told her she didn't like the noodles she had made and had thrown them all away. Before leaving, she complained that our house "smelled *of Asian food*." She must have told the other neighbors, because the next day, one of them stopped by with a can of air freshener. Mom was mortified. She stopped cooking food for the neighbors and never invited them over again. Soon, she stopped attending school functions, or really any outside events.

While my sisters and I were learning to adapt quickly, in a few short years, my parents went from boisterous and hopeful to shadows of their former selves. They had crossed the world to pursue a bigger life. Instead, it felt like they were growing smaller and smaller with each interaction.

CHAPTER 3

DR. CHEN

If *Wheel of Fortune* was Dad's America, *The Brady Bunch* was mine.

It was Joyce's job to notify me when it came on, a task she took seriously.

"Bradys!" she'd yell, her tiny fist rapping the bedroom door. We would settle cross-legged on the soft carpet and watch as the grid of nine fresh-scrubbed faces popped up on the screen. I zoomed in on the girls—three of them, just like me and my sisters. Our names even sounded American, like theirs, no matter that they'd been picked the way that most Asians chose their American names—from old 1950s English learning textbooks. Uncle Kenji, Mom's brother-in-law, picked ours at random: Nancy, Jane, and Joyce.

Physically, the Brady girls looked nothing like me and my sisters. But I could see us in them. Marcia, the oldest, was a natural leader. Powerful and buoyant with quippy little comebacks, she seemed not to need anything from anyone, just like Nancy. Since we'd come to America, Nancy had so much responsibility. She'd become our de facto English translator, learning the language quickly to keep up at school, and helping our parents with everything from placing phone calls to filling out government forms. She made sure permission slips got signed, figured out how to get us into honors classes, and generally kept the house from burning down. As the eldest, she had a long list of duties and little time for sentimentality or sisterly affection. I hardly remember playing with her at all.

Once when Joyce was three or four, she got into Nancy's desk and stole all her erasers—tiny pastel erasers shaped like fruit. Nancy went ballistic.

"What's more important, your sister or your erasers?" my dad screamed at her.

Without a second thought, Nancy snapped back, "My erasers!"

On a rare family trip one summer, we drove to Yosemite in the station wagon. After five hours in the car, Nancy wouldn't get out to look at Half Dome. "It's a free country!" she barked. "Isn't that what America is all about?" She did so much for the family that I suppose forced fun was her only place to opt out, to exert control over her own life. For as long as I can remember, her main objective was to get through, then *get out*.

Then there was Jan, the middle sister. Like me, she was spunky, but in a nerdy way. She was earnest and enthusiastic, which I related to. When I loved something, I *loved* it. One summer, I wore neon colors for thirty days straight. Another time, I had a yellow backpack that I loved so much I refused to take it off during school, wearing it all day even while sitting at my desk, like a turtle shell. When the B-52's song "Love Shack" came out, I recorded an entire cassette—sides A and B—with just that song, and played it constantly, until Joyce threatened to destroy it. Whatever I did, I did with gusto. I related to Jan's feeling of being overlooked as the middle child, sandwiched between a bold, confident sister (*Marcia, Marcia, Marcia!*), and a sweet younger one who got away with everything. She was insecure about having freckles and wearing glasses, and worried she would never be seen as pretty. I knew *exactly* how that felt.

And finally, Cindy. Sweet, pigtailed Cindy. She was soft and earnest and emotional just like Joyce, who was carefree, but could cry in an instant. Joyce clung closely to Mom; I was a close second choice.

"First you laugh, and then you cry!" my mom would exclaim in Taiwanese, as the teasing between Joyce and me inevitably devolved into fighting. But we always returned to each other, giggling as we wriggled into the narrow nook behind the couch that barely fit our two small bodies. Back there, we invented secret languages that only we held the legend to.

" 'Hello' is 'gabayabadaba,' " I declared as we crouched knees to chest.

"Okay. And 'Michael Jackson'?" Joyce asked.

"Hmm." I cocked my head. " 'Manktamaha.' "

Joyce nodded solemnly, mouthing it back to herself. *Manktamama.*

"No, no," I said. " 'ManktamAHA.' "

She repeated it till she got it just right.

"Hello" was always the first word we came up with in every new language, and "Michael Jackson" was always the second. I think in our minds, he wasn't just a pop star—he was the very essence of America. After "hello" and "Michael Jackson," we usually ran out of steam. So the only conversation we could've had was enthusiastically saying, "Hello, Michael Jackson!" over and over again.

Joyce and I soothed and protected each other in ways that our parents couldn't. Once, a neighborhood boy hit her with a hockey stick and she came home crying. I took her hand and marched over to the boy's house, ready to kick his ass. Lucky for him, his mom answered the door. I never got to avenge my sister, but he didn't mess with her after that. One year, when my parents completely forgot Joyce's birthday, I made her a peanut-butter-and-jelly sandwich with a side of potato chips. She hummed quietly while eating the sandwich, and I could tell she felt better.

Joyce was my confidante and emotional conduit, the soft spot to my hardening shell. I'd unload my anxieties onto her—my worries about not being chosen, about social dynamics at school, and conflicts with friends—and she'd listen to it all, nodding empathetically. She'd never consented to the role, exactly, but it was a clear sisterly exchange. I protected her from neighborhood bullies and came up with the best games, and she was a sponge for my growing worries and fears about the world around us.

As much as I could imagine my sisters and me as an Asian version of the Brady girls, Mr. and Mrs. Brady stumped me. Their simplistic lessons and sweet, affectionate nature left me with a yearning I couldn't put into words. In one episode, Jan made a mistake and lost an academic competition. My fists clenched nervously as I watched, waiting to see what her punishment would be. Poor Jan, I thought. I hoped Mr. Brady would go easy on her. But her dad didn't say a word. In fact, it was Mrs. Brady who stepped in. And not with a lashing or to berate Jan. But to give her . . . a *hug*.

"Sometimes when we lose," said Mrs. Brady, as she stroked Jan's hair, "really, we win."

When we lose, WE WIN? What did that even mean?

The difference between the Chens and the Bradys, between my Asian family and our American neighbors, wasn't just the cornsilk hair and the sky-blue eyes. It wasn't the turkey sandwiches versus seaweed and rice balls. Those differences, outsized as they felt when we were children, were ultimately superficial. The real difference was that in our home there was little space for softness, no room to mess up and try again, encouraged by sweet platitudes from our parents.

In our home, there was no reward for effort.

Unlike Jan, I would learn, again and again, that mistakes were not growing pains or opportunities for improvement, but grave and impermissible failures. They were not something to be understood but to be punished.

By the time I was seven, Dad and I had a running call-and-response routine.

"What's your name?" he'd ask.

"Dr. Chen!" I'd chirp, thrilled to have this private game with him. It could have been sweet comedy, a father-daughter shtick. Except it wasn't a game. It was career planning.

Not going into medicine was Dad's big regret, one he carried across the world and foisted on me. Joyce was too young. And Nancy, too sassy. She lacked the obedience for medical school, Dad said. Which mostly meant that she spat back. Dad saw my aptitude early, he'd tell me later. Since the poetry contest and the spelling bee, he'd seen the potential of our family legacy in me.

While they weren't paid well, doctors in Taiwan were culturally revered. Deified, almost. In the time of poverty and political turmoil my parents grew up in, respect may have been the most valuable currency. Born during World War II, Dad embodied both sides of Japan's colonization of Taiwan. In its push to make the island a model colony, the Japanese government sent thousands of its citizens to live and work there. My grandmother, a nurse from a small fishing village in southern Japan, was among them. She met my grandfather, a prominent doctor, at the hospital where he worked in Kaohsiung. Although doctors held high status, it was still understood that my grandmother, as a Japanese woman, was marrying down. The Japanese government tried to forbid the marriage, but she went ahead with it anyway. The family took her last name, Tanabe, instead of my grandfather's. After the war, when Japan lost control of Taiwan, they quietly swapped Tanabe out for my grandfather's surname, Chen.

Dad was the youngest of six kids—four boys and two girls. His family lived in a modest home with my grandfather's cousin, his wife, and their four kids. Dad said he knew he was relatively well-off because there was enough food to eat at home and he had a book bag, while other kids wrapped their books in a towel.

My grandfather was a skilled doctor beloved by his patients and community. He was known for his ability to diagnose illnesses without so much as an X-ray—an impressive feat, especially in a time and place where such tools weren't yet available. He worked such long hours that he mostly slept at the hospital, coming home only for dinner. His patients were his priority, and he had little time for his family. His children had to fight for a shred of attention. Love was even harder to come by. Still, he expected my father to excel in school. Anything that might distract from his studies—even a class field trip—wasn't allowed.

Dad was only five years old when his father was taken away by the KMT. Taiwanese people struggled to adapt to the new regime, as frustration grew over corruption and authoritarian rule. Private property was seized arbitrarily. Citizens were barred from political participation. Tension boiled over on February 28, 1947, when a Taiwanese widow was beaten by government agents for selling contraband cigarettes. Angry bystanders jumped in, and the agents opened fire into the crowd. A civilian was shot and killed. By the next day, protests had erupted across the island.

The KMT's response was swift and brutal, resulting in a bloody two-month slaughter of Taiwanese citizens. In what became known as the 228 Massacre, thousands of Taiwanese people were arrested, murdered, raped, and disappeared. Some were publicly executed; others were taken away and never seen again. Bodies were left in the streets as a warning to anyone who dared to speak out. The number of deaths was estimated at between 18,000 and 28,000. For decades afterward, speaking of the incident could get you jailed or killed. This marked the beginning of nearly four decades of political repression in Taiwan.

During this time, Dad's father and a group of concerned citizens came together to write a letter to the government, pleading for a peaceful resolution. They debated for days over whose address to send the letter from and finally settled on my grandfather's. As a doctor, he was a figure of respect, and they thought he would surely be granted leeway. But they were wrong. The KMT came for him anyway and threw him in jail. Every morning, guards plucked prisoners from their cells at random and marched them to the street, where they were publicly executed.

Dad and his family lived in fear that each day would be my grandfather's last. All they could do was wait. My aunt, A-go, who was the eldest daughter, biked past the prison every morning and waited for my grandfather to wave from behind the bars. It was her job to report back if he was still alive. Eventually, my grandmother sold everything she owned and gave the authorities money in exchange for his release. The only reason they spared his life was because he was a doctor.

My mom's father, a doctor with the Red Cross, was also jailed during that time. He provided medical care to citizens who were shot during a protest in front of the city council building and was arrested and imprisoned for aiding anti-government forces. At mealtimes, the guards tied the prisoners' hands behind their backs, flung uncooked rice onto the ground, and forced them to peck like chickens for their food. It was my grandfather's Red Cross emblem that eventually got him released.

It would be easy to trace Dad's desire to become a doctor to his father. But I think it was more nuanced. Doctors were the most respected profession in Taiwan. After seeing who survived the KMT, I think he came to equate respect with survival. There was only one medical school in Taiwan. Even though Dad did well academically, he didn't score high enough on the entrance exam. His older brother was already attending medical school in Japan, so he applied to the same one and was accepted. But when he arrived in Tokyo, he realized they'd assigned him a tourist visa instead of a student visa. He had to take a Japanese language test to stay in the country. The score to pass was 60. He scored 59.

"It was destiny," he would say later. *Yuanfen.*

He returned to Taiwan and studied chemical engineering instead, then went on to work for a plastics company. As my father moved from one career to the next, and eventually, across an ocean, he was restless. I don't think he ever found his purpose. Still, he clung to a fierce sense of independence. Even if his country wasn't free, he would be.

If Dad couldn't be a doctor, at least he could father one. If there's one thing doctors needed, it was strong math skills. The summer between fifth and sixth grade, Dad enrolled me in summer school to improve my math. More interested in rollerblading than equations, I was a reluctant student. One night, Dad decided to monitor my study session. I sat at the desk in my room, and as I calculated fractions, he sat on the bed next to me with a wooden back scratcher in his hand. Every time I made a mistake, he cracked it down on the top of my head.

"Gong ga be xi!" he'd shout. It was a Taiwanese slang phrase that loosely translated to *you're so stupid you should die!*

I kept pushing through equations, rivulets of snot and tears running down my face. "Wipe your face!" Dad ordered. I shuffled to the bathroom and blew my nose as slowly as I possibly could, dreading the return. That snotty moment was my only respite. Dad never explained *how* I might solve the problems. He just hit me when I got them wrong. By the time I finished the worksheet, my head was throbbing. I went back to summer school the next day as if nothing had happened, turning in my homework with a smile. I learned less about fractions that summer than about the danger of mistakes. Making them, especially in front of others, led to pain and humiliation.

I never talked about getting beaten at home. Corporal punishment was part of our culture. Americans wouldn't understand, my parents told us. According to them, it was both totally normal and something to hide. As I got older, I became a world-class compartmentalizer. I could get slapped one minute and slap a smile on my face the next. *Everything is fine. Everything is normal.* At some point, I started to believe my own story.

Where Nancy fought back with ferocity, I dropped into a steely reserve, pretending like nothing affected me. Joyce, however, remained tender. She let her tears fall freely, letting out full-bellied sobs. I watched her in awe the way I might a beautiful animal at the zoo, both envious of and confused by this strange behavior. She had access to a whole world that I didn't.

Did her tears help? Did they make it hurt less?

After Joyce sobbed, she always seemed lighter. Free to laugh and skip and let the world roll off her back. I yearned for that. Sometimes, when I was overwhelmed, I'd sit on the floor of her room and tell her the saddest stories I could think of. I'd watch her lip quiver, her brown eyes pooling with tears. As they spilled over and slid down her face, I felt some approximation of relief.

Dad wasn't going to let anything distract me from becoming a doctor. Even my hobbies had to support my academic future. Violin was acceptable because it bolstered college applications. Dad drove me to my competitions, and whether I won or lost, he would take me out for ice cream after. We always got the same thing: a scoop of mint chocolate chip for Dad, and Gold Medal Ribbon for me. If I wasn't winning gold medals, at least I was eating them in a waffle cone.

But any other dabbling became a threat. Around the math summer-school era, I went through a baking phase. Every day, I'd roll out of bed at sunrise to make cinnamon rolls. I'd wake Joyce up and force her to keep me company. She would begrudgingly drag a sleeping bag into the kitchen and curl up on the floor while I pulled flour, sugar, and spices from the cabinet. I'd buzz around the kitchen—measuring the vanilla, sifting the flour, and chopping the nuts. It looked chaotic, but I loved that everything alchemized into a delicious treat at the end.

One morning, Mom walked into the kitchen to find me flour-dusted, fingers sticky with sugar.

"Xiao Yu, time to put it away," she said, gesturing toward the counter.

"Yes!" I chirped. "Almost done. I'll clean up after."

"No, no. Dad says no more."

I turned to face her, wiping my hands on my apron. "What do you mean?"

"Stop baking," she said. "Focus on studies."

"But . . . it's just. It's just fun."

I think Dad couldn't bear to see me in an apron once he'd envisioned me in scrubs. I was crushed, but I shelved my disappointment at the back of the cupboard along with the sugar and flour. I took off my apron and pasted on a fake smile where the real one had once been.

CHAPTER 4

WEAPON OF CHOICE

If I couldn't win my parents' approval with sugar and flour, I'd earn it with good grades. So I threw myself into academics. Meanwhile, it seemed like overnight all the girls in my junior high school class had suddenly started to care about their appearance. They plucked their eyebrows into oblivion and got up early to cake on face powder and shimmery eyeshadow. Joyce was in on it too. For her tenth birthday she'd begged me to get her a book by celebrity makeup artist Kevyn Aucoin, and spent all her spare time in her room teaching herself how to do makeup. I thought it was absolutely nuts.

I'd never been seen as beautiful, so I rejected the beauty standards entirely, rebelling against them in my own way. While other girls carefully curated their outfits, I showed up to school in baggy sweatsuits every day. I had an alter ego that only Joyce knew about: Nerdy Birdy. Back in elementary school, I'd draw comic-book sketches of her. She was gawky and awkward, with oversized glasses and a mouth full of braces. The boys never paid attention to her. But one day—like the iconic makeover scene in every teen movie—she'd whip off her glasses, shake out her hair, and reveal a knockout underneath. In real life, I kept the glasses on and leaned into being a nerd.

I had math class with a Vietnamese American girl named Thao. She had olive skin and long black hair streaked with blond highlights. One afternoon, I was waiting in the school parking lot for my parents to pick me up when she bounded over.

"You're super smart, right?" she asked, grinning.

I shrugged, caught off-guard. "Uh . . . I guess?"

"Well, I'm coming over," Thao announced. "I need help with the math homework."

"Okay . . ." I said. My parents were lax about having friends over, so long as we were doing homework. When we got to my house, Thao kicked off her shoes and breezed into the living room like she'd been there a hundred times before. She turned in a slow circle, her eyes sweeping over the grand piano tucked into the far corner and the stiff, pearl-colored couches that we never sat on except to entertain guests.

"Nice," she said. "Got anything to eat?"

"Sure," I said. I went into the kitchen and rifled through the pantry, pushing past giant expired boxes of crackers and peanut butter. Dad had a habit of buying bulk food from Costco that we never finished.

"Raisins?" I asked, pouring a handful into Thao's palm. They were probably three years old. She popped a few in her mouth.

"Ew," she said, laughing. "They're hard!"

I giggled.

We sat down to do our homework and proceeded to get nothing done, laughing and talking about everything but geometry. Thao told me about her family. Her parents had immigrated from Vietnam during the war. She had two brothers and a sister, and her parents ran a small photography shop. They were always working, so Thao and her siblings were latchkey kids.

Thao despised rules and had a magnetic charm that could win anyone over. She had a rebel's spirit and a way of getting what she wanted before you knew what was happening. When we weren't hanging out, Thao and I would spend hours on the phone, even when I was supposed to be doing homework. If I heard Dad's footsteps on the stairs, I'd shove the cordless phone into my desk drawer. My room was directly below my parents', so if we were talking late into the night, I'd sit on the kitchen floor, whispering into the phone. One night, during one of those marathon midnight chats, Thao and I got onto the topic of discipline.

"My dad has torture methods," she said matter-of-factly.

"Like?" I asked, intrigued.

"He makes us kneel on the ground in the front yard with our arms out. We have to hold them like that until he says stop. Especially my older brother. It actually really hurts."

In many traditional Asian households, kneeling was a form of discipline—a way to instill obedience and demand remorse.

"My dad makes me kneel too," I whispered. "Not to do the arm thing, but just kneeling in front of him when he hits me."

"What's his weapon of choice?" Thao asked.

"Hangers, belts, back scratchers," I said. "Oh, and once, the mini-blind rod fell off and he stashed it as a future weapon."

Thao giggled. "Okay, okay. Top this: My dad scours the yard for skinny, flexible branches that'll make 'good whipping sticks.' He brings them in and waves them around. 'New weapon!' he says, trying to scare us."

We burst out laughing. It was funny imagining her dad waving little sticks around.

"He stores them on top of the fridge in a crazy pile," she said. "There's a whole forest up there."

"What about your mom?" I asked.

"Her only rule is 'Don't hit the girls above the waist.' Don't kill the pretty, right?"

"My dad hits our faces," I said. "Or sometimes on top of the head. A good thwack. But my mom hates that. 'That will make them stupid,' she says. 'And they won't do well in school!'"

"Jesus. All they care about is school.

"One day," Thao continued, "I just looked my dad in the eyes. Deadpan. Cold, you know? Like I felt no emotion. And I said to him: 'I know this is making you feel better more than it's actually teaching me anything.' That freaked him out. He called to my mom and started ranting about how I was a devil child. He stopped hitting me after that."

We laughed like it was the funniest thing in the world.

CHAPTER 5

LOVE IS KIND

In junior high, I started going to a Presbyterian church with a Korean friend and her family. I was captivated by the idea of God. One Sunday, the pastor gave a sermon on love, reading 1 Corinthians 13, 4–7:

> Love is patient, love is kind. It does not envy, it does not boast, it is not proud. It does not dishonor others, it is not self-seeking, it is not easily angered, it keeps no record of wrongs. Love does not delight in evil but rejoices with the truth. It always protects, always trusts, always hopes, always perseveres.

I became enamored with the idea of a love "not easily angered" and that "always protects"—foreign notions in my volatile home. Going to church became my regular Sunday routine. Afterward, I'd come home and share everything I learned with Joyce. When I started to pray, so did she.

Dear God, I'd start, clasping my hands as we huddled together under the covers. *Thank you for this day. Thank you for everything you have given us. Please bless Mom, Dad, Nancy, and Joyce. I hope tomorrow is a good day. Amen.*

Dear God, Joyce would follow. *Me too. And please give me a new Barbie.*

Joyce would request presents, but I never asked God for anything. I only gave my thanks, acutely aware that his favors weren't to be cashed in casually. I'd come to think of God as a benevolent bureaucrat, like a judge who sat at a throne or a fancy desk considering requests from humans. He might not take all cases, but those he did would be dealt with in a fair and correct manner. So, I prayed every night, hoping that I was earning goodwill with him.

After school one day, I was doing homework with my friend Mandy, who lived down the street. It was a warm, idyllic day. The sky was a crisp, cloudless blue. Usually, I did my homework inside, at a desk. But Mandy suggested we do our history reading outside. We settled onto a blanket on the front lawn, a wide strip of green bordered by tall hedges. About an hour into our study session, Dad pulled into the driveway. Moments later, I heard the familiar jangle of keys as he strode across the lawn. Dad always carried more than a dozen keys on a metal clip around his belt loop, so you could hear him coming from afar.

"Tell Mandy to go home," he barked in Taiwanese. She didn't speak Taiwanese but *get the fuck out of here* is universally understood. Mandy grabbed her books and bolted home.

Inside, my father unleashed. "Kneel!" he ordered. I knelt on the kitchen floor, feeling the hard linoleum against my knees. My father loomed over me. His eyes were lit with rage.

"How dare you read your book in the yard! Homework should be done at a desk. Apologize for what you did."

He drew his arm back and released it, slapping me hard across the face. I flinched but remained straight-faced. In our culture, you take punishment like a soldier. You aren't allowed to cower or to protect yourself.

"Admit that you're wrong!" he screamed.

But I knew I wasn't. There had been no rule against reading on the lawn. I hadn't been goofing off or getting the house dirty, or any other minor sin that a suburban tween could possibly commit. I'd spent years being wrong at my father's hands, certain that I'd messed up. That I deserved his hand, his belt, his disdain. I'd taken the beatings and worried about how I could be better. But that day, for the first time in my life, I knew I wasn't wrong.

He slapped me again, harder. My new purple glasses flew off my face as tears streamed down my cheeks. The world became a blur. He paused, offering me a moment to surrender. I could have stopped him right then. All I had to do was nod and acquiesce. To agree that I was wrong. But I knew with certainty that it was he who was wrong. Wrong in ways that I didn't have words for.

He slapped me a third time, landing the hardest blow yet. My braces cut into the soft inner skin of my cheeks. The metallic tang of blood flooded my mouth. I grunted, turning the other cheek. Still, I refused to apologize. Instead, I clasped my hands together and started to pray out loud: "*Please, Lord, help me understand what I have done wrong so I can apologize. Help me understand why this is happening.*"

This is what I'd been saving my requests up for. If ever there were a time to call on God, it was now. I wasn't praying for him to rescue me; I was praying to understand. Nancy and Mom were watching TV in the adjacent room the whole time, their backs turned to me. They weren't looking, but they could hear everything.

"What's Jane doing?" I heard my mom ask.

Nancy glanced over her shoulder. "Praying," she said.

I kept praying. And Dad kept hitting me, until eventually he tired and walked away. Relieved, I got up. My sweatshirt was covered in tears and snot. My knees ached from kneeling. I went to my room and curled up on the bed. Standing up for myself for the first time gave me confidence that I could hold my ground, even against my father. But it also crushed my burgeoning faith. Not just in God, but in the idea that anyone would protect me.

"Night," Joyce said softly as we lay side by side in bed that night. I could tell she was worried by the way her face scrunched up. "Night," I said, setting my arm on hers, offering a quiet understanding that what had happened was wrong, but we were okay. We never talked about the beatings, but we both stopped praying that night.

I wouldn't utter another prayer for twenty-five years.

CHAPTER 6

BLEEDING HEART

I didn't become Dr. Chen or get into my dream school—Yale. But I still followed a respectable immigrant path, attending Pomona College, a competitive liberal arts school. After I graduated, Nancy helped me land a job with the prestigious management consulting firm where she worked. After I bombed my first interview, she convinced them to give me a second chance. Eventually, they hired me, offering me a position in their Hong Kong office.

By twenty-one, I was living in an apartment with a skyline view in Hong Kong's glitzy Central District. Most of my time was spent jetting around the world, parachuting into companies to help come up with business strategies. On weekends, I sipped cocktails with my coworkers late into the night. The work was intellectually stimulating, and from the outside, my life seemed glamorous. But I was miserable. We were expected to work 24/7 and pull regular all-nighters. Between the lack of sleep and constant travel, I was exhausted. And even though my job performance was objectively solid, I could never shake the feeling that I didn't deserve to be there because I felt like I hadn't gotten the job on my own. Beyond all that, the work felt hollow. It meant nothing to me. I couldn't imagine grinding for years like that just for money.

One morning, about a year into my time in Hong Kong, I was scrolling through *The New York Times* when an article about an HIV/AIDS outbreak in rural China caught my eye. China had been facing a blood shortage, and the government had run a nationwide collection campaign. It was pushed especially hard in Henan Province, one of the most populated and poorest parts of central China. Farmers were offered $5 for a bag of blood—a small fortune in that area. But the blood-collection process was unsanitary. Blood was pooled together, plasma was extracted, and the remaining red blood cells were reinjected back into people's bodies based on the erroneous belief that it would allow them to generate new blood more quickly. Instead, it led to a massive outbreak of HIV/AIDS. The exact numbers were unknown, but the article estimated that over a million people across the province had been infected. In some villages, the infection rates were estimated to be as high as 60 to 80 percent.

I was in disbelief as I read the article. HIV/AIDS transmission was well understood—how could this have happened? How could they have been so careless with all those lives? The article said that instead of offering help or medication, the government was flat-out denying the problem. Stigma and ignorance about HIV/AIDS made the situation even worse. Those who were infected were ostracized by neighboring communities, and many refused to trade food with them. The disease was spreading so fast that entire family lines were dying off, leaving behind a generation of orphaned children.

I found an interview online of an elderly Chinese farmer from the area who had contracted HIV. His skin was weathered, probably from a lifetime of labor under the sun. His frame was slight, his body hunched and frail.

"We've sold everything we have to pay for basic necessities," he said in the local dialect, his voice trembling. "There's nothing more we can do now. We're just waiting to die." He'd been trying to hold back tears, but as the camera zoomed in, they streamed down his face. He wiped them away with the back of his callused hand. I stared at the soft crinkles around his eyes and saw the resignation on his face. And before I knew it, I was crying too.

These farmers were too poor and powerless to change their situation. The disease was basically a death sentence. It was as if their lives didn't matter. The injustice of it all made me sick to my stomach. I imagined my grandfathers and the fate they might have suffered if they had not been doctors. They, too, had been treated as if they were expendable, their dignity stripped away. In another life, it could have been me and my family suffering and dying deaths we didn't deserve.

Throughout my childhood, there were so many times I wanted to cry but couldn't. But suddenly this story—this man— unlocked a well of emotion that had been dormant for decades. I didn't fully understand why it affected me so deeply, but I couldn't turn away. At work that day, I went through the motions, but all I could think about was the farmers and their children. At lunch, I couldn't eat. During our team debrief, I was distracted and distant. I had to do something. And I had to do it *now*.

For the rest of the week, whenever I could slip away, I holed up in a tiny private phone booth and called every HIV/AIDS organization in Hong Kong I could find. I was desperate to track down anyone who was working on the crisis in Henan. Finally, I found a single nonprofit that had a program dedicated to securing education for the children orphaned by AIDS. *Yes,* I thought. It wasn't everything, but it was a start.

I started volunteering with the nonprofit. Within a few months, I left my consulting job, forgoing my cushy salary to become the program director of the Henan Orphans Project.

When I told my mother, she was livid.

"If you want to help people, you make good money, then donate," she screeched. "Not spend your life poor trying to help the poor!"

"Mom, you don't understand," I told her. "I've never felt more strongly about anything."

Bleeding hearts were not part of our cultural lexicon. In our culture, achievement and financial security were markers of a good life. It was your duty to make enough money so your parents wouldn't worry. Nonprofit work was an alien concept. With my limited Taiwanese and my parents' limited English, I couldn't explain the deeper drive behind what I was doing. I didn't know how to say that something seismic was happening. Something bigger than career or money or my parents' ideas of success. That I felt the injustice deep in my bones and was brimming with the desire to help. That I was electric with purpose.

When Mom realized she couldn't change my mind, she recruited my cousins in Taiwan to convince me not to throw my life away. In truth, it didn't matter what they said or if they understood. There was no stopping me—not for money, not for pride, and certainly not for family honor. But I couldn't explain any of that in words my family would understand.

A few months later, I traveled to the "AIDS villages" in Henan for the first time. A volunteer drove me through the countryside, where fresh grassy mounds rose from the land like giant molehills.

"What are those?" I asked.

"Graves," she said somberly. "People are dying so fast there's no time for proper burials."

I visited an orphanage and met some of the children we were sponsoring. They were rail-thin, their tattered, baggy clothes hanging off their small frames. I asked one boy how old he was. He looked no older than seven but said he was ten. When I asked the kids what they liked to eat, they screamed, "Meat!"—which they got only once a week if they were lucky.

We asked the children to draw pictures and write essays about what they wanted to be when they grew up. The answers were heartbreaking and inspiring.

I want to become a doctor, to cure AIDS, wrote one boy.

A thirteen-year-old girl who'd lost both parents wrote that she wanted to *find a cure for this terrible disease and be the hope that shines the way forward.*

More than half of the children aspired to become doctors or to find a cure for the disease that had ravaged their families. I wanted to help them in any way I could. The intensity of emotion and the life-and-death stakes filled me with purpose like nothing had before.

Within two years, the notoriously impenetrable Chinese government had taken notice of our work and implemented a policy to ensure all children orphaned by AIDS in the region would receive an education. Our efforts became a beacon, lighting a path forward. *The South China Post* wrote an article about me, and I sent a copy home to my parents. They laminated it and sent it to our family in Taiwan—the same family Mom had once enlisted to talk me out of pursuing this work.

It was empowering to realize that a simple goal, pursued with heart and conviction, could change the lives of others. Even though I hadn't become a doctor, I realized I could still help people in meaningful ways. That week, I noticed a quote from Steve Jobs on someone's office wall: "The people who are crazy enough to think they can change the world are the ones who do." Yes! That was it. I was compelled to keep going, to do more, to tackle bigger challenges. I'd thrown myself headfirst into the HIV/AIDS work, learning on the fly. But if I wanted to create change on a larger scale, I needed more skills and more knowledge.

I needed to go back to school.

I decided to apply to graduate programs and looked into both business and public policy schools. My parents were back in Taiwan; they had been spending a few months there every year since my sisters and I had left for college. I took a month off and stayed with them to work on my applications. By then, Taiwan had become a democracy. In 1996, the island held its first open presidential election. My parents flew back to cast their votes in every election that followed. For them, democracy wasn't a slogan—it was a hard-won right, a privilege they didn't take for granted.

I had few memories of living in Taiwan as a child, and my parents rarely talked about their life before moving to America. As kids, we had visited Kaohsiung every three or four years but being back as an adult was different. During my visit, Mom was maternal in ways she'd rarely been in America. It was funny little things. She insisted on holding my hand whenever we crossed the street. When I wanted to join a gym, she called around to find one, then took me herself to sign up—something she would have no idea how to navigate in California. One afternoon, she brought me to a glitzy department store to buy a new bra. The saleswoman brought out a few options, and Mom scoffed.

"Don't you have anything more appropriate for a young girl?" she asked.

"Mom!" I exclaimed, sorting through the bras. "I'm twenty-five years old!"

"It's a shame that you girls didn't grow up in Taiwan," she said wistfully as we walked home. "Here, I know how to do things."

In the evenings, we wandered through the bustling night markets. Food stalls lined the narrow streets, each one specializing in a single dish. The recipes were passed down through generations; many vendors inherited their stalls from their parents, carrying on the family legacy. We visited our favorite vendors who served classic Taiwanese staples: sticky rice, minced pork stew, and fish-ball soup. My favorite was gan mian—handmade flour noodles that were perfectly chewy, tossed in a soy-based sauce with a rich umami flavor and a hint of sweetness. The noodles were topped with thin slices of tender pork and a sprinkle of fresh cilantro. It looked deceptively simple, but the flavor in each bite was exquisite.

Some nights, Dad came along. He would always grumble about the prices as he eyed the menus. "A dollar twenty-five?" he'd exclaim. "Those noodles used to cost fifteen cents a bowl!" He happily slurped them down all the same. As I ate happily, he would watch me with a satisfied smile. "Gam jia ba?" he'd ask. *Are you full? Do you want another bowl?* Eating the same food cooked by the same families since my parents were children made every meal more than a meal—it imbued each bite with a sense of history, a common anchor that we didn't share in America.

By the end of the summer, I narrowed down my applications to programs at Harvard and Stanford. Nancy, who had gone to Stanford Business School a few years earlier, helped review my essays and application materials. As the older sister, she was always ready to assist with the practical things.

"The cat gets in and then helps the kittens!" she quipped.

As I approached the end of my trip, I booked my flight back to Hong Kong. At dinner one evening, I reminded my parents I would be leaving in a few days.

"What terminal will you fly out of?" Mom asked.

Dad overheard her question. "Gong ga be xi!" he barked. *You're so stupid, you should die!*

I froze, my stomach knotting.

"Why are you saying that?" I snapped. "She's asking a perfectly good question. Why do you have to speak to her like that?" Dad grunted and buried his face in his newspaper, dismissing me entirely. Mom didn't say a word.

"Why does Dad have to speak to you like that?" I asked her after dinner. "Can't he just speak to you respectfully?"

Since my sisters and I had left for college, it seemed as though Dad had redirected his fury toward Mom. Anytime she spoke, he'd lash out, calling her stupid or worthless. I didn't notice it as much at first, maybe because I'd become numb to his verbal assaults. But now, after spending my days fighting for dignity and justice on behalf of people who had no voice, something had changed. His words felt visceral and violent.

"He doesn't mean it," Mom responded, sighing as she rinsed a dish. "He's a good man. If there was only one piece of bread left in the world, your father would give it to me."

I wanted to say more, but I bit my tongue.

Over the next few days, I tried to muster up the courage to confront Dad about the way he spoke to Mom. But every time I opened my mouth to say something, the words weren't there. What I really wanted to express I didn't know how to say in Taiwanese, and he wouldn't understand in English. I fantasized about secretly filming him during one of his tirades. Maybe if he saw himself, he'd realize how cruel he sounded.

On my last night in Kaohsiung, Dad and I went to pick up dinner on his moped. It was just the two of us; he drove, and I sat behind him, gripping the back rail with one hand and wrapping the other around his waist. The air was hot and sticky. Cars swerved around each other, horns blaring out greetings and warnings. As Dad wove through the chaos, I could feel the heat of his back. I could count the times on one hand that we'd ever been so physically close.

At a red light, he stopped and planted his feet on the ground to balance the bike. The engine idled as we waited. *This is your chance,* I told myself. *Before the light changes. Say it now. Now!*

I revved myself up, getting ready to speak to him with conviction. But when I opened my mouth, all I could say was, "Dad, please be nicer to Mom." The words came out soft and hesitant. Dad shifted forward in his seat and let out a low chuckle.

"Di xiao e," he said, without turning around. *You're crazy.*

The light turned green and Dad palmed the gas, leaving the moment behind.

CHAPTER 7

UNDER THE ACACIA TREE

I was admitted into all the programs I applied to. I got my Stanford MBA program acceptance first and called home immediately.

"Hi, Dad!" I said when he picked up.

"Xiao Yu. How much money you have in bank account?" he asked.

Taking a financial headcount was his standard greeting. I ignored the question.

"Dad, I got into Stanford!"

"Oh, wow!" he exclaimed. "Goody-goody!"

When Nancy had called to tell him she'd gotten into Stanford a few years back, I had never seen him smile so big. "I proud," he said in English, grinning ear to ear. It was the first time I'd ever heard him say those words. I imagined that same look on his face now, the same pride welling up in him as he heard my news. Just before we hung up, he said my name, softly.

"Xiao Yu . . ."

"Yes?" I said.

"Now that you get acceptance . . . think you can transfer to medical school?"

I was also accepted to the Harvard Kennedy School to study public policy. When it was time to choose what program I would attend, I couldn't make up my mind. Then it hit me: what if I could attend *both* schools? I decided to petition for a dual-degree program. My petition was approved. The schedule was berserk: a year in Palo Alto, a year in Cambridge, and the final year split between the two schools. Maybe two degrees would make Dad proud enough to forgive the fact that I hadn't become a doctor.

From day one at Stanford, I was convinced admissions had made a huge mistake. Stanford was the big leagues. The campus pulsed with ambition. Surrounded by a mix of former investment bankers, Navy SEALs, and Olympic athletes, I felt like an imposter. I was sure all my classmates were smarter and more accomplished than I was and that it was only a matter of time before someone stated the obvious: I didn't belong.

During the first quarter, for World AIDS Day in December, I was invited to give a talk on my work in China. Talk '08 was a monthly event featuring speakers from each year's class. I was excited to share the work I'd been so passionate about but terrified of speaking in front of all my classmates. I wanted it to be perfect. Putting the talk together was simple. I knew the material inside and out, and had the slides committed to memory.

The evening of the talk, I walked to the front of the packed room. My heart hammered against my chest. I took a deep breath and began, my voice shaking. Partway through my presentation, the room started to warp and shrink. My chest tightened. I couldn't get enough oxygen. And then—my mind went completely blank. I tried to recall the script I'd practiced dozens of times. But my mind was an empty hall. As I looked out at the audience, their faces morphed into a single scowling blur.

I heard the words I had heard my whole life: *Gong ga be xi! You're so stupid you should die.*

Only this time, it wasn't my father's voice echoing in my head. It was my own.

I gasped for a breath, mumbled an apology, and ran out of the room. A friend chased after me.

"Slow down. Take a deep breath," she said.

The night air was cool against my burning cheeks.

"You have to go back," she said gently. "You have to finish."

"I'd rather die," I told her.

"I know," she said, her voice full of empathy. "But it's not that big of a deal, I swear. Everyone will forget about it by tomorrow. What you have to say is too important."

I couldn't imagine going back into that room. But she was right. This wasn't about me. It was about the cause. I took a few deep breaths, steadied myself, and followed her back into the room. After I finished my talk, everyone applauded, and people gathered around to tell me how moved they were. Some said it was the best talk they had heard that year. But I was mortified at my public failure. All I could think was *Everyone can see you now.*

The next day, everyone had already forgotten about my blackout. Everyone but me. A shame cloud trailed me as I white-knuckled my way through classes. I was terrified that at any moment, the thread would unravel, and I would come apart. Talk '08 was the first glitch. I'd lost control. The fear that it might happen again kept me from speaking at all. Even saying *My name is Jane* during class introductions had me on the verge of a panic attack. It was humiliating to feel like an anxious grade schooler among the nation's best and brightest. I couldn't shake the relentless, taunting voice in my head that only grew louder. *You should be ashamed. Loser, loser, loser.*

I set out to tackle the issue head-on, trying every tactic to rid myself of my fear. I joined Toastmasters, committing to giving weekly speeches in front of strangers. I experimented with hypnosis. I even signed up for acting classes.

"What's the worst that could happen?" the teacher asked when I explained my fear. "You throw up? Then let yourself throw up."

That didn't seem practical.

That summer, I landed a high-profile internship at Pepsi, called the Leadership Development Program. I was tasked with doing market research to figure out whether customers cared about the company's environmental initiatives. At the end of the internship, all the interns would give a final presentation to executives at the company. All summer, I had anxiety dreams about it. I prepared obsessively. The only way I could avoid error, I determined, was to become a perfectly practiced machine. I slipped into the rote memorization of my past, committing every line to memory. *Two by two.*

But I still couldn't quiet my nerves. What if I blacked out again?

A musician friend, who'd been performing for years, suggested I try beta-blockers—a blood-pressure medication used off-label to reduce physical symptoms of anxiety. A lot of performers and athletes took them to calm their jitters, he said. I got a prescription from a doctor. On the day of the presentation, thirty minutes before my allotted slot, I slipped into a bathroom stall, broke one tiny blue pill in half, and swallowed it with a gulp of water.

The conference room was freezing and lit harshly with fluorescent lights. When they called my name, I panicked. My heart was going wild. I stepped to the front of the room and looked out at all the executives. *Don't fuck this up.* My presentation came up on the screen. I started talking through the slides. By the time I got to the third slide, the buzz of cicadas in my mind stopped. I could think clearly. I wasn't sweating or stuttering, but moving fluidly through every word. And before I knew it, it was over. Everyone smiled and applauded, looking pleased.

The beta-blocker had worked. I wouldn't use them forever, I told myself. Just to get through school. Just until my confidence came back.

It was just one little pill.

My secret weapon.

I enrolled in a class at Stanford's Design School (referred to as the d.school) called "Design for Extreme Affordability." The class partnered with nonprofits around the world and identified challenges for student teams with the goal of creating low-cost technologies to solve pressing global problems. Students from the prior year had developed a super-low-cost solar light that was now being distributed across Africa. I was intrigued as soon as I learned about the course. I loved the idea of building a tangible product—it brought me back to my childhood obsession with baking, to the joy of creating and experimenting.

One of the challenges issued in the class that year: design a baby incubator for less than 1 percent of the standard cost, which at the time, was about $20,000.

"Fifteen million preterm and underweight babies are born worldwide every year," Professor Patell told us. "Three million newborns die within the first twenty-eight days of their life."

One of the biggest problems these babies faced was regulating their body temperature—they were too tiny to produce enough warmth on their own. And death wasn't the only risk. When a newborn's temperature drops, their bodies must work harder to stay warm, consuming precious calories and oxygen needed for growth and development. This can compromise vital organ systems, increasing the risk of respiratory distress, infection, brain injury, and other long-term complications. Even if these babies survive, they can face lifelong health issues. Traditional incubators were prohibitively expensive in developing countries, leaving countless newborns without the care they desperately needed.

In contrast to the world's endlessly complex problems, keeping a baby warm seemed so simple. So intimate and human. If we could figure it out, we could potentially help save millions of lives. We had twelve weeks to come up with a concept. We could use any materials. There were no limits on approach. Wild ideas were encouraged.

We formed teams, and I was placed at random with three other graduate students. Linus was a hilarious computer scientist who'd already made a million selling his first app, "You're a Hottie." Linus liked to say that there were three things in life one should do: *Make money. Help the world. And find love.* He was on number two. Razmig was an MBA student from Armenia who'd worked in strategy consulting and at the United Nations. Rahul was a PhD candidate in electrical engineering, who had grown up in India and Kuwait. He had attended an IIT, which was like the Harvard of India, but even more difficult to get into. At Stanford, he ran a religious roundtable and threw legendary parties. He was one of the smartest, most dynamic people I'd ever met.

The class was centered on "design thinking," which was a framework for innovation. The central idea was that in any creative process, you begin by first understanding the problem as deeply as possible rather than just coming up with solutions. To truly understand, you need to have empathy for the people living with the problem. Which means that you must take the time to learn about their lives, cultures, and mindsets. Instead of projecting your own assumptions, you listen and imagine yourself in their shoes. Solutions rooted in the needs, challenges, and desires of the communities they are meant to serve have staying power.

To come up with the right solution, we'd need to witness the problem firsthand. Rahul and I flew twenty-four hours to India to visit hospitals and clinics. We discovered that their incubators were often broken or unusable, due to inconsistent electricity. Some were used to store documents instead, keeping them secure and away from bugs. We connected with a local NGO that trained women in villages with practical skills, like weaving silk, to improve their livelihoods. We decided to visit one of the villages, traveling by car for hours along dusty, bumpy roads lined with palms. As we got closer, the road narrowed and we passed rows of colorful, single-room homes. Through open windows I caught glimpses of straw mats on the floor, wood stoves, and in every third house or so, a single lightbulb dangling from the ceiling. It reminded me of the villages I'd visited in Henan.

The car finally stopped at a clearing on the side of the road. Twenty women in bright saris gathered around to greet us as we climbed out. Behind them, a tattered blue tarp was tented up for shade against the baking sun. The women ranged in ages from twenty to seventy. Even the youngest had faces weathered from years of working in the fields. Under the tarp, more women sat barefoot and cross-legged on a straw mat. Rahul and I slipped our shoes off and joined them. Their voices rose and fell as they watched us, their eyes sparkling with curiosity.

"It's unusual to have foreign visitors here," our guide explained.

With his help, Rahul and I explained the project and why we were there.

"How do you deliver babies?" we asked.

The translator posed the question. The group broke into chatter, speaking in Kannada, the local language. Hands gestured toward the colorful homes we'd passed on our way in.

"Most give birth at home," the translator explained. "With the help of a local midwife."

The women kept talking, getting louder.

"The nearest hospital is over ten miles away," the translator added.

I paused, then asked, "Has anyone here lost a baby?"

The translator repeated the question and the group fell quiet. Finally, an elderly woman spoke.

"Sujatha," she said quietly. "You must speak to Sujatha."

Everyone turned toward a woman in a bright green sari with brass bangles adorning her wrists. She looked up hesitantly. Her long, elegant face was framed by deep-set brown eyes that seemed to hold a quiet sadness.

I approached her gently and invited her to speak with me privately. I told her we were there to help. She nodded and led me, along with the translator, into the shade of a nearby acacia tree. A warm honey aroma filled the air. Before we began, I asked if I could record her story to share with my team.

She nodded.

With the camera set up and running, I took a deep breath.

"Can you tell me about your children?"

"I've lost three," she said. "The first came two months early. But the government hospital was too far. I didn't have money to get to the hospital, so my baby died." Her voice was steady, almost mechanical.

"My next came very early too. My husband raises silkworms for a living. He put our baby into a box with a light on top to keep her warm—the same way he keeps his worms alive."

My heart dropped. The image was devastating.

"A few days later, she died too," she said, her tone unwavering, as though the pain had long been numbed. Her third child suffered complications at birth and died just before his first birthday.

I nodded, my chest tightening with every word. Sujatha told me there had been no time to grieve. Survival had left no room for mourning. "We are expected to go back to work immediately after each death, to support the family," she said. "Here, we, the women—get blamed for the deaths. The world doesn't care about the death of a child. As mothers, we bear the burden."

I couldn't imagine anything more devastating than being helpless to save your own child. But when I looked in Sujatha's eyes, they seemed vacant. She recited the litany of loss as if it were simple fact, showing almost no emotion. As I listened, I felt that same pulse, that same ache I'd felt watching the farmer's story in Henan. I needed to do something to help. Anything. And in Sujatha's eyes, I recognized my own ability to shut down, to endure when there was no other option.

What holds a child best?

That was the question that kicked off our brainstorming back at Stanford. Talking to the mothers in India, it was clear that we didn't just need a cheaper version of a traditional incubator. We needed to entirely reimagine what an incubator was. These women needed something simple and reliable that could work in bare-bones village clinics or even in their homes. It had to be portable, easy to operate, and function without stable electricity.

High on ambition, espresso, and late-night pizza, we hunkered down in the design lab. The room buzzed with energy as we scribbled ideas onto dozens of neon Post-its.

"People use papooses, right?" Linus asked.

"Yes, something cocoonlike," said Rahul.

"A sleeping bag?" I suggested.

How do we keep the bag warm?

Premature babies need to maintain a consistent temperature of 98.6 degrees Fahrenheit to survive. How could we do that without electricity? One night, tossing and turning in bed, I remembered something from my childhood in Taiwan. During colder months, street vendors in the night markets sold gel hand-warmers—small pouches with a metal button inside. When you clicked it, the gel crystallized and stayed warm for hours. Maybe something like that would work. The next morning, I shared my idea with the team.

"Brilliant!" Rahul said. "It must have been phase-change material." He explained that phase change happens when matter transitions from one form to another—like ice melting into water. During that shift, the material stays at a constant temperature: ice melts at 32 degrees Fahrenheit, holding that exact temperature until fully liquefied. If we could find a material that melted at human body temperature, we'd have a solution. We could use enough of the material so the phase change would last for hours, allowing us to keep a baby warm without the need for electricity.

We started the prototyping process, trawling Goodwill for baby dolls and swaddles. We stuffed Ziploc bags with sticks of margarine, the closest substitute we could think of for a phase-change material that melted at human body temperature. We stayed up all night, cutting and sewing a swaddle with a pocket in the back, where the pouch of phase-change-material could be tucked. We put a doll into our first prototype, and Rahul carried it around campus in his backpack, its head sticking out and bouncing around. Campus cops, who thought the baby was real, stopped him to investigate.

Over the next few weeks, we iterated and improved our sleeping-bag design. Design thinking was the inverse of what I'd internalized my whole life, a process in which *mistakes were permissible*. In my home, there was no room for error. In design thinking, mistakes were not only expected—they often yielded the most interesting results. In fact, they weren't seen as mistakes at all, but discoveries and opportunities to stumble into unexpected breakthroughs. There was no failure. Only trying and trying again. Wild ideas were encouraged, gut instincts valued, and empathy prioritized over action. It was liberating to imagine what was possible instead of spending all my energy worrying about getting it wrong.

By the end of the semester, through collaboration and creative thinking and lots of screw-ups, we had a solution. It was a tiny, hooded sky-blue sleeping bag, made from a soft nylon. A small pocket in the back held a sealed pouch of wax—our phase-change material—that melted at 98 degrees Fahrenheit and maintained that temperature for four to six hours before it needed to be reheated. It was simple and elegant.

We called it *Embrace*. Because that's what a premature baby needs to survive.

What all children need, really.

To be warm.

To be held.

To be safe.

After the class ended, Linus kept telling us that Embrace had legs. That it could work in the real world. Other Stanford class projects had gone on to become world-changing products or ideas. Like the little search engine that could (Google!). But none of us had imagined that we'd come to graduate school to build a baby incubator. After class wrapped, we'd all moved on. Rahul was on track to get a job at Google and make a mountain of money. Linus had plans to develop his next app, and maybe dabble in part three of his life plan: love. Razmig was going to launch a tech start-up. And I was still working out my next steps, thinking about where global health and business might collide.

I spent half of the next year at Harvard. There, I sat in on a class at the medical school with Paul Farmer, a doctor who'd treated AIDS patients in Haiti through his nonprofit organization, Partners in Health (PIH). AIDS had disproportionately devastated communities in developing countries, where treatment was often out of reach. In the '80s, antiretrovirals, the medications used to treat AIDS, were incredibly expensive. The stance of the public health world had been to funnel money toward prevention, effectively resigning those already infected to death. But Farmer rejected the idea that some lives mattered less than others. He believed in the goal of treating *all* patients—no matter how poor, remote, or sick—and working backward to figure out how to make it possible.

During one lecture, he projected a photo of an emaciated man who was in the late stages of AIDS. "How does poverty enter the body?" he asked the class. I mulled over the question for weeks. I thought about the farmers in Henan who had contracted HIV, about babies in India dying because their parents couldn't afford $2 for a bus ride to the hospital. They hadn't chosen their circumstances. The world had been set up unjustly, but we could do something about it.

Paul's team gathered rigorous data to demonstrate that patients in resource-poor settings could successfully adhere to complex HIV treatment regimens. They worked with global health agencies, governments, and grassroots movements to pressure pharmaceutical companies to lower the prices of lifesaving drugs and expand access to generics. Eventually, through relentless advocacy and strategic partnerships, they helped make antiretroviral medication accessible to some of the poorest patients around the world. Everyone said it was impossible. But they did it. And countless lives were saved as a result. Paul's quest was not just about providing medical care—it was about fighting for social equity and human dignity. His work was rooted in solidarity, not charity. It was an "antidote to despair."

Listening to Paul flooded me with inspiration, reigniting the hope I'd felt working with the orphans in China. No matter how daunting the systems were, no matter how many naysayers, we could make a difference. There were tangible ways to make the world better for the most vulnerable people. If we could merge Paul's grassroots approach with Silicon Valley's spirit of nimble innovation, maybe Embrace really could save lives. Maybe it could be our *antidote to despair.*

I was fired up again about the possibility of Embrace. So, when Linus encouraged us to apply to an elevator-pitch competition back at Stanford, I was all in. We'd have sixty seconds to pitch our idea. Linus would deliver the pitch. "The key to not getting nervous is to clench your butt cheeks," he told us as we prepared. The clenched glutes worked. Linus nailed the pitch, and we were floored when he won. The prize money was $2,000.

Linus's belief was infectious. We started to dream about what might be possible with real funding. Between classes, we worked on applications to any business-plan competitions we could find. We lost every single one. But the camaraderie of trying—of believing in our vision enough to go for it—cemented our bond.

A month before graduation, things looked grim—we hadn't raised another dollar. I hadn't applied for any jobs and had no backup plan. Then, in the last week of school, we won the Stanford BASES (Business Association of Stanford Entrepreneurial Students) award, with a prize of $35,000. It was a pittance compared with what most of our cohort would go on to be earning. But winning wasn't just about the money. It was a huge vote of confidence for our idea. We were surrounded by the tech entrepreneurs of tomorrow. *If you can dream it, you can build it* was the Silicon Valley mantra.

"Yahoo! and Google came out of Stanford," one judge told us. "We're waiting to see something of that scale in the social-enterprise world. And we think you guys could be it."

A buzzy phrase still in its infancy, "social entrepreneurs" were a new wave of founders focused on serving the world's most marginalized people. David Brooks captured their ethos in *The New York Times:*

> These days some of the very noblest people have assumed the manners of the business world even though they don't aim for profit. They call themselves social entrepreneurs, and you can find them in the neediest places on earth.

The same day as the BASES announcement, we got even bigger news: we won the Echoing Green fellowship, one of the most prestigious awards for early-stage social entrepreneurs. It came with $90,000 in seed funding over the next two years. We were elated. We created a nonprofit organization and determined official roles. With Rahul's expertise in tech, he was a natural fit for Chief Technology Officer. Linus, who clearly thrived in operations, took on the Chief Operating Officer role. Razmig was starting another company, but would stay on as an adviser. And everyone agreed that I should be CEO. I had the vision, the passion, and a newly minted MBA. We went out for dinner and beers that night to celebrate. But back home, tipsy and alone, doubts flooded my mind.

Who are you fooling? You? CEO?

A CEO was charismatic and polished. He was strategic and inspirational, and could command a room with ease. He was a *he*. And he was most certainly white. The "girl boss" hadn't been born yet. Sheryl Sandberg was just on the verge of leaning in. Who was I to think I could play the role? I was no visionary Jobsesque leader who could inspire a cult following. I was an Asian American immigrant who could barely say *My name is Jane* without trembling. How was I going to convince people to believe in me—let alone our mission—if I didn't even believe in myself?

CHAPTER 8

LITTLE KID DRIVING A BIG CAR

My first year at Stanford, desperate to beat my fear of public speaking, I'd started seeing a therapist. A German man named Dr. Theodore.

"I just can't shake this feeling that I don't belong," I told him in one session. "I'm honestly not sure if I'm smart."

He nodded in that calm therapist way.

I told him how I was convinced that I'd landed the consulting job in Hong Kong based on a boost from my sister, and that I'd gotten into Stanford and Harvard based on hard work, not intelligence.

"Tell me more about your upbringing," he prodded.

I sighed and ran quickly through the basics—the expectations, the rigor, the violence—in a bloodless recitation.

"You tell these stories with so little emotion," Dr. Theodore remarked.

"That stuff is in the past," I replied dryly. "Yes, it sucked. But it doesn't affect me anymore, so why dwell on it? Can we move on to why I'm here? I need to overcome this speaking thing. And I need to do it *now*."

"It's not so simple," he said. "The present is intertwined with the past. It doesn't sound like your parents were very supportive."

"I mean, my dad called me stupid growing up a lot, but . . ." I shrugged.

"Do you think that may be why you *feel* stupid?"

"I don't think so," I said, waving off his look of concern. "That's how Asian parents are." *You wouldn't get it.*

Dr. Theodore cocked his head. "Can I give you a suggestion?"

"Sure."

"Ask other people for their opinion."

"You mean . . . ask them if they think I'm smart?"

"Yes. You like data. Do some data collection. Before our next session, get objective feedback from someone whose opinion you value. That's the homework."

It sounded mortifying.

Dr. Theodore cleared his throat. "I fear you may have a skewed self-perception. *Achievement dysmorphia.*" He explained that it was a persistent distortion in how one views their accomplishments—the sense that no matter what you achieve, it never feels like enough. You downplay success, dismiss praise, and live with the constant feeling that you're falling short. Who I was and what I saw might be two entirely different things, irreconcilably at odds.

Later that week, I emailed the smartest person I knew: Rahul. I couldn't believe I was doing this. I asked if he thought I was smart. Rahul responded a few days later with a detailed explanation of why *I* was one of the smartest people he knew. The next week, he brought me a book called *Mindset* by Stanford psychologist Carol Dweck. In it, she explained the difference between a growth mindset—the belief that intelligence and abilities can be developed through effort, learning, and persistence—and a fixed mindset, where those traits are seen as static and unchangeable.

"It's not always the people who start out the smartest who end the smartest," Dweck wrote.

It was contradictory to everything I believed about intelligence up until that point. My whole life, I'd believed intelligence was fixed. The idea that something so foundational and core to my identity could be changeable was shocking. Starting Embrace and becoming a CEO were going to require a growth mindset, but I was operating on a fixed mindset.

Maybe if I changed my mindset, I could do it.

Maybe I could *grow* into the role.

In my last session with Dr. Theodore before graduation, I told him a story about my dad slapping me when I was seven over something trivial. I breezed through the incident, devoid of emotion.

He held up his hand, stopping me.

"That's *sad*," he said.

"Yes, I guess," I replied.

He leaned forward in his armchair, locking eyes with me.

"That's *really, really sad*," he said, as if imploring me to agree. I stared, stunned, as tears welled up in his eyes.

"Let's talk to her," he suggested.

"Who?"

"You. Yourself at seven."

He stood and placed an empty chair directly across from me.

"Imagine her sitting there," he said gently. "What would you say to her?"

I played along, closing my eyes, and tried to picture myself at that age. Short, glossy hair. Probably wearing a neon outfit. Her purple glasses perched on her nose.

"What would you want her to know?" he asked.

As I pictured her face, *my face*, a sudden wave of sadness washed over me.

"It's, it's . . . it's not your fault," I blurted out, bursting into tears.

It was the first time Dr. Theodore had seen me cry. The corners of his mouth lifted slightly as he offered me a tissue. Dazed, I took it and leaned back in my chair. I didn't know why the words hit so hard—or what they even meant.

My parents came to my Harvard graduation. It was a crisp summer day in Cambridge. After I walked the stage and flipped my tassel, officially becoming a double master's, they found me in the crowd exchanging congratulations with my classmates. Mom sighed wistfully. "I wish you hadn't come here," she said, scanning the boisterous crowd. "Then you might be doing what I want you to do."

"And what is that, Mom?" I snapped. My parents had been acting like this since I told them that I was going to pursue Embrace. They couldn't believe I'd gone back for all this prestigious schooling only to return to *charity work*.

"Get a corporate job," she said. "Make money. Stay in California. Near your parents. Like a good daughter. Like Jackie."

Mom kept bemoaning that I should have been a mortgage broker like my friend Jackie, who'd barely graduated college. "At least she's making a lot of money," Mom said. Where Dad demanded I achieve at any cost, Mom was always comparing me to others. Growing up, she'd nag me for not being more like my most studious friend, Karin Li, who *did* end up becoming a doctor.

"What do you know about starting a company, anyway?" she said, shaking her head. "You're like a little kid driving a big car."

I was about to take the biggest risk of my life, and I needed her support. I wanted to be mad at her, but a part of me thought the exact same thing.

My parents weren't the only ones who doubted me. Shortly after graduation, Rahul and I met with a woman named Denise, who was the head of a prominent foundation in charge of vetting us for a grant. During the meeting, I was nervous, my throat tight, my mind fuzzy. I stumbled through the pitch and choked on my answer to her questions.

Afterward, Denise held a private meeting with Rahul and told him that he should be CEO. He was confident and charismatic, she said. Articulate. Rahul had what it took to sell *the story* of Embrace. Not me. She said the foundation would be *exceedingly comfortable* backing the company with Rahul at the helm.

When Rahul told me what happened, I was crushed.

"Don't worry," he assured me. "I told her no."

But Denise's words were confirmation of what I already believed. CEOs didn't stutter or screw up. Even momentary weakness was impermissible.

Denise expressed her opinion to our board of directors. Thankfully, everyone stood behind me.

"We'll get the money somewhere else," Linus assured me. "Screw 'em."

"That means a lot," I said. "More than you know." I was touched that my team believed in me enough to turn down money when we barely had any. It ratcheted up both my confidence and the pressure. If my team was ready to back me like that, I didn't want to let them down.

But I couldn't get what Denise had said out of my head. I remembered a conversation I'd had with my classmate Logan, who was great at public speaking.

"I wish I had your courage," I told him. "I wish I could just stand up in front of an audience and speak without fear, like you do."

Logan smiled and shook his head. "I enjoy public speaking, sure. But that's not the same as courage. Courage is when you are afraid, and you still try anyway. There is no such thing as courage without fear."

I'd never thought about it that way before. Logan was right. I might not have the skills or the charisma, but I could still find the courage to try, even if I was afraid. Maybe that was enough to start.

A few weeks later, I worked up the courage to request a one-on-one meeting with Denise. When I finally walked into her office, her greeting was polite, if clipped.

"Thanks for coming, Jane," she said. "What can I help you with?"

"You know," I said, "I've been thinking a lot about our meeting. And I have a question for you. What do *you* think is the role of a CEO?"

Denise stared at me, silent. She tapped her foot, pinching her brow in thought. I gave it a beat. Then another. Denise's face was blank. *She didn't know. This woman, trying to knock me off, didn't even know.* Now I was heated. No one was going to tell me that I was shit. Except for myself.

"Well, here's what I think," I said, trying to force confidence into my voice. I counted the roles off on my fingers: "Hiring and inspiring a team. Raising money. Coming up with a strategy." I paused, holding her gaze. "But more than anything, it's about having a vision of what's possible and turning that into reality."

She didn't say a word. "And those are all things I can do," I added. With that final point made, I walked out of her office. As soon as I closed the door behind me, I let out a huge breath. My hands were shaking. *Did I just do that?* I wasn't sure if I had all those skills yet, but sometimes a growth mindset just means you fake it until you make it. And that I *did* know how to do.

We organized a founders' retreat in Marin to come up with next steps for Embrace. We had funding, a prototype, and the team. Now we needed a plan. We decided that to finish developing the product, we had to be on the ground, where the need was most dire, so that we could get real-time feedback from the communities we were trying to serve. We needed to go back to India, where 40 percent of the world's premature babies were born.

The first morning of the retreat, we sat in a circle on the living-room floor of the townhouse we'd rented, sipping tea and nibbling on pastries.

"To kick off," Rahul said, "I think each of us should share why we're doing this and what's personally motivating us."

We all glanced around, waiting for someone to go first.

"Okay, okay." Rahul laughed. "I'll go. Growing up in India, I saw abject poverty and suffering every day. I always knew that coming from a long line of privilege, I wanted to return one day and help my people in a very concrete way." As he spoke, Rahul's eyes sparkled with determination, his hands gesturing passionately.

One by one, the others followed. Linus, Razmig, and Nag—who'd been on a different team in the Stanford class and joined us afterward—shared heartfelt personal stories as well. Stories about where they'd come from. What they'd seen. Then it was my turn. I cleared my throat and set down my croissant.

"I want to bridge healthcare disparities around the world," I said. "I saw the injustice firsthand through my HIV/AIDS work. With Embrace, we can improve people's lives on a mass scale. My goal is to ensure access to healthcare for those who need it most."

Pleased with my speech, I leaned back and took a long sip of my tea. Rahul stared at me blankly from across the circle. "Nope."

I blinked. "*Nope?*"

"It's not clicking for me," he said. "That felt canned."

I turned to the others, but they nodded in agreement.

"Why are *you* doing this?" Rahul asked. "Not Inspirational Speech Jane, but you, Jane. The person. There's got to be something more personal."

I stared at him blankly. I hadn't grown up in India. I hadn't experienced extreme poverty. I wasn't a mother. Closing my eyes, I tried to dig deeper, to come up with something. There was no direct or immediate personal connection to the work that I could put my finger on. But I *felt* it. I felt the purpose and meaning deeply in a way that was sub-language.

I shifted in my chair, finally throwing up my arms. "I don't know."

But Rahul's question lingered. What others might have experienced as compassion, or in Rahul's case, a moral duty, felt like something entirely different inside me. It was an urgency— a fire—that burned with the force of rocket fuel. I didn't understand it. I just knew it was there. And I didn't know how to explain—to them, or even to myself at that point—that it wasn't just a calling. That it was, in fact, deeply personal.

After an awkward silence, Linus went to the white board. "Let's move on to the next agenda item. Moving to India."

"Well," said Rahul, "it's monsoon season now. Probably too soon to get the move arranged." It was September and we still needed to refine our prototype and set up clinical studies. "I say we shoot to be in India by mango season." Mangoes ripened in March, he said, and the season ended in August.

Mango season, I wrote on the white board. Linus grabbed the red marker and drew two ripe little fruits underneath.

He smiled and chuckled.

And then we all started laughing. Somehow those little fruits made it all more real.

"We're doing it," I said. "We're really doing it."

In that moment, it seemed anything was possible.

The plan was to refine and launch the product in one year. Once things were up and running, and the incubators were being distributed around the world, I would move back home. Then I could think about getting married and starting a family, like most of my other classmates were doing. Like all my old friends were doing. Like my parents wanted me to do.

But first I was going to move halfway around the world to save lives. It was only going to be a year.

How hard could it be?

CHAPTER 9

INDIAN STANDARD TIME

Nothing could have prepared me for India. Visiting had been one thing. Our research trip had been a single focused week. But building a home and a company in the land of a thousand gods was an entirely different undertaking. By the time I moved to India, I had traveled to more than thirty countries. I was no stranger to different ways of life, to languages I didn't speak or norms I didn't understand. But India was different from any place I'd ever been. It was a shock to my system.

We set up a base of operations in Bangalore, a city of 7 million in the southern state of Karnataka, known for its mild climate and manicured gardens. Bangalore was the Silicon Valley of India, home to tech giants like Infosys and Wipro—companies generating billions in revenue and helping to fuel India's booming economy. The city was a kaleidoscope of brightly painted buildings, intricately decorated rickshaws, and elaborate temples. Men wove through crowded streets, chattering in rapid-fire Kannada. Women in shimmering silk saris breezed past, leaving scented trails of rose and sandalwood. In one breath, the air carried the sweet scent of frangipani mixed with the acrid fumes of exhaust; in the next, it was thick with the spiced aroma of cumin and cardamom wafting from ramshackle roadside stalls.

Auto-rickshaws, cars, and motorcycles converged in a flood of traffic, seemingly moving in all directions at once. Horns honked constantly, cut through by the occasional bellow of a cow. Vehicles hurtled toward each other, looking like they were about to crash—only to swerve at the last second. It looked chaotic. And yet there was a rhythm to it, a fluid dance. Every movement was part of a greater pulsing organism that somehow made space for everyone.

The one thing everyone agreed on: braking for the Holy cow. In Hindu culture, the cow is sacred, a tenet taken more seriously than seemingly any other in the country. As for the rest, everything was a negotiation and open to interpretation. *Yes* could mean *maybe*. Red lights were optional; deadlines were merely suggestions. India was a place where extravagant wealth was slammed against abject poverty. A place that would test all my assumptions and push me to edges I didn't even know I had.

All the things that might have made India enchanting as a visitor made living and working there exhausting. Blackouts were so frequent I adapted to working by candlelight at night, flames flickering over my laptop keyboard. In the mornings, I timed my showers to three minutes so the hot water didn't run out mid-shampoo. Monkeys perched on my windowsill, peering in like nosy neighbors. And I had to dust the apartment every day to keep it clear of the heavy film of dirt that settled in from the city's constant construction.

And the ants. God, the ants. If I killed a hundred, three hundred more appeared in their place. They marched endlessly through the apartment in perfect formation, hunting down any microscopic crumb of food left behind. Every morning, I fished dead ant carcasses from my bedside water glass. I bought pest spray and sprayed down the house constantly, then swept up piles of tiny bodies. It worked for about twelve hours, until I had to spray again. My life became two modes—ants, no ants—just having sprayed, needing to spray. Eventually, I surrendered. Bleary-eyed in the mornings, I'd sit up in bed, wave to my window monkeys, reach for my glass, close my eyes, and chug the water down, ants and all. At least they were organic.

Time, I quickly learned, was a loose concept. Shortly after I arrived, I ordered a bed for my apartment. It was scheduled to be delivered the following Wednesday. When it didn't come, I called the store.

"Madam, please, what's the problem?" the clerk asked after I had just explained the problem.

"Well, I'm waiting for the bed?" I repeated, confused.

"Madam, most people, when they say Wednesday, they mean Saturday," he replied matter-of-factly, making it clear that *I* was the problem.

It wasn't just the bed. Everything operated on Indian Standard Time. Late was on-time. People rarely said no outright or admitted something couldn't be done. Often, they'd give a distinctive head bobble—a subtle side-to-side motion that could mean yes, no, maybe, or all of the above. I don't know if it was the chaos of the sheer number of people coexisting together, but Murphy's Law seemed magnified in India—exponential, almost. If anything *could* go wrong, it *would*. And it would certainly be delayed. Until Saturday. Which, apparently, was also Wednesday.

Our team had arrived bright-eyed and idealistic. Stanford degrees in tow, we were ready to change the world. But the first time I walked through a NICU in Bangalore, the grim reality of the situation hit me. We followed a nurse down a long stone corridor into a small room at the end. The air smelled like antiseptic. The room itself was windowless, its walls cloaked in peeling white paint. There were no traditional incubators here—only a few radiant warmers. Each machine had a metal frame with a padded mattress and a canopy that radiated heat to warm the babies. Three skeletal infants were crammed together into a single machine meant for one. Their tiny, wrinkled bodies looked impossibly fragile. Their eyes were scrunched shut and diapers hung loosely around their bony frames, barely clinging to their waists. Ants crawled across their exposed bellies.

The nurse led us farther into the unit. A cluster of clear plastic boxes pushed along the far wall caught my eye. I squinted to make out what was inside. And then it hit me. There, stacked in matching plastic boxes, were two infant corpses, their bodies still and lifeless. I gasped and rushed past the group, into the courtyard, desperate for air. I took a few deep breaths, trying to steady myself.

The situation in rural village clinics was far worse. We saw infants being warmed under old space heaters or cradled in boxes under lightbulbs, like Sujatha's baby. We heard story after story of babies being burned by malfunctioning heaters, of lightbulbs shattering over their bodies because of problems with circuits. We met families who'd sold everything they had to pay for medical care for their babies. Many were left destitute. The stories were endless, each more harrowing than the last. Everyone was doing the best they could with what little they had.

During one trip to a village, I met Chandu, a twenty-one-year-old woman whose premature baby had died a few months after birth. "When she died, I felt so much pain and agony, it was unbearable," Chandu said, her voice cracking as tears streamed down her face. "I held her close to me for hours and wept. I think about her every single day. What happened to me should never happen to anyone else." And yet it did, again and again. In some villages, it was customary not to name a baby until they were at least a month old—in case they didn't survive. Name or no name, the loss was no less real.

For months, we traveled around the country, showing our incubator prototype to mothers, doctors, and local healthcare workers, gathering their feedback. Designing a product simple enough to be universal turned out to be much more complex than we had imagined. If several doctors raised the same concern, we'd go back and refine our design, incorporating their suggestions. The changes weren't just functional. There were cultural adjustments too. Even something seemingly objective, like temperature, couldn't be assumed to be understood universally.

One weekend, we conducted a focus group in Uttar Pradesh, in north India. We showed a group of mothers in a village various features of the incubator, including the temperature gauge on the wax pouch. There was a numerical indicator, and when it fell below 98 degrees, the wax needed to be reheated. When we explained this, one mother bobbled her head and said in Hindi, "I don't trust Western medicine. If a doctor prescribes medication for my child, I cut it in half because Western medicine is too strong. Maybe 36 degrees Celsius [98 degrees Fahrenheit] is too warm for my baby. I'd keep the pouch below that."

The other women bobbled their heads in agreement.

Rahul and I shot each other a look. We'd never considered that temperature might be subjective. I scribbled notes in my notebook, underlining them in bold red ink. It was moments like this that reinforced why we had uprooted our lives and moved to India. Sitting in Palo Alto, designing in a bubble, we never would have uncovered such critical cultural nuances.

With this feedback, we replaced the numeric temperature indicator with a simpler, more intuitive one: a happy face and a sad face. When the pouch was at the correct temperature, the happy face lit up, and when it dropped below 98 degrees, the sad face lit up. A binary system left no room for interpretation.

As we were packing up to leave that day, a frail young woman in a tattered red sari approached us, cradling a newborn. Her face was creased with concern, her anxiety palpable.

Through a translator she explained, "My baby is just a week old. He's had a fever for days."

I looked down at the tiny bundle in her arms. Wrapped in a dirty cloth, the baby looked barely over two pounds. She explained that she didn't have 100 rupees—less than $2—for bus fare to the nearest government hospital. *Just like Sujatha.* But her baby was still alive. There was still a chance. Frantically, I dug through my wallet and handed her 500 rupees, about $10. With tears in her eyes, she thanked me.

"Of course," I murmured, trying to muster a reassuring smile. "Hurry. Go now."

As I watched her disappear into the distance, I couldn't shake the heaviness in my chest. I knew it might already be too late. Life felt so tenuous, so fragile. As we got in the car to leave, I was rattled, my limbs heavy with the weight of what might happen to that baby.

That night, I headed to Delhi, where I had planned to spend the weekend with some Indian friends from business school. They had invited me to a birthday party. After the sobering experience in Uttar Pradesh, going to a party was the last thing I wanted to do. Reluctantly, I swiped on some lipstick, slipped into a dress, and waited outside of the hotel for my friends. Soon, a fleet of black BMWs pulled up, and my friends waved me over.

As we stepped through the door of the hotel suite that had been rented for the party, it felt like I had entered an alternate universe. The floors were smooth white marble, and the chandeliers were waterfall tiers of dripping crystal. A DJ was stationed at the back, spinning hypnotic EDM beats that pulsed through the room. Waitstaff glided between guests with trays of absinthe and Champagne. In the center of the suite, people were dancing, while others lounged on velvet couches, sipping cocktails. The women were decked out in glamorous designer dresses and sparkling jewelry. The whole room shimmered. I'd felt fancy just putting on lipstick; back in Bangalore, I lived in Indian kurtas— long, comfortable cotton tops that felt like glorified pajamas. The contrast from that morning was startling.

"How's Embrace going?" asked a friend of a friend whose name I couldn't recall. The question hung in the air, impossible to answer. How could I sum up what I had just experienced? I evaded the question, turning to small talk instead. Everything felt hollow, unreal, meaningless. I slipped out onto the balcony to get some air. The Delhi skyline was a hazy rainbow of city lights and smog. Beyond the hotel's border, the light faded abruptly into darkness, dotted by faint flickers of candlelight. I leaned over the railing, squinting to get a better look. On a hillside below, rows of ramshackle tin structures with blue tarps for roofs leaned against each other like dominoes, each holding up the next. A shanty-town.

Inside, the bass thumped. I turned to see a woman dancing barefoot on the coffee table, holding a Champagne flute over her head. Laughter erupted from a group nearby, their voices rising above the music. I felt a rush of sadness. The cost of the party— every designer dress, every imported bottle of Champagne, every extravagant detail—could have fed that shantytown for weeks. Months, even.

It was hard to accept that these worlds existed right next to each other. And it was getting harder to understand which world I belonged to.

CHAPTER 10

AIRTIGHT COMPOSURE

Our one-year timeline to launch the Embrace incubator was laughable. There were so many things we hadn't anticipated. That first year, we went through dozens of iterations of the prototype. To demonstrate the safety and efficacy of the product, we helped organize a clinical study across three major hospitals in Bangalore—a logistical feat that took over a year of planning and coordination. We were elated when the results showed our product worked as well as radiant warmers, which were the standard of care. We couldn't find a local manufacturer that met international medical standards, so we set up our own manufacturing facility. From scratch. Something I never expected to do, and which none of us had experience in. But it was the only way to move things forward. After that, we went through the rigorous process of obtaining international regulatory approval. What had started as a small-team project had become a full-blown multi-tiered operation. We faced countless setbacks, but I was determined to blast every mishap and roadblock out of the way.

Most days, I tried to shove my anxiety down. But some days I thought my mother was right: I was a little kid driving a big car. To prep for team meetings, I wrote meticulous scripts, thinking carefully through every word I was going to say. One day, Rahul pulled me aside.

"Are you writing down everything you say?" he asked, raising his eyebrow.

I lifted my chin, defiant. "It helps organize my thoughts."

His eyes narrowed. "Mindset, Jane," he said, tapping his temple. "It's all up here."

Easy for you to say, I thought. He acted like mindset was a switch I could just flip. My mind felt more like a beehive, buzzing with self-doubt. For the mission, I could push past any negativity. But for myself, there was an endless stream of self-criticism. There was no use explaining that to Rahul. He wouldn't get it. I gave him a curt nod and grabbed my gym bag.

It was five P.M., my nonnegotiable hour for myself. I'd signed up for a gym on my block, where I ran on the treadmill every day and then spent ten minutes in the small steam room in the back. The steam room was always empty, and it became my sanctuary—the only place I could really let go and clear my head. I'd set an alarm and when my ten minutes were up, I'd go straight back to work. I worked seven days a week, fourteen or fifteen hours a day. Every morning, I woke up groggy, vowing to get six hours of sleep that night.

It never happened.

It soon became clear that we'd need to be in India much longer than expected. Everyone else settled in for the long haul, adopting a more sustainable pace. The rest of the team went out to dinners together, made friends with locals, or toured the gardens and temples. I just worked more. I figured the sooner we could get to the finish line, the sooner I could move home and get my life back. Every weekend, I planted myself with my laptop at the same table in the ITC Gardenia Hotel's open-air restaurant, drinking masala chai, becoming increasingly isolated and exhausted.

Between the time difference and my grueling schedule, it was difficult to keep in touch with family and friends back home. Even when I did talk to them, I was so drained that I didn't really want to talk about work. The life I was living and the problems I was facing were so far removed from their world, it seemed fruitless to try to explain.

Aside from running operations in India, fundraising was a key part of my job, and it was a constant effort. We were often down to our last month of payroll. As founders, we made sure everyone else was paid first, sometimes forgoing our own salaries. Every few months, I had to fly back to the States to solicit donations. Starting with Stanford's network and following every lead I could find, I attended ladies' luncheons in suburban Connecticut and spoke at Rotary Clubs. I shared our story, passed around the incubator, and made my pitch. The donations I gathered would sustain the organization for a few months before I'd have to come back and do it all over again.

One evening, a board member invited me to a dinner event at Stanford, where Bill Gates was the keynote speaker. After his talk, I made a beeline for the stage and pulled an incubator from my purse. I never left home without one anymore—opportunity could be around any corner

"Do you want to keep it?" I asked Gates after delivering my rapid-fire, sixty-second pitch.

He looked at me like I was a deranged infomercial host trying to sell him a ShamWow.

"Um . . . no thanks," he replied.

When I was back in San Francisco, Nancy let me crash in her guest bedroom. She'd gotten married, bought a house, and given birth to my first nephew, Kyle. On those trips, I worked all day, and when it was nighttime in California, I started taking calls with my team in Bangalore. The team would have been fine without me for a week, but my sense of duty was unrelenting. The only breaks I took were to spend time with Kyle. I'd hold him on my lap and read him stories, his soft, chubby limbs slack and warm against mine as he smiled and cooed.

Nancy came into the nursery one night to find me rocking Kyle and reading aloud from Jeff Sachs's *The End of Poverty*. "What the hell?" she asked.

"I want him to understand the social inequities of the world!" I laughed. "I think he gets it."

Nancy tossed me a picture book about pandas. "Try this."

"Okay, Okay, pandas it is," I said.

Kyle's eyes lit up at the panda book.

"I'm eating bamboo," he crowed, munching on his fingers. Kyle became the only source of lightness and play in my life. He loved to crack jokes. Nancy taught him to say "Arigato," which is Japanese for *thank you*. But he'd say "Arigatee!" instead, knowing it was one sound off and giggling every time. When we gave him his first bite of ice cream, his whole face lit up—and, watching him, mine did too. I loved seeing the world through his eyes. I taught him to call me Best Friend, which he thought was my actual name. When I was back in India, Nancy would send me videos of Kyle chirping messages into the camera. "Hi, Best Friend!" he'd say. When I was homesick, I'd watch them on repeat in my apartment, reminding myself why I was doing this work. So that babies all over the world could grow up healthy and happy, like Kyle.

The travel time from San Francisco back to Bangalore was twenty-four hours door-to-door, and it took me days to recover from each trip. The worst part was returning to India. My flight always landed in Bangalore at three A.M. I'd stand in a long line to get through customs, the fluorescent lights buzzing overhead, my body aching from the journey. Then I'd roll my suitcase through the echoing halls of the airport. I'd exit into the thick darkness outside, exhausted and already bracing for the challenges ahead. I'd get to the office by nine A.M., paste a smile on my face, and start tackling the endless list of demands.

Even as I gained confidence in my role, I couldn't shake the sense that I had something to prove. To me, being a leader meant I had to keep myself composed at all times. Someone could barge into my office with a full-blown crisis that had me on the edge of meltdown, and two minutes later, I'd be leading our all-hands meeting with a practiced smile. I could have won an Academy Award. *I'd like to thank my father for teaching me how to take an ass-beating like a soldier. And thank you to my mother for teaching me how to hide all challenges and pretend everything is fine.*

One day, between a particularly emotional field visit, a disagreement among the founders, and the latest series of vendors failing to deliver on their promises, I broke down crying in a meeting. The tears came suddenly and I couldn't stop them. Afterward, I was mortified.

The next day, Raghu, our head of marketing, stopped me in the hallway.

"Thank you for being vulnerable yesterday," he said.

"Oh!" I brushed my hair back, flustered. I'd hoped everyone had forgotten. "I'm sorry. I'm usually together."

"No," insisted Raghu. "I mean it. Seeing you soften is what we needed. It gives us permission to be vulnerable as well."

I looked at him blankly.

"We see you as this super-person," he explained. "Always so composed, never needing a break or sleep, never fazed by anything. But for the rest of us, it's unattainable."

He went on to tell me that everyone was tired. That the work we were doing was taxing, not just logistically but emotionally. Everyone felt it, but because I was at the helm and maintained such airtight composure, they felt they had to do the same. I stood there, letting his words sink in.

In trying to keep it together, I'd been inadvertently teaching my team what I'd been taught growing up: that emotional expression was dangerous. That showing vulnerability was weakness. I'd received these messages my whole life—as a woman, as an immigrant, as an Asian. To prove I could lead, I'd prioritized composure above connection. True leadership, I realized, wasn't about perfection or invincibility. It was about authenticity. And authenticity required vulnerability.

"Thank you for your honesty," I told Raghu.

What I did not know how to articulate to him, or even admit to myself at the time, was that I didn't actually know how to be vulnerable. And showing weakness was a skill I had never learned.

*

Joyce came to visit at the end of my first year in India. She was living in San Francisco and had just broken up with her boyfriend. I hadn't taken a single day off since arriving in India, so I decided her visit was a good excuse to take a break. I wanted to give my sister the real "Indian experience." I decided to center the trip on two things: spirituality and tigers.

First, I booked us a three-day "Art of Living" course at a guru named Sri Sri Ravi Shankar's ashram, outside of Bangalore. The course website promised to provide practical knowledge to deal with the daily challenges of life through yoga and relaxation exercises, meditation, and breathing techniques. *Perfect*. Post-ashram, I arranged what I imagined would be a glamorous tiger safari at

Bandipur National Park, a sprawling reserve five hours away, famous for the highest tiger and elephant populations in India.

First stop: enlightenment.

Shortly after Joyce arrived, we headed to the ashram, which was situated on a lush, sprawling property. The main meditation hall was a lotus-shaped building adorned with intricate wood carvings. Out front was an open-air courtyard flanked by towering trees and surrounded by small meditation rooms, yoga studios, and modest bunkhouses. Joyce's enthusiasm plummeted the moment she realized there was no hot water or toilet paper.

We headed to orientation, where an instructor detailed the course rules.

"Number one," she said. "Eat only food served in the cafeteria. No junk food, no meat, nothing 'impure.' The canteen on the grounds is for tourists only." She glanced around the room, making sure we were listening. "Rule number two: pay attention and observe all the learnings of class."

Our days consisted of multi-hour meditation sessions and a breathwork technique called Sudarshan Kriya—long, deep breaths, followed by quick, forceful exhales through the nose. "Breath is the main source of prana—the vital life-force energy," the instructor explained, circling the room. "And prana is the basis of health and well-being. When prana is high, one feels alert and energetic."

My prana must have been on empty. The second I closed my eyes, I fell asleep sitting upright. Every time we sat to meditate, I dropped into a narcoleptic trance. Instead of achieving enlightenment, I looked like a tranquilized meerkat. During one session, we were instructed to bow to the four cardinal directions, placing our foreheads gently on the ground with each bow. The moment my forehead hit the ground, I was out cold.

The assistant shook me awake gently. "Madam! Sorry, madam?"

"Huh?" I jerked upright, pretending I had been bowing with spiritual fervor. From the corner of my eye, I saw Joyce snickering.

So much for rule number two.

Rule number one didn't take either. After a day of bland dhal—unseasoned, soupy lentils—and overcooked rice, Joyce and I started plotting a trip to the forbidden canteen. When the afternoon meditation ended, we slipped away from the group. Like outlaws in yoga pants, we donned oversized sunglasses and darted around trees and buildings to blend in with a group of tourists shuffling down the corridors. We snapped photos and nodded solemnly as the guide spoke about Sri Sri's awakening.

"Ooooh!" Joyce said suddenly, pointing at a coconut vendor beyond the fence.

Glancing behind us to make sure we weren't being watched, we scurried away from the group and dashed through the ashram's gates.

"Why do I feel like we're escapees?" Joyce asked.

We were giddy as we approached the cart.

"Two coconuts, please," I said to the vendor in my best Indian accent, bobbling my head side to side. He flashed a big grin, hacked off the tops of the coconuts with a machete, stuck a straw in each, and passed them over.

"Why are you talking like that?" Joyce asked as we walked back toward the ashram. "You're faking an Indian accent!"

"Helps me blend in," I told her, taking a sip of my coconut.

"I'm not going to lie. It's impressive," Joyce said. "I also didn't know you could sleep while sitting upright *and* chanting."

"Me either." I shrugged. "There's a lot of things I didn't know I could do before this year."

"You sure you're okay, though?"

"Yeah, what do you mean?"

"You're basically narcoleptic," she said.

I waved away her concern. "We just have to get through this next push."

"That's what you said last month."

"This is what it takes to run a company, okay?!" I snapped.

"Jesus," she muttered as we walked back through the ashram gates. "I'm just . . . I'm worried about you."

"I'm fine! You're the one going through a breakup. Why are we talking about me?"

Joyce groaned. "Ugh, I'm so miserable here, I had almost forgotten about my broken heart."

The next morning, I woke feeling more refreshed than I had all year. I heard Joyce groaning next to me. I rolled over in bed and gasped. Overnight, she'd been bitten by mosquitoes, and the bites on her chin had swelled into one huge, pus-filled welt. We went to the main hall and told the teacher that while we were so looking forward to another day in paradise, my sister was unfortunately not feeling well, and we would have to leave at once.

He nodded empathetically. "A blessing for the ill before you go?" he asked.

Joyce shrugged. Touching a hand gently to her forehead, he recited a Sanskrit mantra.

"May you be in great health and happiness," he concluded with a bow and Namaste.

"Teacher," I said sweetly, "could I also receive a blessing?"

He nodded. "May you be well," he said flatly, giving my forehead an abrupt tap.

I couldn't blame him for rushing my blessing. I'd been an awful student.

We bowed and said our thanks, then rushed toward the parking lot, where a cab was waiting to take us back to Bangalore.

A few days later, we headed to Bandipur, which was considered one of India's most beautiful national parks. It had once been the private hunting grounds of Indian kings, but was now 200,000 acres of protected land, home to antelope, deer, elephants, and tigers. The ashram hadn't been the relaxing experience I'd hoped for. But Joyce loved animals, and I couldn't wait to see her face light up at the sight of a real tiger in the wild.

Rahul had recommended a luxury resort in the area, and I'd asked my assistant to book it. "So glad we're doing this," I said as we settled into the back of the cab for the long ride south. "And it's supposed to be five-star. No more cafeteria gruel." Visions of plush linens, gourmet meals, and infinity pools danced in my head.

As the pocked highway stretched on and on, we passed grand resorts, each more lavish than the last.

"Oooh, maybe that's ours?" we'd exclaim.

But the driver kept going until, finally, we arrived at our destination: a decrepit inn clinging to the edge of a rocky mountainside. Scraggly trees dotted the barren landscape.

"Sir, I'm sorry," I called to the driver. "There must be a mistake."

I repeated the name of the hotel. He shook his head. After some back and forth, we figured out that there were two hotels with the same name. My assistant must have booked the wrong one. I groaned and slid down in my seat.

"Who cares?" Joyce chirped. She jumped out of the car and yanked her bag from the trunk. "At least we'll get to see tigers!"

I shrugged and followed her lead. After we checked in and freshened up, we met our guide, Santi, in the lobby. "I will be your guide on safari," he announced, bobbling his head enthusiastically. He led us to an old white pickup with tires that looked one pothole away from imploding. We climbed into the bed of the truck, where they had installed makeshift benches. After about an hour, the surrounding trees hadn't thickened at all. There was scrub brush covering small hills, with an occasional boulder. The only things we'd seen were a crumbling old temple and a banyan tree.

Suddenly, Santi held up his hand. "Now we are entering the deep forest," he said, his voice dropping into a hushed, dramatic tone. Excited, we looked around. Nothing had changed. Just more scraggly trees. Joyce and I rolled our eyes and kept chatting. She was telling me about what had happened with her ex.

"I couldn't see it at first," she said. "He was super unreliable, you know?"

I nodded. "It's hard when you can't trust someone to be there."

"NOW!" Santi interrupted, his voice booming. "We are entering the deep, *deep* forest!" We looked around again, scanning for something new. But it was more of the same.

"Are we going to see any animals?" I asked, trying to mask my annoyance.

"Ohhhhhhh *yes*!" Santi proclaimed. "You may see some wild . . ." His voice dropped to a mysterious whisper. Joyce and I leaned in. "Dogs!"

Joyce stifled a laugh.

"And up ahead," he went on, with the gravitas of a Shakespearean actor delivering a monologue, "is . . . a COW!"

"Cows are everywhere," I said flatly. "It's India."

"Yes, madam, you are correct," he said. "But this is a special cow, with *poooooowerful milk.*"

Joyce and I exchanged looks. It was at that moment we realized this "safari" was nothing more than a slow car ride through the bushes. We'd been duped.

That night, back at the hotel, we weren't served dinner until ten P.M., because the male guests were served first. By the time we ate, the food was cold. After dinner, we tried to make the most of it and sat around the outdoor fire pit. As the logs crackled and I breathed in the rich, woodsy smoke, I tried to relax. I'd been so excited for Joyce to see the animals and bummed that I couldn't deliver. But I'd lost sight of what was important. We were here, together. I ordered a Fanta, hoping for something sweet and fizzy to lift my spirits. The server handed me a cold bottle, and when I took a sip, I got a chilled mouthful of chemically orange syrup. The soda was totally flat. I looked at the expiration date on the bottle. Over two years ago.

The expired Fanta broke me. I launched into a tirade, screaming at the hotel guide, at the front desk, at the hotel manager, at anyone within earshot, demanding a refund for the room, the fake safari, the cold meal, the flat Fanta. They barely flinched. Everyone went back to business as usual, avoiding eye contact.

"Let's just go," Joyce said quietly, ushering me away. "Come on. We can leave in the morning."

On the drive home, I called my assistant and barked at her for booking the wrong hotel, even though it was an innocent mistake. Later, I snapped at Joyce over something petty.

"I'm so sorry," I apologized after.

Why was I taking my frustrations out on my brokenhearted sister, who'd flown halfway around the world to see me? She was the only one in my family who cared enough to visit and under-stand what Embrace was really about. I'd wanted to be there for her during her breakup. Instead, I was lashing out. I felt like shit.

She accepted the apology, but her face was leaden. "You better change something," Joyce said. "This is going to wreck you. You need to set some boundaries."

I knew she was right. But I understood boundaries about as well as I understood weakness.

I didn't hear my body yelling, *Stop, stop, stop* until it finally had enough.

And by then, it was already too late.

CHAPTER 11

ANTIDOTE TO DESPAIR

"This better save lives," Triloki, one of our junior engineers, muttered under his breath. "Because it ruined mine." He'd been pulling all-nighters for weeks. We all had. Almost two years after we'd landed in Bangalore, it was finally launch day.

Our progress had been slow and circuitous. Every imaginable issue had cropped up in the final weeks leading up to the launch. The wash tags on the sleeping bags were sewn on incorrectly. The electricity in the manufacturing facility cut out in the worst moments. The temperature indicators got stuck in customs—the officials threatened to toss them into the Bay of Bengal unless we paid a bribe. We refused, and after days of pleading, they were finally released. It felt like a miracle when all the pieces came together.

We were finally ready to hand-deliver the incubator to our very first customer, a doctor who operated a small clinic outside of the city. He'd placed his order months earlier, after we'd demonstrated the product at a local medical conference, and had been waiting patiently since. But first, the puja. Our Indian team wanted to hold a spiritual blessing for the incubator. In Hindu tradition, pujas were done for special events, like the birth of a baby or the beginning of a new venture. In some ways, this was both.

The energy was electric as our team of thirty clustered around an altar we'd built on top of a stack of boxes. Someone lit a stick of sandalwood incense, and the smoke snaked through the air as we draped strands of marigolds over the boxed incubator. Sajju, our head of operations, lit a candle and then crushed a whole melon on the floor, which was meant to ward off evil spirits. He launched into a melodic prayer to bless the incubator.

After the puja, we hired a driver to take us to the doctor's clinic. I set the box gently in the trunk of the car, as nervous as if it were an actual baby. Four of us climbed into the taxi, including Rajan, the first engineer we had hired out of Stanford. We were giddy with excitement. As we drove outside the city, the streets grew bumpier. We turned down a narrow, potholed road. Suddenly, there was a loud *thunk,* and the car lurched to one side. The driver slowed to a stop.

"You've got to be kidding me," Rajan groaned. He jumped out of the car. "Flat tire!"

I started to laugh. It was either that or cry.

We clambered out of the car, staring at the sagging wheel. A few minutes later, we flagged down a passing auto-rickshaw. The four of us squeezed in; I sat in the center, the incubator nestled in my lap. The rickshaw sped off as fast as its little motor could go, puttering down the road riddled with potholes. It felt like a slapstick version of *Indiana Jones.* There we were, crammed into a clown car, carrying precious cargo and a dream. As we bumped down the road, a hot, dusty wind blew through the rickshaw. I looked at the faces of the guys around me, bleary-eyed but pushing on. I felt a surge of gratitude, for this moment and for every person on our team who had helped us get to this point. Without their tenacity and commitment, we wouldn't have made it this far.

Thirty minutes later, we pulled up to the clinic, tucked away on the edge of a dusty road. The young doctor greeted us and led us through a narrow corridor to the supply room, where he cleared a space on the cluttered counter. I carefully removed the incubator from its box, placing it down gently. Then, step by step, I walked the staff through how to use it.

The doctor stepped out, then returned a moment later, carrying a baby swaddled in a soft white cloth. "She was born this morning," he told us. He placed her in my arms. She was tiny, with golden-hued skin and a full head of glossy brown hair. I carefully placed her into the incubator, securing the Velcro fasteners. Her eyelids fluttered closed, and she drifted into a peaceful sleep, cocooned in warmth. My heart flooded with love for our tiny first customer.

Shortly after the launch, we returned to the first village we had visited to do our research. We brought the incubator to show the women who had helped shape its design. They gathered around it, examining every detail. I pulled Sujatha aside. During that first visit, we had filmed her sharing her story. We had edited the footage and I wanted her to see it. I opened my laptop and pressed play. Sujatha's face filled the screen as she recounted the stories of the babies she'd lost. At first, she watched in silence. Then her hands began to tremble. Moments later, she erupted into deep, wrenching sobs.

My eyes filled with tears as I watched her witnessing herself— as I saw her recognize the weight of her own story. The raw emotion was such a contrast to the stoic composure she'd had when I first met her. And in that moment, some part of me understood. Surviving trauma and confronting its aftermath are two different experiences. Some of us never get beyond mere survival. Sometimes, we have to step outside of ourselves to really understand what we lived through—to extend the same compassion to ourselves that we might offer someone else. It seemed, in that moment, that Sujatha was truly feeling her grief for the first time.

"If I had this incubator," she said through tears, "maybe I could have saved my children."

Her words pierced me. I was too late to help her, but I vowed not to be too late for others like her. No matter what it took. I hugged Sujatha, and as we embraced, I couldn't tell where her pain ended and mine began.

Orders started to trickle in for the incubators. Then, we got a call from the producers of the news show *20/20*. They were running a series on global health and wanted to film a segment on Embrace. They sent a reporter to India, who spent days capturing our journey. The production team filmed us walking through the streets as I recounted our origin story and mission: *That any family who needs an incubator will have access. That no premature baby will die from being cold.* The reporter interviewed the rest of the team, local doctors who had tested the product, and Sujatha, who graciously shared her story again.

When the segment aired, we watched it together as a team. After so many years of hard work, it was a proud, surreal moment. I couldn't believe how far we had come.

Joyce called me after watching it.

"I am *so* proud of you!" she shouted. "I've been playing it every morning when I get ready for work. It's so inspiring!"

Nancy sent a video of Kyle.

"Hiiiii, Best Friend!" he said, sticking his face close to the camera and waving chaotically. "You're a very important person!"

Old classmates and professors from Stanford reached out to congratulate us. Embrace had become the darling of the d.school. Stanford University's president, John Hennessy, started talking about Embrace in his speeches to alumni. In rapid succession, we were featured in major news outlets, including *Time, National Geographic, The Wall Street Journal,* and *Forbes.* With all the press, requests for donations of incubators came in from Africa, South America, and across Asia.

One of the first requests was from an orphanage in Beijing, where we donated a few incubators. Shortly after they arrived, the orphanage reached out to tell us they'd rescued a two-pound baby who'd been abandoned on a street. He'd already gone for days without food and water, and they weren't sure if he was going to make it. They kept him warm in our incubator for weeks. He survived, and was growing stronger by the day.

A few months later, I was in Beijing for a conference and arranged to visit the orphanage. When I walked around the nursery, one of the caregivers lifted the baby from his crib and handed him to me. I cradled him to my chest, rocking him gently. I could feel his heartbeat against mine.

"Look at you," I whispered. He gurgled in response, his bright, curious eyes meeting mine. "You beautiful boy. Just look at you."

"He loves to be held," the caregiver told me with a smile. "He gets upset anytime we're *not* holding him."

A few months after my visit, I received an email from a family in Chicago who had adopted the little boy. They named him Nathan. *We're so grateful for your organization and the role you played in saving his life. Thank you.*

I was overcome with emotion. This baby hadn't just survived—he now had a family and a chance to live a full life. That single thank-you made every struggle and sleepless night worthwhile. Nathan's story touched our entire team. A picture of him crawling and smiling became the screen saver for our communal office computer. It was a reminder of why we were doing this work. We hoped this could be our *antidote to despair*.

Even with all the attention, we were constantly on the brink of running out of funds. We needed a more sustainable model to keep going. Back in Silicon Valley, a new breed of "impact investors" was emerging. These investors funded for-profit companies with a mission to create social impact. Suddenly, everyone was talking about purpose. Customers wanted products with purpose, and they wanted their money to make a difference. Companies like TOMS shoes and Warby Parker were having success with their one-for-one models, weaving purpose into the core of their business strategy. A few impact investors had expressed interest in funding Embrace, but our nonprofit structure made it impossible.

We decided to make a bold move and spin out a for-profit arm. A for-profit entity would allow us to raise capital from impact investors, giving us financial resources to grow more quickly and ultimately deliver more incubators to communities in need. Our plan was to have two separate but complementary organizations: the nonprofit would continue raising donations to distribute free incubators to the most vulnerable communities, while the for-profit would focus on product development, manufacturing, and selling the incubators to paying customers like private hospitals and governments. We believed aligning profit with purpose was our best shot at achieving long-term impact.

To announce the change, I wrote an article for *Harvard Business Review:*

The challenges that social entrepreneurs are trying to solve are some of the most formidable problems in the world, in areas with significant market failures, poor governance, and a complete lack of infrastructure. Effectively tackling problems in this environment may require leveraging both capital and expertise from grant makers and private investors alike.

We hired a new team to manage the nonprofit, while our existing team pivoted to lead the for-profit. To raise money for our for-profit, we approached Vinod Khosla, the iconic founder of Sun Microsystems, and one of Silicon Valley's most influential venture capitalists. Vinod was a visionary investor who wanted to reinvent social infrastructure. He was on the lookout for "Black Swan" technologies—high-risk innovations with the potential to create massive social and environmental impact. To support initiatives like ours, he had recently launched the Khosla Impact Fund. After turning me down for months, he finally agreed to meet. I was ecstatic—and nervous. During the three-hour discussion, he asked us a defining question: "If you had to choose one, would you make money or impact?"

"Impact," I answered, without a second thought.

It was a risky response. Though the culture might have been shifting toward purpose, investors still prioritized financial returns. But my answer was honest. If we had valued money over impact, we wouldn't have chosen this path. With our education and skills, there were far easier ways to make money. Almost *anything* would have been easier than what we were attempting.

A few days later, Vinod made an offer to invest in our company. With him as our lead investor, we attracted other major investors and quickly raised $5 million. Up until then, we'd been scraping by, begging for every penny, piecing together just enough to keep the company running. Suddenly, doors I'd been knocking at for years swung open with ease. We were now part of the inner sanctum of Silicon Valley, seated at tables like Vinod

Khosla's CEO Summit. Every year, he invited his partners and start-up founders to a fancy hotel in Marin for a weekend of networking and insight.

Rahul and I drove to the event together. When we arrived at the hotel, the valet greeted us with a polite smile.

"The spa is just down the hall past the elevators, ma'am," he said.

I bit my tongue and nodded, then picked up my room key and headed to the executive mixer. The room buzzed with the energy of Silicon Valley's elite—the Who's Who of the tech world. But out of at least 100 CEOs attending, there were only a handful of women. It was 2011, and only 8 percent of all venture-backed CEOs were women. Even fewer were women of color.

Vinod graciously introduced us to his VIP guests, including Tony Blair, the former prime minister of the United Kingdom. He even arranged a private meeting with Bill Gates, an investor in his fund. After giving our presentation, I offered Bill the incubator once again. This time, he smiled and accepted it.

I figured that once we had funding secured, I could relax and breathe for a moment. *Wrong.* Instead, it raised the stakes even more. Now that we had investors to answer to, the pressure mounted. A start-up is like a premature baby. Every day can mean the difference between life and death. The odds were daunting—75 to 90 percent of start-ups fail within the first five years. As CEO, you're focused on one critical number: the *runway*. This is your lifeline. It's the cash you have, divided by your monthly expenses, which determines exactly how many days you can keep going. To survive, you must generate enough revenue to offset your expenses before your money runs out. Decisions need to be made quickly. Delays aren't just setbacks, they're existential threats. Time is literally money.

To push forward, we hired sales representatives across India to market and sell the product. They went door-to-door to private doctors and knocked on the gates of government agencies. Securing government contracts was critical to getting our product distributed across the country, especially the most remote areas, but the process was bureaucratic, opaque, and often corrupt. In parallel, we started to develop add-on technologies to the incubator, like sensors for diagnostics. Our goal was to eventually develop a portfolio of products.

As we grew our team in India, we needed a bigger office. We found the cheapest building that met our needs—a bare-bones structure with just four walls and a roof. It had no flooring or windows. We laid Astroturf ourselves and hired contractors to build the office from the ground up. Week after week, I'd visit the site, only to find it in chaos. Wires hung from open sockets, piles of drywall were stacked in the corners, and there was plaster everywhere. After months with no visible progress, I stormed in, my patience gone. "If this is not done in the next week," I shouted, "every single person in this room is *fired*!" A few weeks later, it was done. In India, I had to be patient yet assertive; diplomatic yet ready to slam my foot on the gas when needed.

When I first arrived in India, my singular goal was to launch Embrace. In the process, I learned how essential it was to build a strong, cohesive team. We hired dozens of people from different religions, castes, and socioeconomic backgrounds. My cofounders and I defined a core set of values: *Passion to change the world, Empathy, Respect, Boldness, and Innovation.* We encouraged taking risks and learning from our mistakes. Every Friday, we held a "Meet, Think & Solve" session, where we tackled challenges together, brainstorming solutions as a team. Empathy had been the driving force behind developing our incubators, and we tried to infuse this into every aspect of our work. At our weekly meetings, we recognized team members who went above and beyond in showing kindness and care, whether toward colleagues or customers.

One day, one of our junior engineers from Bihar, one of the poorest states in India, told me how working at Embrace had inspired him to live out these values in his own life.

"I've never been in a place where everyone's opinion is heard and respected," he said. For the first time, he felt seen, and that sense of recognition had started to ripple outward, shifting how he viewed the world around him.

"Just the other day," he told me, "a rickshaw driver was being beaten by someone from a higher caste for something petty. That sort of thing happens all the time. And no one does anything . . . we all just watch." He looked down for a moment.

In many parts of India, the caste system—though officially outlawed—still shapes daily life. People from lower castes often face discrimination and violence. Generations have grown up learning to stay silent—to not challenge the system.

"This time," he continued, meeting my eyes, "I stepped in and stopped the beating. Now I believe it's my duty to stand up for those with less power."

"Yes," I said. "You're right. It's something we can all do."

It was so easy to get lost in the endless tangle of logistics and firefighting. But moments like this helped me see that our impact wasn't just about incubators. It was about empowering people by helping them believe they could make a difference.

As Embrace's visibility grew, so did mine. As the CEO, and the only woman on the leadership team, I became the face of the company. Suddenly, I was thrust into the spotlight, fielding interviews, speaking on panels, and being featured in the news. While I always emphasized the collective effort of our team, the media often gravitated toward a singular hero narrative—the scrappy CEO leading the way. In rapid succession, I was named a TED Fellow, a Young Global Leader by the World Economic Forum, and one of *Forbes*'s Impact 30. I received a string of other honors that I'd never dreamt of. We hadn't started Embrace for recognition, but after all the hard work, it felt validating. Especially on the hard days.

Embrace was being showcased not only at Stanford, but in technology museums and textbooks around the world. At the Clinton Global Initiative in New York, I pinched myself when Queen Rania of Jordan mentioned Embrace as an example of social innovation on the opening panel alongside Bill Clinton, Jim Kim (then president of the World Bank), and Ban Ki-moon (then secretary general of the United Nations). I was even invited to meet with the princess of Serbia—in her castle. Mom's table-manners training came in handy. When I told her about the royal visit, I made sure to mention that I did *not eat with my knees up*, like the vegetable sellers in Taiwan.

I was thrilled to receive an invitation to the World Economic Forum meeting in Davos, Switzerland. This exclusive gathering brought together the world's elite leaders, sprinkled with celebrities, set against the stunning backdrop of the Swiss Alps. The event was glamorous beyond belief. I crashed Bono's party, unabashedly fangirling as I professed my love. I attended a surprise private performance by Mary J. Blige. I even danced with the crown prince of Norway. Everywhere I turned, I was brushing shoulders with someone famous.

Since blacking out during my talk at Stanford, I'd come to rely on beta-blockers to calm my nerves anytime I had to speak in front of an audience in a high-pressure setting. And now I was constantly in high-pressure settings, so I'd started to lean on them more. With each new tier of success came new fears. Being shot into the public eye started to take its toll. I felt myself disappearing into performance. I could show up, sit down, smile, and speak on cue. As long as I had my magic pills.

On the outside, everything was fine.

On the inside, I was exhausted and terrified of failing.

But we were going full speed, and there was no getting off the ride.

CHAPTER 12

PRANAYAMA

I flew home that Christmas. Our first few years in America, my parents had gone all out for the holidays. But over time, our celebrations had petered out. Not just Christmas, but celebrations of any kind. Even our birthdays were acknowledged at random, if at all. Some years, we would get a cake and presents. Other years, the day would pass without a word, like any other.

As kids, Joyce and I would buy each other Christmas presents and set them under a wooden table in the hallway that we pretended was a tree. But eventually, I grew to loathe the holidays, always bracing for the inevitable letdown. By sixth grade, I'd banished Christmas from my heart altogether. No one could take away my holiday spirit if I didn't have any.

I don't know if Mom felt bad about the sporadic holidays of our childhood, but after we left for college, she'd started to throw celebrations every year. When I got home that year, Joyce had set up a beautiful, bushy tree in the living room. Underneath it were tidy piles of presents with big gold bows, mostly for Kyle, who was now three. Stockings for everyone were hung on the mantel, and a CD of generic Christmas classics played on the stereo. It was everything I'd wished for as a kid.

I dropped my bags by the door and wandered into the kitchen, where a savory aroma filled the air.

"Hi, Mom," I said.

"Xiao Yu!" she beamed, her face lighting up as she stirred a pot on the stove. She was making you fan—sticky rice with pork, mushrooms, dried shrimp, and fried shallots—traditionally served at family gatherings and celebrations. Mom had spent all day preparing our favorite dishes. As she finished making dinner, Joyce and I set up the dining table.

Dad emerged from the garage with a box of chintzy crystal goblets that he'd scored on sale. Dad couldn't resist a deal. He'd drive across town just to save 5 cents per gallon on gas and kept hundreds of rolls of cheap toilet paper stacked high in the garage as if preparing for the apocalypse. He especially loved buying discounted special-occasion items. He stashed his treasures away for safekeeping, bringing them out only on the holidays.

"Jia bung!" Mom shouted from the kitchen. *Time to eat!* We all filed in to help carry dishes to the table. I brought out the plate of turkey Dad had carved and set it in the middle, next to Joyce's creamy mashed potatoes and Stove Top stuffing. Nancy set down the sticky rice, and her husband carried the pork-rib soup and fried rice noodles. Joyce followed with a big plate of freshly steamed shell-on shrimp. Dad popped bottles of Martinelli's sparkling apple cider and filled our glasses. "Goody-goody!" he exclaimed with a big smile.

"Happy Christmas," we cheered, raising our glasses in a toast. The room went silent, except for the sounds of pleased grunts and the tinkle of silverware and chopsticks against plates. Mom had taken only a few bites of her food before she started to peel shrimp, methodically, one by one, and set them on our plates.

"Mom, I can peel my own," I told her. "Eat your food!"

She just smiled and kept peeling.

"Your uncle from Taiwan went to Paris for the first time and got pickpocketed," Mom shared with us.

"There's an easy solution to that," Dad chimed in, his face serious. "Just keep crabs in your pocket, and you will never be pickpocketed."

"Who has spare crabs to keep in their pocket?" Joyce asked, as we all burst out laughing.

Joyce inhaled her plate, then retreated to the couch and fell into a food coma. I ate slowly, biting into one sweet, tender shrimp after another. I hadn't realized how much I missed my family, our food, and these moments together. Maybe it was because Nancy had a child now, but everyone seemed more excited to be together. I'd been in India for nearly three years. I was so tired. Tired of the chaos, tired of working around the clock, tired of being so far from home.

After we finished eating, Nancy cleared the dishes and I got to work on dessert, pulling cinnamon and sugar from the cupboard. Every year, I made an apple pie with a puff-pastry crust. While I worked, hands deep in dough, Mom sat down at the piano in the living room and sang "O Holy Night," her favorite Christmas song. She'd started attending a Taiwanese Presbyterian church and had joined the choir. Many of the women were first-generation Taiwanese immigrants. My mother had never believed in God when we were growing up, but now she attended church every Sunday and prayed daily.

"They say I'm the best singer in the group," she beamed after she finished the song.

It was nice to see Mom stand a little taller. She had become a pillar of her church community, the person everyone turned to when they needed support. If there was a crisis—big or small—Mom was the one they called. She always listened patiently and offered thoughtful advice. If someone was sick, she brought them homemade Taiwanese food. I loved that she had found a group of friends who appreciated her generosity and kindness—and her cooking.

After pie, we gathered around the Christmas tree. Kyle tore the paper off his presents in great big strips. When he saw the toy car hidden underneath, a huge smile spread on his face and he jumped up and down with excitement.

"Mine next!" I said, handing him another box. He tore it open and pulled out a small, baby-blue terrycloth robe with "BF" embroidered on the chest.

"What do you say?" Nancy asked.

"Thank you, Best Friend!" Kyle shouted, flinging his arms around my neck in a big hug. I hugged him back, until he wriggled out of my arms, giggling. His happiness was contagious.

Later that night, I followed Nancy as she put Kyle to bed, lingering in the doorway. We stood in silence, watching his eyelids droop and flutter, the slow rise and fall of his chest. I imagined getting all the sleep I wanted, like my nephew, and felt a twinge of envy.

"He's so big now," I whispered.

"Aw," Nancy said. "You want a baby."

I shrugged. "I don't know . . . I just love Kyle."

"It'd be such a shame if you didn't have a kid," she said. "You'd be a great mom."

Watching my nephew grow up made the passage of time painfully clear. I wanted to get married and have a family someday, but I always figured it would just happen when the time was right. Now I was approaching thirty-five, living abroad, and working hundred-hour weeks with no serious romantic prospects. I'd tried a couple long-distance relationships, but nothing stuck. My last boyfriend had complained that I was married to Embrace.

Later that night, while everyone slept, Mom stayed up stuffing our stockings and writing letters from Santa Claus—a tradition she'd started since we'd left home. Santa's English wasn't perfect, but it improved every year. He said the things that Mom couldn't say to us directly. In my twenties, I'd been dating a guy casually, and Santa's note that year read something like: "Your mom told me that you're dating someone new. Don't go too far before you get to know him. *You know what I mean.* Ho! Ho! Ho!"

The next morning, we rushed to our stockings as soon as we woke up. I pulled out my letter from Santa. It was longer than usual:

Dear Jane: You parents and I are very proud of what you did. We never thought you will go so far and your dreams are so big. It must be very difficult to be a CEO. Sometimes we are worry about your health. You always stay up too late, but you are a big girl now. Hope you will take good care of yourself and hope you will find a good husband soon. I think your parents are very lucky to have such a nice daughter. You are very kind, understanding and generous. Hope you can come back to America soon. You live too far away now. Your mom miss you very much all the time. Have a nice new year and happy holidays. Ho! Ho! Ho!—Santa

It was touching to have Mom, via Santa, acknowledge my work. I tucked the letter away for safekeeping. Maybe Santa was right. Maybe it was time to come back to America.

After the holidays, I mustered the courage to tell the board that I wanted to move home and step down as CEO. I would transition to the role of Chief Business Officer and work remotely from San

Francisco, where I would be responsible for securing partnerships, managing investor relations, and serving as a spokesperson for Embrace. I was eager to step away from running day-to-day operations.

We hired a search firm to help us find a new CEO. I wasn't going to leave my baby to just anyone. The ideal candidate had to embody the values of the company and care about our team as much as I did. We needed a CEO with a balance of business acumen and heart. Someone who understood this wasn't just a business—it was a mission. We searched the entire country of India for candidates, but no one seemed to fit the bill. At the time, purpose-driven work wasn't the norm. Many candidates we interviewed had practical business skills, but lacked the vision and passion for the social impact we aspired to achieve.

Six months into the search, I was despondent. I called Sanjiv, a grandfatherly mentor who'd recently come on board as an adviser. A retired executive from a multinational medical device company, he had both the skills and the heart for the role. I had approached him before, but he had turned me down; he wasn't looking for another job. Still, I was convinced he was the one.

"You're the only one I can trust," I told him. "Would you please, please consider taking the role?"

Sanjiv finally agreed to discuss it with his wife. Early the next morning, he called me back. "I'll do it," he said. I leapt up from the couch in joy. "Thank you, thank you, thank you!" I cried before hanging up and sprinting circles around the apartment like an overexcited golden retriever.

During my final weeks in India, I felt a million pounds lighter. Counting down the days until the transition, I did my work with renewed energy and found myself reflecting nostalgically on the last four years. We had faced so many challenges. Living amidst so much death and poverty had been incredibly hard. But for every tragedy, I realized, I had seen something equally beautiful—moments of resilience, kindness, and unexpected grace. I teared up thinking of all the people who had come together over the years to bring Embrace into the world. I thought about the doctors I'd met in villages who saw patients late into the night. Doctors who, like my own grandfathers, had put the well-being of others above everything else. But what I'd been most privileged to see up close, again and again, was the boundless love a parent has for their child. Every day, I witnessed parents—no matter how little they had—go to extraordinary lengths to save their babies. Their love and determination were unwavering, even in the face of impossible odds.

We get to choose the lens through which we see the world.

I wanted to choose the lens of beauty.

At the last team meeting I led in India, I stood in front of our team of nearly eighty people. They had become like family to me.

"It has been the greatest honor of my life to lead this team," I said, my voice raw with emotion. "I still remember when we were first setting out on this journey. Rahul said to me, 'No matter what happens, we're going to make our mark on the world.' And that's exactly what we've done. Each of you has made a mark—by saving lives, by helping others, by showing what's possible with passion, dedication, and purpose."

Looking at the team, I felt both pride and gratitude. I thought back to the conversation with Denise, who didn't believe I was fit to be a CEO. In the years since, I had proven otherwise. I had built and inspired a team. I had raised millions of dollars. I had launched a lifesaving product, crafted a strategy, and, together with this fiercely hardworking team, we had saved more than 50,000 lives. *Fifty thousand lives.*

I had done all the things I once believed I couldn't because I stayed committed to our mission. Even when I didn't feel worthy, and even when I questioned my own abilities. "I can't tell you all how grateful I am to each of you," I said. "And while there's still a lot of work ahead, I am certain we will reach our goal of saving one million lives—and beyond."

My last week in India, I got a tattoo on my arm.

Pranayama. The Sanskrit word for breath. In yogic philosophy, it also meant *the expansion of individual life force into universal energy.*

My time in India would forever be marked by just that—the potential for good that comes when people join together in service of something bigger than themselves.

Pranayama.

Breath.

I could finally breathe again.

CHAPTER 13

ENJOY THE MOMENT

Back in San Francisco, I felt like a mole who'd emerged after years underground. I was still working with my team in India, but immediately had more balance in my life. I was bursting with appreciation for all the little things I'd once taken for granted. I skipped across the street freely without worrying I'd be run over by a rickshaw or fall into a pothole. At the grocery store, I strolled leisurely through aisles of neatly arranged food, relishing the fact that everything I could possibly want was at my fingertips. I rented an apartment in the Marina District, went for runs along the ocean every day, and took pictures of every sunset with the Golden Gate Bridge glowing in the background.

I made new friends who lived nearby and quickly bonded with Uma, an Indian American woman whose family was from Bangalore. Uma became my new partner in crime. We went to parties, explored bars, and engaged in the typical escapades of single thirtysomethings in the city—things I hadn't done in years. Uma was as passionate about social-justice work as I was and had a great sense of humor. We could have meaningful conversations one minute and be doubled over in laughter the next. After trying so hard to keep everything together, it was nice to let loose.

I even started dating again. Just before my thirty-fifth birthday, I was invited to speak at a philanthropy conference in Switzerland, hosted by UBS Warburg for their private wealth clients. They hosted a black-tie dinner at the end of the conference. I pulled together my most glamorous look—a long black strapless dress, a gold bracelet I borrowed from Nancy, and bold red lipstick. After dinner, I wandered over to the bar. As I waited for my drink, I felt someone's gaze on me. Turning just as he approached, I saw a man with chiseled features. His dirty-blond hair was perfectly tousled, and his suit was crisp.

"Pierre," he said, introducing himself with a thick French accent. We chatted for a few minutes. He was a real estate mogul and was on the board of a women's education nonprofit. He asked if I would have dinner with him back in Geneva. I said yes.

A few nights later, Pierre took me to a gorgeous restaurant, where he insisted on ordering for us both—a very European move. When the bill came, I offered to split it. Pierre laughed like it was the most absurd thing he had ever heard. It was fun to be wined and dined, to feel feminine and desired again after years of focusing so little on how I looked or indulging in the more sensual side of life. I couldn't remember the last time I'd let a man do things for me. And Pierre did all the things. If you plugged "romance" into the algorithm, out would pop Pierre. He sent me dozens of red roses. A month after we met, he invited me to Paris. When I arrived at the hotel, a new leather jacket was laid out on my bed—a surprise gift from him. I wore it the next day to lunch with his friends at the hotel restaurant, an eclectic mix of European artists and entrepreneurs. We were in the middle of our entrees, talking about travel and work, when Pierre pulled out his computer and started playing my TED talk.

"She's saving babies!" he exclaimed. "Magnifique, non?"

His friends nodded politely, but I was mortified. It felt like my work was a party trick to impress his friends.

That night, we went to a black-tie caviar party. Everyone looked glamorous in their designer dresses and tailored suits. I wore a form-fitting blue dress and threw my new leather jacket on top. Tinkling jazz piano floated through the air, and clusters of people gathered around caviar stations, sipping languorously from Champagne flutes. I sipped mine, too, and tried my best to blend in. Pierre kept disappearing into the crowd. He would introduce me to people by talking about my work at Embrace, then leave me to navigate awkward small talk as he flitted from group to group. By the end of the night, I felt less like a partner and more like a trophy for my résumé and good deeds.

Pierre never asked me about where or how I'd grown up, what my dreams were, or even silly things like my favorite song. It felt like Embrace was of more interest to him than I was, though he never asked me why I did it or what it meant to me. I broke up with Pierre shortly after I got back to San Francisco. After him, I went on a string of dates with other successful Silicon Valley men, but many of them felt the same.

Empty.

"Now, relax into Savasana." The yoga instructor's soothing voice broke through my thoughts. As I lay on the mat, my limbs melting into the floor, I exhaled deeply. A knot in my chest loosened, and tears welled up in my eyes. Every time I went to yoga, lying in corpse pose at the end, I felt an emotional release. I'd been back from India for months, but no matter how much I slept, I still felt bone-tired. It was as if my body were catching up to the years I'd spent pushing through. A friend of mine had worked for years at a human-rights nonprofit, and when I mentioned my exhaustion to her, she reminded me to be easy with myself.

"There's a human cost to this kind of work," she said.

She told me her organization offered employees a sabbatical every five years to recuperate—physically and emotionally. I'd been so concerned about the mothers and babies, I had little space to consider what it had cost me to bear witness to so much trauma. To carry—even indirectly—the weight of a child's survival on my shoulders.

Now that I was back home, I needed to move at a slower pace. To plant both feet on the ground, to feel rooted. After years of international flights and the relentless demands of work, I craved simplicity. Even the thought of travel, once thrilling, now filled me with dread. I didn't want to get on a plane, a train, or even into a car.

For the first time in years, I longed for stillness.

When I was invited to President Barack Obama's White House for the first ever Maker Faire—a showcase of American "tinkerers, inventors, and entrepreneurs"—I almost turned it down. It was a once-in-a-lifetime honor, the sort of recognition we'd worked so hard for. But all I could think about was the exhaustion of flying across the country for what I feared would be another dog-and-pony show. When I told a friend that I was thinking about skipping it, he flipped out.

"Jane, you're crazy!" he exclaimed. "This is an amazing opportunity. You *must* go."

"I'm so tired, though. Does any of this stuff really matter?"

He scoffed. "Matter? Who cares if it *matters*? It's the fucking *White House*. Just enjoy the moment."

Enjoy the moment?

That felt like a foreign concept.

But I went.

The day of the Maker Faire, I was selected as one of ten people to meet with President Obama. I showed him the incubator and shared some of the stories of babies we had helped to save, including Nathan. We took a photo together, standing side by side, each with a hand on the incubator. Both of us smiling.

As soon as I received a copy of the photo, I sent it to my parents. Later, Joyce told me that they'd called our family in Taiwan and told them about it. For the first time since we'd started Embrace—or maybe since winning the kindergarten poetry contest—it felt like my father was proud of me.

CHAPTER 14

SEVEN DAYS

Our incubators were groundbreaking, but it was challenging to sell enough for the business to be viable. In India, the government was our biggest customer, but the contracts were incredibly slow and mired in bureaucracy. We needed to generate more revenue, which meant breaking into markets beyond India. We wouldn't be able to pull that off with our small team. We needed a partner. One that already had global reach.

The answer to our problem was Philips Healthcare, a multi-national company with over $13 billion in revenue and a reach of more than 100 countries. At a World Economic Forum event, I had the chance to meet the CEO. Philips was looking to diversify its product offerings in emerging markets like India, and she loved our incubator. After a few conversations, Philips made an incredible offer: they wanted to invest $5 million in Embrace and become our exclusive global distributor. This meant our incubators could finally be distributed on a massive scale. It was the kind of deal I could have only dreamed of—one that would secure Embrace's future.

For years, I'd operated under the mantra "Embrace first, me second." With Embrace's future secure, I could prioritize my self-care and take the break that I desperately needed. I negotiated a three-month leave with Sanjiv, which would begin after the deal was closed. My first stop would be Italy. I daydreamed of lounging in the Tuscan sun, savoring a glass of spicy Chianti, indulging in leisurely lunches filled with local delicacies, and—most of all—taking naps. Naps were my ultimate fantasy. I just needed to push myself for this final stretch. The finish line was in sight.

The next nine months were a whirlwind of meetings, negotiations, and endless legal documents. Finally, the paperwork was almost complete. In just about a week, the deal would be signed, sealed, and delivered. I'd finally cross that finish line.

Then, one morning, while brewing a cup of tea, I scrolled through the news. A *Wall Street Journal* headline cut off my air supply: "Philips Health-Care Chief Steps Down; Move Follows Disappointing Second-Quarter Results." *No. This could not be happening.* The CEO who was stepping down was the key champion of the Embrace deal.

A few days later, I got the call.

They were killing the deal.

I felt punched in the gut. Our runway was down to seven days. *Seven days of cash left in the bank.* I had already taken out two bridge loans from our investors just to keep things afloat long enough to close the deal. Now the deal was dead. And we were about to lose it all.

Suddenly my sabbatical didn't matter.

Nothing else mattered.

We had to save the company.

Seven days and counting.

It was two A.M. I couldn't sleep. My eyes were red from three straight days of crying. Desperate, I made a list of every person I'd met over the last several years at all the events, galas, and conferences. Every venture capitalist, tech entrepreneur, and anyone who had the means to save us or even keep us going for just another day.

One of the names was Marc Benioff, the billionaire CEO and founder of Salesforce. We had met at the World Economic Forum conference in Davos. Despite my jet lag, I had dragged myself out of bed early on the first morning to attend a guided meditation. Out of over 2,500 attendees, only seven showed up. By chance, I sat in the front row, right next to Marc. After the meditation, we introduced ourselves. I told him about Embrace, and he shared that his daughter had been born prematurely. He was in the process of gifting $25 million to the Gates Foundation to create a global program addressing premature births.

We marveled at the serendipity.

Now sitting at my desk, I swallowed my nerves and drafted an email. "I want to update you on an urgent situation," I began. I explained how the Embrace deal with Philips had fallen through due to circumstances beyond our control and that we needed immediate funding to stay afloat. I hovered for a second, then pressed Send. And waited.

The next few days were excruciating. I was stuck in a loop—a literal loop, playing the song "We Had Today" on repeat. Embrace was my baby, and it was dying.

That Friday, just before the close of business, my inbox dinged. It was an email from Marc. "Jane, I will fund you . . . aloha." I burst into tears. In the span of a week, I'd gone from thinking we were completing a deal that would secure Embrace's future, to being sure that it was over, to Marc's miracle investment saving us.

But the challenges weren't over. Without a global distributor, we needed a new long-term plan. Given all the uncertainty, Sanjiv stepped down as CEO. I was forced back into the role. My long-awaited sabbatical was out the door.

Embrace first; me second.

I didn't know how much further I could push myself. I was running on fumes.

At dinner one night, Nancy asked me, "Why are you still doing this?"

"What do you mean? How could I stop?"

"You've given this your all," she said, looking concerned. "Just give your investors any money that you have left and quit. This is destroying you."

The thought of quitting was intoxicating. But I couldn't. Embrace wasn't just my baby. It was my identity. Too many people were counting on me, and for some it was literally a matter of life and death.

Walking away wasn't as easy as Nancy made it sound. If Embrace failed, I failed.

It was as simple—and complicated—as that.

CHAPTER 15

STOKE

With the holidays around the corner, Nancy took matters into her own hands.

"You're barely hanging on," she said. "Let's spend the holidays together. All of us. Somewhere tropical. You need to take a break."

Family vacations were not something we did growing up, but now that Nancy had a second son, Joey, she was creating her version of what family should be. She knew my weakness: my nephews.

"They need to spend time with you. Nobody works at Christmas," she added.

We decided on Honolulu. It was a five-hour direct flight from California and had something for everyone: ocean, shopping, great Asian food. Nancy found a spacious oceanside rental. From our deck, you could look out to the Diamond Head surf break, its turquoise waters framed by lush greenery, palm trees, and volcanic cliffs.

In the early mornings, I'd step outside with a cup of tea, letting the salty breeze wake me up as I watched the surfers glide across the waves. The way they moved was so rhythmic and graceful. The more I watched, the more I longed to try it myself.

For Christmas, my mom, sisters, and I exchanged certificates for massages at a local hotel. Joey and Kyle eagerly tore into their presents—snorkeling gear we had picked out for them. "For scooty diving!" Joey squealed, holding up his new treasure.

The next day, we went for lunch at Ala Moana Center, a sprawling outdoor mall in the heart of Honolulu. We decided to grab lunch at the food court, which was filled with Japanese food stalls. Dad was craving udon soup noodles, so we began our search.

"Thirteen dollars? Crazy!" Dad scoffed as he examined the menu at one stall. At each stop, he scanned the prices and grumbled about how overpriced everything was. We wandered from stall to stall, Dad shaking his head at every menu we passed. Finally, he settled on a bowl of noodles that cost $11.

After lunch, we strolled through some of the shops. As we passed a boutique, a wallet caught my eye. I asked the sales clerk to take it out, running my fingers over the soft leather. It was beautiful, but when I glanced at the price tag, I hesitated.

Dad noticed me lingering.

"Do you want that?" he asked in Taiwanese. Before I could shake my head, he took the wallet from my hands and walked toward the register.

I was touched. We'd just spent thirty minutes examining every menu so he could save two dollars on noodles, but he was willing to splurge on a spontaneous gift for me. He'd always been like that. Unwilling to spend a cent more than necessary on himself, but when it came to Mom and us girls, he could be endlessly generous.

"Thanks, Dad," I said quietly, tucking my head in gratitude.

Later that afternoon, my mom, sisters, and I went to get our massages. I was booked with John, a local guy about my age, who happened to be a surfer. During the massage, I mentioned

I was dying to learn how to surf. He generously offered to teach me. The next day, he picked me up in a Toyota truck with two surfboards in the back, and we drove to the Diamond Head surf break. When we arrived, John pulled a long multicolored board from the bed of the truck and handed it to me.

I carried it awkwardly and followed him down a steep trail to the shore. Halfway down, I was already panting.

"You good?" John asked, looking back.

"Yes," I answered, trying not to slip on the rocky path. "Just didn't realize surfing was hard work before you even get in the water!"

We finally reached the beach, where we kicked off our flip-flops and surveyed the waves. The water was a shimmering blend of aqua and green, lapping softly against the shore. The ocean was glassy, the winds light.

"Perfect conditions," John said. "Let's start with some beach work."

I raised my eyebrows and set my board on the sand.

"Let's try practicing some pop-ups," he instructed, lying his belly down on his board. I followed his lead as he guided me through a series of drills, showing me how to paddle and how to pop up onto my feet.

"The pop-up is everything," he said. "You have a split second—you can't hesitate."

"How do I know when it's time?" I asked.

"You feel it," John answered.

"But how do I *know* I'm feeling it?"

John ran a hand through his hair, searching for the right words.

"I guess you *learn* to feel it," he responded. "It's a rise. The sliiiiightest lift. Then you go! You're up."

After I popped up successfully a few times on the beach, John led me toward the water.

"Now we watch the waves," he said. "One of the hardest parts of surfing isn't the ride itself, it's learning how to read the waves."

He pointed toward the horizon, where a rolling line was forming in the distance. "See that there?"

I followed his finger.

"It's starting out as a bump out there," he said. "But now it's building . . . and then it's going to feather and crest. That's the moment you want to catch the wave—right before it breaks."

Squinting, I could just make out a growing wave.

"The next one is rolling in slowly," John continued, "so it's going to be mushy and hard to catch. But the one after that is walling up. That's what you want."

The wave climbed higher and started to curl over itself.

"Waves are like people," John said. "They have their own habits, routines, even weird little quirks. Some are mushy. Others shifty. They peel or close out. They change depending on the swell, the tide, the winds, and the reef or the sand below."

"I had no idea it was so intricate," I said.

John smiled. "Now we get in the water," he announced. He picked up his board and walked into the ocean, while I followed eagerly at his heels. The water was lukewarm and soothing to slip into. John went belly-to-board and started to paddle. I dropped to my board and did the same, propelling my arms through the water. My shoulders started to burn after just a few strokes. As if reading my mind, John turned and shouted back, "Most of surfing is paddling! Get ready to rip those delts."

Overhead, the sun blazed. My heart was already pounding. How could water be so dense? I kept pushing. The sea rose and fell in wavy hillocks, and the real world felt somewhere far beyond. We were almost past where the waves began to rise when John stopped and gestured for me to turn my board back toward the shore. I paddled in a clumsy circle, trying to position myself.

"Get ready!" he called out. The next thing I knew, he was shoving my board into the oncoming wave.

"Stand, now!" I heard him shout.

Clutching the sides of the board, I centered my gravity and tried to push myself to my feet. I toppled over immediately, plunging into the water. The wave passed over me in a burst of frothy bubbles. I shot to the surface, gasping for air.

"You okay?" John asked.

I flashed him a thumbs-up, eager to try again.

Wave after wave, I tried, each fall humbling me further. Finally, as another wave approached, I paddled into position. I felt it begin to lift me ever so slightly. Without hesitation, I popped up, knees bent, arms out for balance.

"Waaahhooo!" John hollered, his voice warped by the wind.

As I rode the wave, time slowed to the millisecond, and all the noise in my head faded away. I was enveloped in a symphony of sensation. The *sshhh* of the ocean. The light tickle of wind on my face. The buttery smoothness of the water beneath my feet. There was only this moment, this wave. I was flying. I was *free*.

The wave softened beneath me and I slipped off my board, dunking underwater. As I surfaced, I saw John floating nearby on his board, grinning.

"I just felt the whole world in that wave," I told him with a huge smile. It was like I had just ridden the energy of the universe, like I'd tapped into some cosmic current.

John grinned wider. "You got it," he said. "That's called stoke."

I spent the rest of the day in a euphoric daze. Nothing, not even Dad berating Mom, could pierce it. I played with my nephews and helped Nancy make dinner. I felt light, like something new was possible.

For the rest of the week, John and I surfed every morning. I quickly learned that each break has its own rhythm, its own ecosystem. The ever-changing conditions demanded total presence—you had to read the water in real-time, adapting to what was in front of you. No two waves were ever the same. I'd never imagined surfing was so demanding, so intimate. You had to be in continuous relationship with the ocean. And there was no end goal, really. No goal except the ride.

Stoke.

I fell in love with surfing fast and hard, giving myself to it wholeheartedly. Back in San Francisco, I bought a surfboard and was in the water whenever I could sneak away. Early mornings, I'd pull on a hoodie, grab a mug of tea, and drive out to the nearest break. The water in Northern California was nothing like Hawaii. It was frigid—maybe sixty degrees. I had to wear a full wetsuit, a hood, and booties. But there was something refreshing about the cold water that left me feeling high after every session. Riding a wave was the only thing that motivated me to leave the three-mile radius around my apartment. Nothing made me happier.

I started surfing with my friend Rory, who was just as obsessed as I was. "I can see all your teeth," he said once, teasing me about my smile after I caught a wave. He'd never seen me smile that big.

If I wasn't trying to catch waves, I was talking about them. I kept a surf blog and started writing surf poetry. Before bed, I would binge YouTube surf videos to try to seed my dreams with waves. I watched *Blue Crush* on repeat. A friend had forced me to watch it a decade earlier, and I'd scoffed, dismissing it as cheesy. Now I cried every time at the end when the main character conquers her fear and rides a perfect barrel at Pipeline, one of the world's most iconic waves. Her victory became my lullaby.

Surfing was so visceral, it forced me to be present in a way I had never been. A typical ride on a wave lasts maybe ten or fifteen seconds. A long one could be thirty. But I could recall specific rides, frame by frame, in slow-motion detail. I started noticing the most subtle things: how the wind rippled over the water, how the color of the water deepened or brightened. I could remember what a wave felt like in a particular millisecond, the slight turns I'd taken, the exact push and pull of the water beneath me. Nowhere else did mere seconds feel so cinematic and precise.

A wave was something I could not control. Learning to move in concert with such an unpredictable force taught me to let go, to surrender in ways that I couldn't elsewhere in my life. Everything about surfing stood in stark contrast to the life I'd been living, which was focused on end results and controlled outcomes. Surfing was just pure play. It was all the freedom and joy I was never allowed as a kid and hadn't chosen as an adult.

I started referring to surfing as my one true love—it filled a space in me no romantic relationship had ever touched. With the mounting pressures of Embrace, it became the only way to turn my mind off from the daily stresses of work. Surfing became my lifeline; the ocean, my solace. I learned to stand with steadiness as the world—and the waves—shifted under my feet.

CHAPTER 16

FUMES OF FUMES

Without a global distributor, Embrace needed a new pathway toward becoming profitable. We decided to launch a product line for the U.S. market. Doctors and nurses who used our incubators around the world often reported back how soundly newborns slept in them—so soundly that they had to be woken up for meals. Inspired by this feedback, we developed a line of baby sleeping bags using a variation of our technology. It would be positioned as a consumer product to help babies sleep, rather than a medical device. For every sleeping bag we sold, we would donate funds to help save lives with our incubator.

I was running on the fumes of fumes. But I hired an entire team and developed a new product line—in just six months. We threw a launch party that Marc Benioff graciously hosted at one of his homes in San Francisco. Baby Nathan and his mother Charlene flew in from Chicago to join. Nathan was three now. I'd kept in touch with his family ever since his adoption from the Beijing orphanage; every few months Charlene sent photos and updates on his progress.

At the party, I introduced Nathan and his mom to our team. I couldn't believe how big he'd grown. His thick black hair framed a wide smile that stretched ear to ear. He was bursting with life, despite the challenges he faced. Nathan had cerebral palsy, a neurological disorder that affects mobility and is common in premature babies. He wore leg braces to help correct his gait, slept in a full-body splint at night, and did physical therapy five days a week. His life was filled with routines and obstacles most kids never had to think about. But none of that dimmed his light. His joy was magnetic. "He is grateful to be alive," Charlene told me. "He may not be able to say it or express it right now, but it's who he is . . . he lives life with abandon."

As the party wound down, Charlene waved me over.

"Nathan's wiped. We're going to head back to the hotel, but I have something for you," she said. She pulled a tiny ceramic figurine from her purse. It was an angel standing over a little boy, holding his hands to help him walk.

"This represents you," she said gently. "Watching over Nathan. And all the angels watching over Embrace."

I pressed my hand to my heart as a swell of emotion rose.

"Thank you," I whispered.

In that moment, I knew we couldn't give up.

I wouldn't give up.

Parents raved about our new product, and for the first time, we hit our sales targets. Selling a consumer product online was far easier than the uphill battle of going door-to-door to doctors' offices and government agencies in India to sell our incubators. For a while, everything seemed to be going smoothly.

But then we discovered a critical manufacturing error: repeated washing and drying caused some of the snaps on the sleeping bag to fall off—a potential choking hazard for babies. Although the issue affected fewer than 1 percent of the units, we made the difficult decision to recall the entire line. Between re-calling the product, redesigning it, and then waiting for the new design to be manufactured and shipped, we ran out of money.

Again.

My stress hit an all-time high. I was so beyond burnout, I didn't even know what to call it anymore. I felt like I was swim-ming in a rip current; no matter how hard I tried, I couldn't make progress. I just needed to get Embrace to safe harbor, but safe harbor was a mirage, always appearing and disappearing just out of reach.

One night, desperate to clear my mind, I escaped into a flota-tion chamber. The dark, soundproof tanks were filled with highly concentrated saltwater kept at 98 degrees Fahrenheit—just like our incubators. The saltwater made floating effortless, keeping you suspended in a weightless state. The experience was sup-posed to help you relax, to let go.

I stepped into the tank and placed my tea mug in the metal doorway to keep it ajar, so I could easily find my way out. Over the next half hour, I let my body go limp in the warm vat. At first, my mind quieted. But then morbid thoughts began to surface.

Wouldn't it be easier if I just died? If I just slipped under the water now and stopped breathing all my problems would go away.

When I opened my eyes again, it was pitch-black—the mug I'd used to wedge the door open must have slipped. I screamed, flailed, and kicked at the walls, convinced I was trapped. It was suffocating, like being sealed inside a coffin. I finally found the door, shoved it open, and gasped for air, trembling. The feeling of being locked in was exactly what my life felt like. I felt trapped in Embrace, desperately wanting to save it *and* desperately want-ing out.

It'd been nearly ten years since I started Embrace. I was almost forty. I didn't own a home or have a retirement plan. I'd worked for a decade at far below market rate—a choice I had willingly made. As the years passed, the wealth gap between me and my classmates had become painfully stark. Many of them now owned multiple homes around the world, while I still rented a small one-bedroom apartment and drove the same beat-up Toyota Corolla I'd had in school. I hadn't started Embrace to become wealthy. That was never the goal. But at some point, I knew I needed to consider the practicalities of life. I had already sacrificed so much.

I had disagreements with some of Embrace's investors—big enough that I was ready to walk away. But when faced with the reality of losing the company, I couldn't do it. Every time I tried to step away, I found myself pulled right back in. In a final, last-ditch effort, we found a company in New York interested in our new U.S. baby-sleeping-bag business. Even though the product line had only been in the market for a year, with a rough start, they saw potential. After several phone conversations, they decided to fly out to San Francisco to meet with us. They were interested in acquiring our for-profit arm.

The day of the meeting, I reserved a WeWork conference room with a sweeping view of the bay. This was it. Our final shot. As we went through the specifics of the business, I found my eyes wandering to the shimmering water outside. I imagined smelling the salt in the air. Hearing the crashing waves. Feeling the joy of riding them.

"Listen, we really want you to stay on as CEO," one of the principals said.

I snapped back to the room. "Excuse me?"

"Are you committed to continuing this?" he pressed.

I hesitated for half a second, then nodded convincingly and flashed a warm smile. The way I had learned to do as a child when I headed to school after a beating. *Everything is fine.*

"Yes, of course I'm committed," I responded.

My yes convinced them to move forward.

The acquisition offer was small, but it would give Embrace a home—and a way to continue its mission. Over the next several months, we negotiated the terms and drafted reams of legal documents.

I began dreaming again about taking that long-overdue sabbatical once the deal was complete. A friend who was very into manifestation suggested I make a vision board. She brought over a stack of magazines and instructed me to cut out images that inspired me. "Don't think about it rationally," she told me. "Just find images that stir up any feelings in your body." I had heard of vision boards but never took them seriously. I went along with it, grabbing a surf magazine and cutting out images of surfers on the world's most epic waves.

"Now," my friend said, "you have to feel in your body what it will feel like when these things actually happen."

I closed my eyes and felt the skin-tingling ecstasy of gliding across the water, the freedom of flying through the air—untethered from Embrace, untethered from everything. It felt like hope, and a small step toward reclaiming my life.

I had to balance the woo-woo with the practical. So, in true CEO fashion, I started a spreadsheet and titled it "Bucket List."

The first item on the list: *Surf in Indonesia.*

A few weeks later, we signed all the documents for the acquisition. The bank transfer was the final step. On the day it was supposed to go through, we refreshed our online bank account every hour, ready to celebrate. But by two P.M. California time, which was closing time in New York, there was nothing. Then we got an email requesting a conference call. Dread flooded my body. *Not again.*

On the call, the investors said they were having issues transferring the money from an international account. "It should be sorted out in a few days," they assured us. Another day passed. Still, no money. No word.

While we waited, I went to dinner with Rory and his girlfriend, Sharon. Over bowls of carbonara, Sharon talked about the importance of prayer and intentions. "The universe," she said matter-of-factly, "has a larger plan for all of us."

"I wish it had one for me," I said, not sure if I wanted to surrender to a higher power or stab it with my fork.

"Well," Sharon asked, "are you doing anything to stay open to it?"

I shrugged. "Meditation?" I'd been meditating every morning for years. Sometimes it helped, sometimes it just gave me ten extra minutes to stress in silence.

"Ah yes," Sharon said, twirling pasta into her spoon. "Meditation is great to help you *receive*. But you need to balance that with prayer, which is about *asking*." She suggested I read *Outrageous Openness* by Tosha Silver, a collection of stories about what she called "divine intervention." Before I could say no, she insisted on sending me a copy.

A few days later, the book arrived. I settled on my couch and thumbed through the pages. Silver suggested praying with specifics. I hadn't prayed since I was twelve—the day my father beat me for reading on the lawn. Back then, it had felt like speaking into a void. But now, desperate for a lifeline, I figured it couldn't hurt to try.

I took a deep breath, closed my eyes, and clasped my hands together.

"*Dear Universe,*" I began. "*Please help us find a solution for Embrace—one that benefits everyone involved, allows me to continue being a changemaker, and helps the babies and families this product was created for.*"

Over the next few days, I prayed my ass off. I repeated my *Dear Universe* prayer at the end of daily meditation, in the shower, even on my surfboard. I became ravenous for signs from the universe. I started to see God in croissants and crosswalks. The cashier who undercharged me at 7-Eleven was a sign that I was undervaluing the company. The bird that flew into my window and nearly died but then shook itself off and flew away—a sign that Embrace was going to die? Or it was going to *appear to have died,* and then be resurrected? I was losing it.

Finally, the call came. The company that was going to acquire Embrace was shutting down due to its own financial problems. The deal was dead. After we hung up, I sat there staring at the phone. After all the highs and lows, it was just . . . over. All my cards had been played. There was nothing left to do. After ten years of Hail Marys to keep the company alive, we had no choice but to shut it down.

I'd given it everything I had. But in the end, none of it mattered. I'd already cried so many tears for Embrace, I simply had none left.

In that moment, I knew what I'd known when I was twelve. Prayers didn't work for shit.

CHAPTER 17

BURIAL AT SEA

Over the next few weeks, I moved methodically through the painful process of shutting down the company. One by one, I let employees go. I sent emails to investors and supporters who had stood by us over the years, informing them the journey was over. Kai, my director of operations, stuck with me until the very end, even when we weren't sure we could pay months of salary we owed her. I'd wanted out, but not like this. This wasn't just the end of a company; it felt like a death.

Maybe my father had been right.

When Embrace was at the peak of its success, Joyce had called me one evening.

"Don't shoot the messenger," she warned. "Just thought you should hear it from me."

"Oh God," I said with a sigh. "What now?"

"Dad ranked us."

"Huh?"

"In order of success. He ranked us."

"And?"

"Nancy was first."

Of course. Nancy checked all the boxes. A lucrative corporate job. Married with two kids.

"I was second," Joyce said softly. I winced, but given her high-paying job as a producer for an advertising firm, I understood.

"And I was last," I groaned. "The consummate underachiever!"

We laughed. At the time, I'd genuinely thought it was funny. Even my visit to the White House—which had become a source of bragging rights for our relatives in Taiwan—didn't register on my father's scorecard. I was still seen as someone whose career was glorified charity work. In other words, a failure. Now I had just proven him right.

After I pressed Send on the final email shuttering the company, I sat at my desk and hand wrote a long letter to Embrace, hoping to give myself closure. I thanked it for everything—the lessons, the lives saved, even the heartbreak. The final goodbye.

You have been imbued with my love, my heart, my soul. As I start this new chapter, I hope it will be one of hope, beauty, and courage. For now, I ask the universe and the ocean to cleanse and heal me.

Joyce came over and stood sentry as I started a small fire in my garage. I lit a match to the letter, watching as the flames curled and blackened the paper into ash. She put her hand on my shoulder as the words I'd poured out dissolved in smoke.

"It's time," she said softly. "You did all you could." Joyce had seen firsthand the years of sacrifice, and she knew how hard it was for me to finally let go.

When the fire burned out, I carefully scooped the ashes into a Ziploc bag and drove to the beach. I tucked the bag into my wetsuit and paddled out into the ocean, seeking a quiet spot away from all the surfers. Sitting up on my board, surrounded by the vast expanse of blue, I took a deep breath and felt the sun against my face. Slowly, I scattered the ashes. The final remnants of my relationship with Embrace drifted into the wind, blending into the sea.

On the car ride home, I played the Adagietto from Mahler's Fifth Symphony. I'd read somewhere that Mahler had composed the piece as a love song for his wife, and as I listened, I heard tones of sorrow interwoven with the tenderness of love. There cannot be one without the other.

When I told my parents the news, they were surprisingly supportive. Mom tried to console me. "I know you tried your best, Jane," she said, her voice gentle. "I'm proud of what you did. You really wanted to help those babies." Without saying a word, my father transferred six months' worth of rent to my bank account. Money had always been his way of saying *I've got you,* which translated into *I love you.* Their acknowledgment of how much my work had meant to me was deeply touching. And having a financial cushion was a relief. It meant I could take a moment to figure out my next steps.

Technically unemployed for the first time in my adult life, I felt paralyzed, unable to leave the house. The days were hard enough. The nights were unbearable. While the rest of the world slept, I lay awake, trapped in a spiral of dread that seemed to thicken with every passing hour. One day bled into the next, scored by the endless chatter of bad television. As I mindlessly flipped through Netflix one night, a documentary caught my eye. The description said it was a behind-the-scenes look at Tony Robbins's weeklong seminar, "Date with Destiny." All I knew about Tony Robbins was that he was a self-help speaker who had starred in 1980s infomercials sporting power suits and Ken-doll hair. I hesitated, wondering if this was just another empty fix, but something compelled me to click Play.

I poured a glass of Chardonnay and didn't move for the next hour and a half. I watched, transfixed, as Tony conducted interventions with participants. In one scene, he focused on a man wearing red shoes who was on the verge of suicide. Within fifteen minutes, Tony had drawn him out of despair into tears of gratitude and joy. Afterward they embraced, and the crowd erupted in applause as if they'd completed an Ironman.

It was therapy on steroids. Tony could look into a person's soul and immediately locate their deepest pain. When a nineteen-year-old woman said she had problems with her diet, Tony uncovered the real issue within minutes: her fractured relationship with her father.

"For her to heal," he said to the audience, "she needs to claim not only the 'fuck-you' but also the vulnerability she has around her father. Else, it's going to show up with pain for her with men in the future." Turning back to the woman, he said, "As much as you've hated him, he's hated himself more. The role your father played in your life is a gift. If he had been the father you wanted, you wouldn't have the drive you have."

Was it the Chardonnay, or was Tony talking directly to me?

Over the years, I'd been around some of the world's most powerful people, yet few had moved me as deeply as Tony Robbins did that night. He seemed to genuinely care about the people he was helping. He'd come from a traumatic background himself, and his empathy allowed him to break past people's defenses with a rare authenticity. As the credits rolled, I felt uplifted for the first time in months. That's what I needed, I thought. A Date with Destiny.

I opened my laptop and pulled up my Bucket List spreadsheet. Above *Surf in Indonesia*, I added *Go to Date with Destiny*. Then I pulled out my vision board and stared at the images of perfectly peeling waves. I closed my eyes and imagined myself riding them. Maybe I could surf my way out of this emotional sinkhole.

Maybe it was time to do the surf trip I'd been dreaming of. Time had been scarce the last ten years; now it was the only thing I had.

The next morning, I called Karen, a raven-haired New Yorker I'd met surfing, who was just as obsessed as I was.

"Let's do it," I said. "The trip we've been talking about."

"Finally!" she squealed. "I think we should go to the Mentawai Islands."

The Mentawais are a remote chain of islands off the western coast of Sumatra, known for some of the most iconic waves on the planet. Quintessential cinematic barrels that shimmer as they curl into perfect tunnels. What surf dreams are made of.

"It's shoulder season," Karen said. "The waves will be more manageable and less crowded."

"Perfect," I said, already feeling the stoke rise.

"And we should bring Ane and Alex," she added. They were coaches who traveled with surfers. "The Mentawais are no fucking joke."

When you google the Mentawai Islands, one of the first things that pops up is a warning: *The Mentawais are not for learning how to surf!* Karen and I were both still relatively new to surfing, and I agreed that we could use the help.

Planning the trip, I felt excited for the first time in months. I stashed the remote control and hit the water the next day. Each paddle chipped away at the heaviness I'd been carrying, and with every session, I found myself coming back to life. Then I took on that monster wave—and wiped out hard. After being tossed and held under, I was shaken to my core. The next day, a sharp, searing pain shot up my arm, radiating through my scapula. I couldn't even hold my toothbrush without wincing. For days afterward, even the simplest movements were agonizing.

I booked appointments with an orthopedic surgeon and a

physical therapist. The prognosis wasn't good. "Something like this could take months to heal," the physical therapist told me. My flight was in a week. I was crushed. I had waited years to do this trip, and now—after everything—this? Desperate for a solution, I scoured surf chat boards for injury-recovery hacks, looking for anything that could get me back into the water. That's when I remembered hearing a story from another surfer about an intuitive healer in Ubud, Indonesia.

"He's a miracle-worker," this guy had said. The healer's name? *Papa.*

I needed a miracle.

I needed someone to fix me.

And that belief would drive everything that came next.

CHAPTER 18

NO PAIN, NO GAIN

I waited in the thick, soupy heat outside the hut where Papa was supposedly performing miracles. Behind me, a group of American women on a yoga retreat sat on a straw bench under a broad swath of shade. We'd been there for hours, watching the line inch forward with a mix of horror and fascination as people were called in one by one. Every so often, a strangled scream would escape from inside the hut. Thirty minutes later, someone would stumble out in a loopy daze.

"Next, you!" A petite Indonesian woman stepped out of the hut and waved me in. I swallowed hard and entered an airy room with a straw bed in the corner. A faint trace of smoke lingered in the air. The woman pointed to the bed and I lay down, my nerves jangling as I prepared to meet the mystical Papa. I pictured him floating into the room in a flowing caftan, radiating a serene, otherworldly aura. According to the surfer who'd told me about him—and hundreds of glowing online reviews that made him sound like the love child of a shaman and a chiropractor—this guy was the real deal. I was there for my shoulder injury, but open to any life wisdom he had to bestow. Maybe he would whisper something prophetic, or an insight that would change my life.

Papa emerged from the back room wearing a white tank top and a simple sarong. He was small and wiry, with weathered skin and a thick mustache straight out of the 1970s. His dark complexion and square glasses reminded me of my father. In one hand, he held a lit cigarette. In the other, he gripped a small wooden stick the size of a baseball bat cut in half, smooth and rounded at the bottom. He took a drag of the cigarette, then exhaled a cloud of smoke. Not exactly the image of the spiritual healer I'd conjured.

Papa put the cigarette out and sat next to me, gripping the small bat.

"Relaaaax," he hummed.

I nodded stiffly, trying to suppress my fear.

"N-Not too rough," I stammered.

He began slowly, pressing his bat into the sole of my left foot. My jaw clenched. The back of my knees started to sweat.

"Arghhh!" I screamed as a hundred hot rockets exploded from my foot up my leg.

"You have liver problems," he announced matter-of-factly, digging the bat harder into my heel. The sensation was so intense, I couldn't form words to ask what he meant. To tell him that I was here for my shoulder, and maybe a minor prophecy. That it was my heart that was broken, not my liver. As he dug under my toes, I screamed louder, gripping the sides of the mat. Papa pushed and kneaded, twisted and dug, and time went bendy with pain. I gritted my teeth and dropped into it, the way I'd taught myself. The way I'd always gotten through as a child.

"All done!" Papa said suddenly, flashing a grin.

I let out a long, shuddering sigh. My feet were throbbing.

"No pain, no gain," he quipped cheerfully, like he was running a Pilates retreat.

He even sounded like my dad.

Still clinging to the hope of a prophecy, I slipped in a question before leaving. "Do you think I'm going to meet my soul mate this year?"

Papa looked at me blankly. "Lady, I'm a healer. Not a fortune-teller."

I waved a hurried goodbye to Papa and hobbled to the front of the hut, where I set my donation at the foot of a wooden statue of Vishnu, the Hindu god of preservation and protection. As I stepped into the street, I made a silent bid for both. I was ready to take any help I could get.

The morning after Papa's sadistic treatment, I woke up feeling refreshed. I sat in my hotel bed and slowly rotated my arm in a slow circle. *My God.* He hadn't even touched my shoulder, but the pain was completely gone! I let out a squeal and threw open the blinds. The courtyard outside was lush and vibrant, brimming with tropical flowers and vine-draped plants. The sun was already high and bright, and the morning felt full of possibility.

I dressed quickly and wandered outside into an open-air arcade lined with stalls selling vibrant silk sarongs and terra-cotta masks of Hindu deities. Tropical birds chirped from the canopy of a banyan tree nearby, its roots dangling like ropes from the sky. Clusters of pink frangipani, or jepun as the locals called it, sprouted from high branches, releasing a faint, sweet perfume that mingled with the warm breeze. I wove my way through a throng of street vendors selling food. Local families chatted as they waited for nasi goreng, while tourists in sundresses and yoga pants wandered through the stalls. Everything buzzed, but nothing felt rushed.

"Babi guling?" a woman called cheerfully, gesturing to the roast suckling pig. I shook my head and kept walking, but for the first time in months, I was actually hungry. After a light lunch, I headed back to the hotel and found a seat at the bar. I pulled out my book and ordered a cocktail—something with arak, the local liquor. After Papa's treatment and the long trip here, I was exhausted in a good way, and that seemed like something to celebrate.

Next to me, two men chatted boisterously. As my drink arrived, they called over to me.

"What are you reading?" one of them asked.

Me? I mouthed, glancing around.

"Yes, you."

I held the book up, a little sheepish. "*The Alchemist?*"

They hooted.

"Join us now, or else!" crowed the bald one with a golden tan.

The taller one, with dark hair, nodded gravely. "Drinking alone is a crime."

I smiled, tucked the book into my bag, and pulled a chair up to their table.

"Derek," said the tall one.

"Max," said the other, extending his hand.

"First things first," Derek asked. "What are you doing here?"

"Well . . ." I began. "I came to surf. The Mentawais."

"Oooh, a surfer chick," cooed Max. "Are you a pro or something?"

"Hardly." I laughed. "But I am obsessed."

Derek wasn't satisfied. "But the *reason?*" he pressed. "Everyone comes to Bali for *a reason.*"

I dabbed sweat from the nape of my neck.

"The reason . . ." I trailed off, not knowing how much I wanted to say.

I thought of a talk I'd seen recently about *liminal time.*

Dr. Joan Borysenko, an integrative medicine doctor, described it as *the pregnant pause between what is no longer and what is not yet*. It was a transitional space, a journey into the unknown, that comes after a significant event that alters your life irrevocably. An event that is often marked by grief or loss. The landscape is uncharted, and the outcome is uncertain. That's exactly where I was. Embrace had ended, and I had no idea what lay ahead.

"There is no map of the territory," Borysenko said. "But those who make it through return transformed, bearing precious gifts."

I wondered what Derek would say if I told him that I was in liminal time. *Oh, me? Yes, I'm just in a pregnant pause right now— between what was no longer what is not yet.* I decided against it.

"A fresh start," I finally mustered.

"Fresh start." Derek raised his glass. "A classic."

A few days later, feeling refreshed, I met up with Karen, Ane, and Alex in Bali for our flight to Jakarta, where we'd catch a smaller plane, then a boat, to the Mentawai Islands.

"What are your goals for the trip?" Alex asked as we boarded the plane.

"To feel free again," I replied. "To let go of the fear." I recounted the wipeout, telling them how terrified I'd been and how even thinking about catching a wave now felt scary. It had been my first inkling of fear in a great love affair. The inevitable crash. The moment I realized I could get seriously hurt. It was as if a spell had been broken.

My fear was bigger than just that wave—it took over the only space I had left for myself. Every part of my life had beaten me down.

"Forget technique," said Alex as the plane's engines whirred to life. "You need to get out of your head and back to your instincts."

I nodded, turning my gaze to the window. Below us, Bali shrank to a speck of green in the Java Sea. Beyond it, the horizon stretched endlessly.

"The best thing that could happen to you on this trip," Ane chimed in, "is to get clobbered by a wave and get up smiling. Your job is to eat shit as many times as possible."

I already felt like an expert at the eating-shit part.

Two interisland flights and two very rocky boat rides later, we arrived at Simakakang Island, one of seventy islands scattered off the western coast of Sumatra that make up the Mentawais. It was even better than the photos. In every direction, as far as you could see, the Indian Ocean ran to the horizon—an endless cerulean desert framed by clusters of palm trees and cream-colored beaches.

Our resort, Aloita, was on its own island. We stayed in thatch-roofed bungalows with boho-style furniture and verandas that opened to sweeping ocean views. The island had limited electricity, and the neighboring island had none. At night, flashlights flickered in the darkness, tiny pinpricks of light dancing across the inky sea. Between the trill of tropical bugs, the rustle of leaves, and the occasional spark of light across the ocean, it felt like I'd been catapulted back to an ancient era. A time out of time.

Javier, our surf guide, tracked the weather and tides to determine the best breaks for surfing each day. In the morning, we waited for his signal, and when it came, we grabbed our boards, slapped on sunblock, and hustled to the dock, where he was waiting in a speedboat. Once aboard, Javier gunned the engine and steered us into the open water, the sun glinting off the sea. Karen and I sat up front, laughing as the salty spray speckled our faces.

In the Mentawais, you pulled up by boat to a wave that seemed to appear out of nowhere in the middle of the ocean. Unlike paddling out from the shore, you were deep in open water, with no comforting coastline to orient you. The only land for miles was a scattering of tiny islands dotting the horizon, each rising up like pom-poms.

Javier eased off the throttle, and the boat began to slow. When we came to a full stop, he pointed to where the water curled and broke in the distance—that's where we would be surfing. In surfing, landmarks are crucial. A tree, a rock—anything to help you stay oriented so you don't drift too far from the break. In yoga, they call it a drishti, a focused gaze or point of attention to help maintain balance. I looked around, trying to isolate a single palm tree to fix my gaze on, but they kept blurring together like those optical-illusion posters. Just seconds earlier, the sea had felt expansive and enlivening. Suddenly, it was *too big*. There was so much ocean and nothing to anchor me.

I remembered what a good friend said when I told him how rudderless I felt after Embrace ended. "You're lost at sea," he'd said. "You have to get used to this feeling . . . just see where the sea takes you." Well, here I was—lost at sea, no shore in sight, and no road map for what came next. I felt a wave of panic.

We were surfing a break called Ombak Tidur. *Sleepy Wave.* It must have been a local joke, because there was nothing sleepy about it. Ombak Tidur had no channel, the calm stretch of water off to the side that allows you to easily enter or exit a break. Here, you were always in the impact zone. The wave broke in multiple places, so surprise sets could roll through at any moment. And where the waves broke, the sharp reef loomed just beneath the surface. The margin for error was slim; the chances of getting hurt, high.

Alex jumped into the water first and I followed, clutching my board. The conditions were perfect that day, the sort of waves

I'd once fallen asleep dreaming of. I floated for a while, my legs dangling in the water, letting wave after wave pass by. The sea was a vibrant, crystalline blue. I could see straight through to the ocean floor, where schools of canary-yellow and electric-blue fish darted back and forth. I wanted to be like them—playful and serene. Wanting nothing. Needing nothing. Instead, my chest was tight, my heartbeat skittish. I fought back swells of terror as the wipeout replayed in my mind.

"Go! You got this, Jane!" Alex shouted as another perfect wave rolled in. I paddled halfway in, but at the last second panicked and pulled out. Even when my mind said, *Go,* my body refused.

"Okay, okay, next one," Alex called wearily, his deep well of patience running thin. I had traveled halfway around the world to catch perfect waves, only to be paralyzed with fear. Everything else in my life felt like a battle, and now the waves had become a threat too. Once my oasis, surfing was now yet another calculus of risk and reward—the sea just one more thing that could hurt me.

The next day, we ventured out to a new break. Minutes after getting in the ocean, I saw a big wave charging in hard and fast, a towering wall of water surging toward me.

No, no, no.

I froze, eyes wide with panic. *Try to paddle over the crest? Ditch your board?* My three-second analysis was two seconds too long. The wave crashed into an explosion of foam and spray, pushing me under. My limbs flailed and swished inches from the knife's edge of the jagged coral. One move in the wrong direction and I'd slice myself open. Instead of fighting the force of the water, I relaxed and let go. I knew that surrender was my only shot at making it out unscathed. My body turned to jelly, muscles softening, everything slackening and swaying with the current instead of pushing against it.

A few seconds later, I broke the surface. I was fine. I was fine because I'd *let go*. Beaming with relief, I climbed back onto the boat. Alex and Ane flashed me a thumbs-up.

I wrote in my journal that night. *Overcoming fear isn't about running away from the thing that scares you. It's about knowing you can fail and that you'll be okay.*

It was aspirational, but I wanted it to be true.

Every day after that, my confidence grew. With each wave I caught, I beat back a bit of the fear that had been consuming me.

After ten days in the Mentawai Islands, Karen and I flew to Ngalung Kalla, a six-hundred-acre off-grid eco-retreat in Sumba. One of the least developed Indonesian islands, Sumba sat at the edge of the Savu Sea. The waves were supposed to be even more epic than the Mentawais, the water said to be bluer, and the jungle wilder. I hoped the raw energy of the place would wash away the lingering restlessness in my body.

"I just *really* hope there aren't as many bugs here," I said, scratching my arms incessantly during the two-hour ride from the airport to the lodge. We were covered in insanely itchy sand-fly bites. When we arrived, we were greeted by an on-site yoga teacher with sun-kissed skin and an easy smile. As he toured us around the grounds, he casually warned us to "be mindful of the snakes and biting geckos." Karen and I gave each other death stares. *Biting geckos?* she mouthed.

The owners of the resort grew all their own food on-site and foraged materials from the land for the dwellings. Our rooms were completely open-air, with no walls or doors. They were perched atop a dramatic cliff overlooking the turquoise expanse of the ocean, with a view of the break we would be surfing. Nothing like being able to do a surf check from bed. The toilets were outdoor eco-composting pots, and the whole resort ran off solar power that shut down after dinner. At night, it was flashlights only.

Karen and I settled in, admiring the spectacular view from our room. Just before sunset, we were lounging in the dining area when half a dozen shirtless men filed in from the beach, laid down their surfboards, and sat in a circle on the deck. They were tan, scruffy, and glistening with seawater. A burly blond with a shaggy beard broke out in song.

"*Om Namah Shivaya, Om Namah Shivaya,*" he chanted.

"*Om Namah Shivaya, Om Namah Shivaya,*" bellowed a husky man with a crew cut sitting to his left.

"*Shivaaya namaha, Shivaaya namah om!*" A few more joined in, chanting at the top of their lungs until, one by one, all the men were chanting. The air hummed with their warm baritone.

We sat for dinner around a communal table. Feasting on fresh fish and greens seasoned with nutritional yeast, the men shared they had been chanting to Krishna Das, an American-born Hindu devotional singer. It was a ritual they did every night after surfing. Most of them were Aussies who'd met back home in an Alcoholics Anonymous group. They'd recovered together, and now they surfed and chanted together. Many had come from rough beginnings: booze, drugs, abuse.

The more I surfed, the more I encountered men like them. Epic surf seemed to draw a certain breed of wounded souls. If you grow up in a volatile environment, you get accustomed to a certain adrenaline rush—which being on the waves can replicate. You chase upheaval, almost instinctively, until the world's outer turmoil aligns with your inner storm. Surfing becomes a way of coping. Go, go, go, until there's nothing left to think or feel.

I understood that addiction to intensity.

"Why do you all love surfing so much?" I asked, looking around the table.

Robert, a man with dark chin-length hair and a crescent-shaped scar under one eye, spoke first. "Surfing connects me to my true essence."

"Which is?" I asked, leaning in closer.

"The essence of pure bliss, freedom, and presence," he said. It sounded ethereal, but I knew exactly what he meant.

To my left, a tatted guy with a pierced ear introduced himself as Mick. Addiction to dope had nearly destroyed his life, and surfing had saved him. "Surfing taught me to stay calm," he said. "And the calmer you are throughout heavy situations, the more you can endure."

"Totally agree," I said, telling him about my wipeout and how when I'd learned to just let go and stop fighting, I found the surface faster.

"Still, the fear is there, buzzing around at the back of my mind," I admitted.

"The more time you spend in your element," Mick said, "the less fearful you become."

I nodded and pushed the greens around on my plate. "That's what I'm hoping."

The next day, I walked out to a thin strip of beach surrounded by rugged sandstone cliffs and jagged outcroppings. The surf was gnashing and wild—twenty feet and up. The waves were far too big for Karen or me to even think about attempting. Even the Australians were wearing inflatable vests. From the shore, I watched them charge wave after wave. Their waves might have been bigger, but all of us were trying to overcome fear in our own ways.

We spent our days at the beach, our evenings catching and racing frogs, listening to the Aussies chant along to old Krishna Das recordings, and trying to avoid the biting geckos and snakes. At night, we could hear giant wolf spiders scuttling around the perimeter of our room. The smaller spiders, meanwhile, had set up their headquarters in the toilet bowls, presumably because they knew it would cause the most inconvenience. I had to spray them away with my water bottle before I could even sit down.

By the end of the week, I was restless and eager to move on to the next leg of my trip. I had decided to sign up for a ten-day silent Vipassana meditation retreat at a center outside of Jakarta. Vipassana means "to see things as they really are," and is rooted in the principles of impermanence and nonattachment. I had done my first Vipassana a few years earlier, shortly after I learned to surf. The practice teaches you to become aware of your physical sensations as you sit in silence and stillness. The idea is to notice that every sensation—good or bad—arises and passes. You learn not to cling to any moment or feeling because it will inevitably change. From that awareness, you can respond with intention instead of reacting impulsively.

As far as I knew, it worked. After my first retreat, I decided to stay behind for a couple of days and checked into an eco-lodge— because nothing says relaxation like a compost toilet. The first night, as I lay down to sleep, I saw clusters of cockroaches crawling on the ceiling. Normally, I would have freaked out. Instead, I stayed calm through the night, even as the occasional cockroach plopped onto my bed. The next morning, I called the front desk and calmly (but firmly) demanded a refund before switching hotels. Ten days of silence and I'd achieved equanimity! Granted, it didn't look like I'd imagined. I hadn't transformed into a glowing orb of bliss, but I could be in a room with cockroaches without flipping out. If that's not enlightenment, I don't know what is.

I yearned for that feeling of peace again.

I needed it more than I realized.

CHAPTER 19

NOBLE SILENCE

As the taxi approached the entrance to Dhamma Java Vipassana Meditation Center, ominous clouds filled the sky. Rain began to pour down in thundering sheets, blurring the landscape.

"We're here," called the driver, braking abruptly in front of a narrow gravel path fringed by palms. The meditation center was about an hour's drive southeast of Jakarta, tucked into the misty hills of West Java. It sat between two branches of the Ciliwung River, surrounded by lush jungle and the soft green sprawl of tea plantations. I pulled my suitcase from the trunk and dashed through the downpour into a reception room.

As I glanced around, I saw people milling around in small groups. There were about sixty of us—half Indonesian locals, the rest a motley crew of American and European backpackers. All of us had come to meditate twelve hours a day, every day, for ten days, in what was called Noble Silence.

Noble Silence, explained the orientation handout, *means silence of body, speech, and mind. All forms of communication with fellow students, whether by physical movements, sign language, writing, and so on, are not permitted.* There was no reading, writing, or exercise allowed, aside from solitary walks around the property at least twelve feet away from anyone else. Even eye contact was forbidden. *Students should cultivate the feeling that they are working in isolation.*

A petite Indonesian woman with a long, thick braid ushered us into the dining area. Tiny cups of syrupy pink guava juice and trays of sweet buns filled with lotus paste were arranged on a low wooden table. The woman guided us to the snacks, then passed around a schedule. I scanned it while chewing on a bun. Each day would begin at four A.M., and we would meditate until ten P.M., with short breaks for meals. But the part that truly scared me: those of us who'd done a retreat before were considered return students and deemed spiritually advanced enough to skip dinner. My last meal of the day would be at noon.

A stout, white-haired Indonesian man floated into the room. "Welcome," he said, his voice melodious but firm. "My name is Wayan. We will have our first group meditation this evening. If you brought a computer or phone, please turn it in here." He pointed to a thin, doe-eyed woman sitting at a small table in the corner. One by one, we lined up to surrender our electronics. Our lifelines to the outside world would be locked away for the next ten days.

I was assigned a room with two women: a German backpacker and a yoga teacher from Spain. The setup was simple—three twin-size beds sat in a row, with a small nightstand next to each. I situated my suitcase in the corner of the room and headed to the evening meditation, starting down the path toward a large Indonesian-style building perched on stilts to protect it from monsoon rains. The meditation hall was on the second floor.

Inside the dim room, we settled onto cushions. The men sat on one side, the women on the other. Wayan sat at the front of the hall and pressed play on an old speaker. A recording of S. N. Goenka's voice crackled to life. Goenka, a Burmese-Indian teacher who helped bring Vipassana meditation to the West, would be guiding each session through these recordings. He gave simple instructions: focus on the breath as it moves in and out of the nostrils. If a thought arises, notice it, then gently return your attention to the breath—no reaction, no judgment. Observing the breath was meant to anchor the mind in the present moment and would serve as the foundation for learning Vipassana.

The first few days felt endless—a great wide yawn. Each hour felt like a day, each day a week. The morning meditation bled into the midmorning meditation and the after-lunch meditation and the evening meditation. We ate fried rice, eggs, and thick, sludgy porridge for lunch. I tried to take in as much as I could, knowing there would be no dinner. But with no real exercise, the food just sat in my gut. At night, I pounded lukewarm tea, forgetting that caffeine sensitivity was why I steered clear of coffee. I needed something—anything—to keep me going and to break up the monotony. Meditating for so many hours was more exhausting than I remembered.

Sitting with myself for twelve hours a day made it painfully clear how addicted to worry I was, and how spectacularly bad I was at relaxing. My thoughts bounced around like Ping-Pong balls in a wind tunnel, ricocheting from old conversations to unfinished to-do lists to a sudden craving for mangoes. I grew antsy, craving my phone or any stimulus outside of my own mind and body, neither of which was a *chill* place to be. I couldn't stop thinking about my email. I really needed to check it. Like, on a cellular level. More than I needed food or sleep or someone to talk to. I finally made up a work emergency so elaborate that they let me into my locker and gave me five minutes with my phone. Scanning through spam never felt better.

Every evening, we sat in a room and watched a grainy old DVD of Goenka giving lectures. Born into a conservative Hindu household in Burma, Goenka had been a successful businessman. In his early thirties, he experienced debilitating migraines. After finding no relief in Western medicine, he sat with a Vipassana meditation teacher. The practice not only cured his headaches, but brought him profound inner transformation. He trained under that teacher, eventually moving to India to open his own center. Determined to make the practice available to people of all backgrounds, Goenka reframed it as a secular, practical technique. He offered it to the world through free ten-day intensive retreats, sustained by donations from former participants.

In our meditation sessions, Wayan spoke minimally, only to share essential instructions for the day. If we had questions, we could sign up for a five-minute slot. I signed up every single day, eager for conversation. Aside from Wayan's sparse directives, the only voice we heard was Goenka's. We hung on to his every word in the nightly video lectures and the recordings that played over the loudspeaker before and after each meditation. His voice was low and raspy, like the croak of a dying frog. He chanted a series of hypnotic aphorisms in every recording, echoing himself after each phrase:

Work diligently. *Diligently.*
Work patiently and persistently. *Patiently and persistently.*
And you're bound to be successful. *Bound to be successful.*

Work diligently. There it was. Again. Even in this place of extreme *nothing-doing*, there was talk about hard work. I knew Goenka meant it in a different way, but the invocations hit a nerve. Work patiently and persistently. *I had, Goenka, I had.* Every day

155

had been a fight. And still, I had wound up here, burned out and broken.

After a few days, flashes from my time in India started to surface—jump-cut images that I couldn't control or predict. Sujatha under the acacia tree. The moment she saw herself on camera. My time in India had moved at such lightning speed that I'd never stopped to process the heartbreaking stories I'd witnessed. *This is the practice*, I reminded myself. Sitting with uncomfortable sensations. Not trying to escape them. Not grasping for something else.

My childhood had been an exercise in repressing my physical sensations. I'd mastered *not feeling*. But after days in the Indonesian jungle surrounded by fifty-nine mouth-breathing strangers, I started to feel *every single sensation*. With each inhale, I felt my lungs expand by the millimeter. I noticed every variation of my heartbeat. I could feel the blood chugging down my limbs, pooling in my fingers and toes. Between the pulse in my veins, the lack of food, and the hours and hours and hours of meditation, punctuated by Goenka's croaking refrains, I started to lose all sense of the outside world.

"Slowly move your awareness, part by part, through the entire body, from the top of the head to the tips of the toes and back again. Observe whatever sensations arise without reaction, without clinging to it or repelling it. Let it arise and pass away," Goenka instructed in the audio recording during the one P.M. meditation. It was day five. Or maybe six? I'd stopped counting. Time was a flat circle, an endless bowl of flavorless breakfast porridge. After four days of focusing on the breath, we'd been learning the Vipassana technique: scan your body, notice sensations without judgment, and don't lose your shit. "If you are aware of the sensations and remain equanimous, you break the old habit pattern of reaction and start coming out of misery," Goenka said.

That day, Goenka added a twist: "sweeping"—a quicker scan meant to supplement the slower practice. "After working part by part, you may try sweeping through the entire body," he said. "Move your attention like a flow of water or a stream of oil, from head to feet, from feet to head." One or two full "sweeps" were recommended before returning to the slower scanning practice.

If sweeping once or twice was good, then surely three or four was better. Maybe I could hack the system and achieve inner peace faster than anyone else! I spent the entire morning meditation sweeping, zipping through my body at turbo speed. Instead of the calm flow of water Goenka suggested, I was more like a busted fire hydrant. After a dozen rounds, my heart rate erupted into a gallop, thumping erratically as my legs started to tremble. I pushed through the last twenty minutes of the session, then quietly slipped away to my room, skipping the afternoon meditation. My overzealous sweeping had unleashed something. Over the next few hours, my body was stuck in overdrive. My heart wouldn't slow down. I did a few illegal sun salutations to calm my nervous system. It didn't help. I had not found inner peace faster than anyone else.

That evening, I rejoined the group for the final meditation of the day. As we walked toward the central building, thunder cracked in the sky and a warm tropical rain came pouring down. I ran down the stone path, covering my head with a scarf. Once inside, I sat on my cushion and settled into lotus position, legs crossed, with one foot perched on top of the opposite thigh. Mist drifted through the open-air room. It should have been refreshing. Instead, I felt trapped. The rain slammed against the tile roof like a loud percussion, sharp and unsettling. As I sank into meditation, my breath became short and shallow. My chest tightened, squeezing my heart in a vise. My pulse was a rat-a-tat, each beat pounding in my ears. The walls around me seemed to warp and bend, closing in on me.

I tried to pace my breathing and push through the sensation. I forced myself to sit even straighter. *Simply observe. This is just part of the process. This is normal.*

But it wasn't. Panic gripped my entire body, and there was nowhere to run. I sat through the hour, but I was freaking out. After the session, I waited for everyone to leave before approaching Wayan to tell him what was happening.

He listened, nodded slowly, and said, "Just stay with the practice."

I wanted to scream, to tell this holy, white-haired man that I was more concerned with staying alive than *staying with the practice*. That I'd never, in a decade of incredibly high-stress work with very little sleep, felt so unhinged. But I bit my tongue because his message was so familiar. *Keep going. Don't stop.* When you are in pain, *no you're not.* Pain is just weakness leaving the body.

Over the next few days, the panic attacks kept coming. I was so tired I could barely function, yet I couldn't sleep, kept awake by my heartbeat thundering in my ears. I lay awake at night glancing jealously at my roommates, their eyelids fluttering as they drifted through what I imagined were soothing dreams of clouds and puppies. They seemed unfazed by the rigor and asceticism of the program. Desperate for relief, I almost cried when I found a NyQuil pill buried deep in my bag. I popped it quickly in secret. It didn't help.

The next afternoon, a pair of yellow eyes started to follow me. I was washing my clothes outside and hanging them on a drying line when the other students around me transformed into zombielike creatures, their faces disfigured, their flesh rotting. One even looked like a mummified version of my mother. I told myself it was all in my mind and took a cold shower to shake off the images. But it was the bugs that did me in. Late one night, I got up to use the bathroom. As I sat on the toilet, three very real mouse-sized cockroaches rushed at me from the corner. Flinging the toilet paper aside, I yanked up my pants and ran out shrieking. The cockroach-level calm I'd cultivated during my first Vipassana was long gone.

The next morning, I packed my bags and told Wayan's assistant I was leaving.

"Only a few days left, no?" she said. "You're so close. Don't you want to *complete* the course?"

My shoulders dropped. I wasn't a quitter. Had they planned this? *What to Say to Ambitious People Who Want to Leave.* The sweet, unassuming assistant had activated my Kryptonite: my inability to quit. For those of us who have been bullied into excellence, who have learned to achieve in order to survive, there is never space to say *enough*.

I pushed through the rest of the retreat, my mind growing more jagged by the hour. On the last morning, in the last meditation, tears streamed down my face for two hours straight. At first, I didn't know why I was crying. The tears felt like water simply leaking out of my body. Then, a vision appeared. Three mothers I'd met in India, all of whom had lost their babies. We were sitting in a circle, holding hands, and I told them I had to leave. That I could no longer fight because I had nothing left to give. I promised I would come back for them. But first, I had to save myself.

When the final bell rang, signaling that we could break silence, I snapped out of my reverie to find my shirt soaked in tears. Around me, the room erupted into friendly chatter. People swapped names and laughed—it was like the last day of summer camp, if summer camp involved mandatory silence and existential breakdowns. I glanced around enviously at the smug glow of the newly enlightened. The thought of small talk made my stomach turn. I slipped out the side door, grabbed my suitcase, and waited for my taxi. As we passed through the gate, leaving the center behind, I shook off the last ten days.

I had done it. I hadn't quit.

Even if my mind felt way worse than when I arrived.

CHAPTER 20

DESTINY

After I left the Vipassana retreat center, I checked into a hotel in Jakarta. I holed up in my room, totally disoriented after ten days of meditation hell. The ground, the furniture—everything felt like it was shifting beneath me. One moment I'd be fine; the next, the floor would turn to air under my feet. I couldn't read more than a few sentences in a book without feeling like I was falling off a cliff. I'd lean against a wall, clutch the side table, or do whatever I could to anchor myself. I was back at sea, no drishti to hold me steady.

Maybe I'd finally pushed it too far and was having a psychotic break. Terrified I was going to have a full-blown panic attack in public, I ordered all my meals to the room. I spent all day trying to ground myself through deep breathing and calming music. Meditation, which had been my go-to in stressful situations, was obviously out of the question. Alone in a foreign country and convinced I was losing my mind, I called Zoe, an old therapist.

I told her about Papa and the Mentawai Islands, about Sumba and Vipassana, about how I felt like I was falling off a cliff—physically and metaphorically.

"Those are all high-stress scenarios," Zoe said.

I nodded. "Yes, my system is definitely stressed."

"No. I mean the things that you *chose* to do to recover from stress are also inherently stressful."

"Surfing?" I asked. "Meditation?"

"You didn't just surf—you went to a remote island to surf intense waves. You didn't just meditate—you signed up for ten days of complete silence in the jungle."

I thought of the chanting surfers. About the line between challenging yourself and pushing yourself to extremes, about chasing the high versus inviting in peace.

"You're trying to recover from years of taxing your body, but you keep replacing one stressful situation with another," she said. "What your nervous system probably needs is to just chill out."

She was right. I should have been parked on a beach and committed to a regimen of mai tais and trashy novels. Instead, I had chosen "self-purification through self-observation," which had left me sleep-deprived, wrung out, and teetering on the edge of a nervous breakdown.

The next day, I committed to doing nothing. I was lying in bed when my phone pinged. I glanced down and saw an email with the subject line: **IMPORTANT: Embrace**. I pushed the phone away and got up to shower. As I undressed, I caught my reflection in the mirror. My eyes were sunken. My skin looked aged and sallow. My arms felt weak as I massaged shampoo through my hair. Then, a familiar wave of adrenaline hit me. The feeling that had kept me up so many nights in India. My email auto-response clearly said I was on leave. Whoever it was would just have to wait.

But . . . what if someone really needed me? What if the message was really *important?*

What if, what if, what if. My siren song.

I'll just take a quick peek, I thought, hopping out of the shower.

The email was from a man named Jonathan. He said he worked with Tony Robbins and wanted to talk about Embrace. *Tony Robbins? The guy from the Netflix documentary?* I harnessed every ounce of self-control and replied: "Thank you for reaching out. I'm currently on sabbatical and will be available next year."

Pressing Send felt electric. And also like I might throw up.

Jonathan responded before I even set the phone down. It was *urgent*, he insisted. And there it was. The magic fucking word. The big red button: **URGENT**.

Delete, delete now! part of me whispered. But the part that was always desperate for *what next* won out. I emailed Jonathan my number.

Two minutes later, the phone rang.

I answered cautiously.

Jonathan introduced himself and explained that he'd been following Embrace for years. He wanted to use our incubator at an upcoming Tony Robbins event as an example of social innovation. Oh, and he and Tony wanted to invest in the company. The company I'd just shut down.

Was this some kind of sick cosmic joke?

"We're not taking investments right now," I said, pacing the room. I couldn't bear to tell him it was too late. "But what a coincidence," I added. "I just watched Tony's documentary on Netflix. It was so moving." I didn't tell him about my bucket list.

"Come!" Jonathan practically shouted. "You're invited as Tony's personal guest."

"Come?"

"To Date with Destiny. And let's meet in person to talk about working together."

I was speechless.

"I'm sorry," I finally blurted out, overcome with emotion.

"The timing really isn't great. To be honest with you, Jonathan, there's nothing left to invest in. It's over."

Jonathan was silent. It was a spacious silence—curious, not threatening. I don't know if it was his presence or the steady timbre of his voice, but I felt like I could trust this man. That I should trust him. When I opened my mouth again, the entire story came pouring out. I told this stranger things I'd never admitted to anyone. I told him that I was burned out, fragile, and having panic attacks. That every day I felt like I was falling off a cliff. Everything I'd concealed behind the glossy veneer spilled out. Not in all my years building Embrace had I talked like this—not to my co-founders, friends, or family. But I had nothing left to lose. I braced myself for a curt goodbye.

"Actually," Jonathan said slowly, as if putting together the pieces, "this is perfect timing."

"Excuse me?"

"If you'd already sold the company, we might not be able to work with you. Now we can come up with a solution together. We would love to be a part of this mission."

My heart was racing like a jackrabbit. If only he'd shown up a few months earlier. We could have saved the whole thing. But no. *No.* I'd been down this road too many times—getting my hopes up, pouring everything I had into a solution, only to have it crumble. It was a toxic relationship I couldn't quit. I had given Embrace a funeral. But here it was, clawing its way out of the grave, tempting me back. Embrace was like a cat with nine lives.

"Before I can even think about it again," I said carefully, "I have to take care of myself first. I'm burned out after ten years of this work, and I have to take a break."

The words were like glue in my mouth. Sticky and painful to get out.

"Well, then," Jonathan said after a moment. "Let's get you right first. Business can wait. Take all the time you need, and please let me know if I can help."

My head nearly lifted off my body. Never in all my working life had anyone said those words to me. *Business can wait.*

"But you should come to Date with Destiny," he urged. "I think it will really help you. We can discuss what to do with Embrace afterwards. I'm confident we can find a solution."

I closed my eyes and pictured myself at Tony's event— thousands of people jumping up and down, cheering, crying, screaming, while Tony loomed over us like a motivational Colossus. I shuddered. My nerves were too frayed.

"I don't know . . . I'm afraid I might have a panic attack around all those people," I admitted.

"We can reserve you a private room just in case. And you can bring a friend along," Jonathan offered. "I used to have panic attacks. I found the best thing to do is to welcome them. Don't resist them."

I told him I would think about it and be in touch.

A few days later, Jonathan sent me an audio message from Tony Robbins. *The* Tony Robbins. His voice was a sonic boom, deep and resonant. "Jane! Jonathan told me about your company and what you're going through. I know just what you need. Please join me at my event, as my personal guest."

I played it over and over in disbelief. Tony Robbins, the world's most famous self-help guru and a complete stranger, wanted to help me. Not my company. Not Embrace. But me—Jane.

How could I say no?

CHAPTER 21

LIFE HAPPENS FOR YOU

I convinced Thao to come with me to Date with Destiny. We'd stayed close friends after high school, and over the years, she'd seen me through all of Embrace's ups and down. No matter what country or time zone I called from, she always picked up. "It's a once-in-a-lifetime opportunity!" I gushed as I tried to sell her on the idea. Pregnant with her second child, she was not exactly itching to renew her purpose. But she was a ride-or-die friend, so she agreed.

When we arrived at the Palm Beach convention center, the scene was electrifying. The line outside stretched for half a mile. People looked like eager students on the first day of school. Inside the big registration hall, the energy was even more frenetic. Thousands swarmed the space, eager to get to their seat, to see *him*. Shrieks of joy were followed by group hugs—reunions of people who'd clearly been here before. These were diehard Tony Robbins fans who saved up every year to attend this annual six-day, twelve-hour-a-day workshop. Every year, they were reborn.

I thought back to watching the documentary in my living room just a few months earlier. I couldn't believe we were actually here.

"Wow," Thao murmured, her eyes wide as she took it all in. "I didn't know what to expect."

"Get excited!" boomed a coordinator, jumping up on a chair and shouting over the din. The crowd broke into an exuberant cheer and started surging toward the doors. Thao eyed me and clutched her belly. As we walked into the room, deafening electronic dance music and freezing air came blasting at us. Thao shivered, rubbing her arms.

"My God, I'm sorry," I muttered, flashing on the welcome email that I glossed over. Tony's events were kept at an "invigorating chill," they'd warned. He didn't want anyone dozing off during twelve-hour days. How cold could it be, I'd thought, tossing a single hoodie into my suitcase. It was Florida.

We made our way toward the stage up front, framed by massive television screens broadcasting the action: five staff members, bouncing up and down, arms pumping in the air to hype the crowd like it was day one at Coachella. Everyone followed along, jumping in place to the music and throwing their hands in the air. At first, I assumed this was an attempt to stay warm. I would soon learn it was just what people did at Tony's events. Not some of the time, but constantly. For days on end. What I'd seen on Netflix was a two-hour highlight reel. But live, it was an endless loop of unfathomable excitement. It was 9:25 A.M. and it felt like we were at a rave. A very sober, very cold, positive-vibes-only, life-altering rave.

An usher approached, glanced at our lanyards, and guided us to our seats in the front row—eye-level with the massive stage, where the music was even louder, the lights brighter, and energy more pulsing. My teeth rattled.

"Come on!!!" shouted the onstage hype-crew, leading us in a sway, then a sidestep, then a clap and twirl, clap and twirl, which everyone joyfully followed. This was bigger than a rock concert. Not in numbers, but in purpose. People were ready to have their lives transformed. In the documentary, I'd watched people undergo what looked like true transformation, but live, the scale seemed too grand for healing. Could you really find meaning in a convention center surrounded by 4,999 strangers?

The house lights dimmed and a hush fell over the room, followed by a murmur of excitement. Beams of red and yellow and blue light flashed across the stage, and a pulsating synthesizer morphed into AC/DC's "Thunderstruck." Tony Robbins came bounding out. Funnels of smoke shot up from the corners of the stage, and when they cleared, he loomed over us. His uniform was subdued: black T-shirt, black jeans, baseball hat. But his presence was anything but ordinary. Up close, he looked seven feet tall, a barrel-chested Hercules with a mile-wide smile.

"Come on!" he shouted, clapping to the beat. It wasn't a typical clap. He spread his fingers wide, but only the base of his palms touched. It was the first of many Tony-isms I'd come to know over the next six days. The crowd went wild, mirroring his every move.

"Welcome to Date with Destiny!" Tony bellowed. "How about ten good mornings? Ten hugs. Introduce yourselves." Everyone seemed to know the drill, turning to their neighbors, arms stretching open for a hug. I forced a smile. Hugging strangers wasn't exactly in my comfort zone—I'd grown up in a home where physical affection was rare. Thao and I exchanged a knowing look, squeezed each other, then turned reluctantly to the people around us.

Pacing the stage in just a few massive strides, Tony launched into his opening address. "We're going to change our lives this week," he said. "But this isn't all positive affirmations. This is real, raw shit. We're going to get to the core beliefs determining how you live your life. If you hear me, say *aye!*"

"Aye!!" the crowd shouted in unison.

Tony jumped down from the stage. "My mother beat the shit out of me. Also, she loved me." Pacing the aisle, he told us about growing up in North Hollywood. He'd been raised by a mother addicted to drugs and alcohol who remarried four times. She once poured an entire bottle of liquid soap down his throat. When he was seventeen, she chased him out of the house with a knife. He never went back—it was the first time that he said, *No. Enough.* Her violence had both scarred and shaped him. "If my mom had been the mother I thought I wanted," he said, "I wouldn't be as driven. I wouldn't have suffered, so I probably wouldn't have cared about other people's suffering as much as I do. It made me obsessed with wanting to understand people and help create change."

"Life happens for you, not to you!" Tony shouted. "If you're with me, say AYE."

"AYEEEE!" came the thundering response.

He laughed and struck a dramatic pose, pulling his arm back like he was about to throw a javelin. Or a lightning bolt. The crowd went nuts.

For twelve hours a day, we chopped through limiting beliefs, identified our core values, and mapped out our goals through a series of worksheets, interventions, breakout sessions, and lots of jumping up and down in the icy auditorium to a whiplash-inducing playlist of EDM, metal, and bubblegum pop. Tony moved through the crowd like a human dowsing rod, zeroing in on the person who needed the most help at that exact moment. Just like in the documentary, he cut through the noise with uncanny precision, diving straight to the root of people's struggles with supernatural insight. He understood human psychology at its core. I had never witnessed someone who could see through others so quickly or completely. He repeated his favorite phrases like a drumbeat:

When you're grateful, you can't be fearful.
Where your focus goes, your energy flows.
Change your state, change your life.

He clapped his giant-paddle hands over his head, his energy never waning. He never yawned. He never sat down. He barely even stopped for a drink of water. Everyone here was so primed for growth, the room could have self-combusted. Rest was not part of the equation. We didn't even take meal breaks—energy bars were handed out by his staff as we powered through.

If you want to change your mindset, change your physiology, Tony said.

In one evening session, Tony paced the auditorium before stopping in front of an Indian woman seated in a wheelchair.

"What's your name?" he asked, kneeling down, his voice booming over the sound system.

"Is that you, Tony?!" she shrieked in disbelief. "Or is this an audio recording? Is it actually you?" She reached out, searching for him with her hands, and it became clear that she was blind. "I've listened to your recordings hundreds of times," she cried, shaking with joy. "I can't believe it's you!"

The camera panned across the faces in the crowd. On the screens above the stage, I could see how deeply her joy was moving everyone. It was infectious.

"Tell us about your life. How did you get here?" Tony asked.

She'd been abandoned as a child in India—her mother had taken her to a playground one day and left her there. A police officer found her and brought her to an orphanage, and she was later adopted by a family in Canada. Throughout her life, Tony's recordings had been her source of inspiration and strength. She had been given a second chance in life. And now here she was, meeting her hero.

The camera zoomed in on her as she spoke. Tears streamed down her face. By the time she finished her story, the whole auditorium was weeping and laughing with her. Tony gave her a hug, and he was crying too. It was remarkable to see this huge man, the epitome of masculinity, so openly show his emotion. His vulnerability seemed to unlock something in others—particularly the men in the crowd. Over the previous few days, I'd seen more men cry than I had in my entire my life.

Tony turned back to the crowd, his eyes still misty.

"You might think she is missing something," he said, his voice raw. "Her sight. Or the ability to walk. But I think each of us can tell as we listen to this story that *we* are the ones missing something. That happiness and gratitude are a choice."

He looked around at the audience, letting his words settle over the room.

"We've all experienced serendipity. Something that happens that defies explanation," Tony continued. "Some call it luck, coincidence, or fate. I call it grace: the acknowledgment that there's more in this world than just ourselves—that perhaps a higher power gives us both the privilege of this life as well as the gifts of insight and guidance. Life happens *for* you, not to you!"

The crowd erupted into applause as he repeated his anthemic phrase. But this time, it hit me differently. Something clicked. If life was happening *for* me, instead of to me, then every experience, no matter how painful, had led me to this moment. I realized the desperate feeling I had when I was twelve years old, kneeling on the kitchen floor, was the very force that had driven my life's work. I had prayed back then to understand why my father was hurting me. Now I knew. That pain had given me purpose. The powerlessness I had felt as a child had seeded my compassion and relentless drive to help the most powerless people in the world.

When I'd prayed for a way to save Embrace—praying for the first time in twenty-five years—I thought it had gone unanswered. But now it dawned on me. Not long after that prayer, Jonathan had reached out to help. Perhaps both prayers—the one I said as a child and the one I said as an adult—*had* been answered. I had lost my faith as a young girl, but maybe grace had been guiding me all along.

I grabbed Thao's hand tightly.

You okay? she mouthed.

I nodded, swallowing the lump in my throat.

I finally knew the answer to the question Rahul had asked all those years ago at our founders retreat, before we moved to India.

I had fought so hard to save those babies because I couldn't save myself.

The next morning, Jonathan met me in the lobby of the hotel to say goodbye. I thanked him for pushing me to attend the event. My mind was swirling with all the revelations, my heart brimming with emotions. I felt like I was on the horizon of a new understanding, of a new way forward.

"You were an angel reaching through to grab me," I told him. "I was in a dark spot. I'm still recovering, but I have more hope for the future now."

He smiled warmly. "You made this happen, Jane. You get to create what you want. And I've got your back. We've got your back."

I was high on the energy of the week and the idea that any-thing was possible. I took a breath. "I've been thinking about your question," I said. "About how we can work together. What if . . . you guys acquired Embrace?"

Jonathan tilted his head, thoughtful. "Hmm," he said. "Inter-esting idea. Let's keep talking. That's certainly not off the table."

I tried to maintain a cool facade, but inside I was squealing with joy.

On the ride to the airport, I sat in the backseat of the taxi, watching the blur of city streets go by as a wave of awe washed over me. Was this really happening? Maybe Embrace *would* be saved. But deep down, I was beginning to understand: this wasn't just about saving the company. This was about finally facing the wounds I'd spent a lifetime outrunning. I couldn't step into what was next without reckoning with what came before. And I knew exactly who could help me do that. Her name was Christine Price.

CHAPTER 22

HAIRBALLS

When I first moved back home from India, I joined an initiative for social entrepreneurs called the Wellbeing Project. It was a support system designed to help people working in social change—passionate leaders tackling some of the world's most intractable problems. In the process, many of them neglected their own well-being. The initiative was founded by a man named Aaron Pereira, who recognized a troubling pattern: changemakers burned bright, pouring everything they had into their work, only to burn out completely. Aaron's observations led him to dig deeper. What he uncovered was startling. Many of these founders carried unaddressed trauma from their own lives. Their pain became the fuel driving their obsessive commitment to their causes, often at great personal cost. Their trauma was both their energy source and their shadow, propelling them forward but slowly consuming them in the process.

Even as I went through the program, I didn't fully understand how it applied to my life. I couldn't yet see how my work with AIDS orphans and premature babies was linked to my own pain. After Date with Destiny, the picture became clearer. Aaron's insight had been right all along: when you are driven by trauma, you may succeed in helping others—but you risk destroying yourself in the process.

My commitment to social impact remained unwavering, whether through Embrace or a future mission. I knew I wanted to help others. But I couldn't do that without helping myself first. For the first time in my life, I understood that confronting my pain wasn't optional.

Christine Price had been the leader of my Wellbeing Project cohort. Christine specialized in Gestalt practice, which takes a holistic approach to understanding a person by tuning into the present moment as a gateway to uncovering deeper truths. Often, the sensations you feel become a portal to the past, revealing buried emotions and experiences that have shaped your current reality. Like Vipassana, it was a method of practicing awareness. But unlike Vipassana, it was done with the help of a practitioner—a steady hand to help you navigate difficult emotions.

Christine had been leading Gestalt practice for more than forty years; she was remarkably gifted and intuitive. I trusted her completely. I called her and told her everything that had happened. She listened patiently and urged me to come to an upcoming workshop she was leading. Which is how I wound up on the floor of a low-lit room, surrounded by ten barefoot strangers, reliving a painful moment from my childhood.

"What does the pain feel like?" Christine asked gently.

I squeezed my eyes shut and tried to block out everyone's gazes. We'd been like this for ten minutes. Them cross-legged and silent in a circle; me, in the center, trying to feel the pain, to locate it. The pain was elusive at first, more of an idea than a sensation. But Christine kept pushing me to "feel into it," to give voice to it. Slowly, it began to move. From my mind, down through my body, until finally, it coalesced in my throat— a woolly lump stuck in my windpipe.

"Like . . ." I said, trying to swallow it down. "Sort of like . . . a hairball?"

"Keep feeling into it," Christine encouraged.

"I want to cough it up," I cried, the lump growing with each word. "I need to get it out."

"Then do it. Cough," she said.

I forced a cough. It sounded fake, like something you feign in grade school at the nurse's office to get out of class.

"Keep going," she urged. "*Be* the hurt. Feel *into* the wound."

I kept coughing. The more I did, the more real it became. My body started to contract, my stomach clenching as I hacked louder and harder. The lump was constricting my airway. I knew that this hairball, which I visualized as big and woolly and black, was both real and not real. But gagging and hacking as tears streamed down my face, I was desperate to get it out.

Suddenly, I was seven years old, sitting at my desk in a third-grade classroom. My face was buried in my arms, tears spilling uncontrollably as my teacher and classmates gathered around me. That morning before school, I'd been beaten for something minor. Between starting a new school for the third time in as many years and the violence at home, I was overwhelmed and broke down. The kids swarmed me. "What's wrong?" they kept asking sweetly, setting their tiny hands on my shoulder to try to comfort me. But I couldn't say. I had to protect my family. I had to keep us safe from people who didn't understand.

My classmates watched me cry that day. But it didn't feel better to be witnessed or comforted. Instead, I was terrified that I'd put my family in danger. I swore I would never cry in front of other people again.

I was fine. I was always fine.

Now, back in the circle, I was coughing harder, trying to dislodge the hairball in my throat. The coughing turned into dry heaving until, in one final retch, up it came—a heavy lug that thudded onto the floor in front of me. There was nothing there, but I could *feel* it. Its texture. Its mass. An invisible buildup of thirty years.

The people around me stared at the floor, then up to me, their eyes wide. Christine's voice drew me back to the moment.

"Tell us, now," she said. "Feel it in your body. Express without analyzing."

"I had to protect my parents, but they didn't protect me," I said, my voice shaking.

Christine echoed me: "I protect you. *But you don't protect me.*"

"I never know what's going to happen when I get home from school," I continued. "I don't get to be a kid. I have to hide what you do to me." A hot flush ran through my body. I was unspooling, a thread pulled loose.

"When I cry, you tell me to shut up. How could you do that?" I shouted, my voice raw with anger.

"Yes," urged Christine. "Keep going."

A pang of guilt hit me. I saw my father's face. Its soft lines. The kind crinkle of his eyes as he warmed my feet on those weekend mornings. And then, those same eyes flashing with rage when he flipped. "But I don't want to forget the good things," I said. "I don't want to speak badly about my parents. I don't want to hurt them."

"This is not about hurting them," Christine said firmly. "This is about letting a thirty-year-old pain come up and come out. Until you face the severity of what happened, Jane, you can't address it."

I nodded and tried to drop back into my body. My breath was ragged. Shallow.

"We cannot heal from what we cannot feel," Christine continued. "That's why we go back and see and feel it. That's why we go back and say it."

I choked down a sob. "You never said 'I love you,'" I whispered as hot tears ran down my face. "You never even hugged me."

And that was it. The heart of the matter.

I broke down, doing what I swore I'd never do again—crying hysterically in a room full of strangers. I shifted into fetal position, resting my head in Christine's lap. "Someone should have said sorry to that little girl," she said softly, stroking my hair. "And since no one did, I'm going to." She looked into my eyes, her gaze steady and loving. "I'm so sorry this happened to you. You didn't deserve it."

Her words hit me like a wave. My shoulders dropped. My belly ballooned with relief. I exhaled deeply for the first time in what felt like years. It had never occurred to me that *I* deserved an apology. My whole childhood, I'd been the one saying sorry. My entire life, I'd believed something was wrong with me.

Slowly, I became aware of the people around me. I must look pathetic, I thought, embarrassed at my raw, blubbery display of emotions.

But for that one trembling moment, I was too heartbroken to care.

Driving home from the workshop the next day, I called Joyce. She picked up on the second ring. My voice was shaky.

"What's wrong?" she asked.

I hesitated, gripping the steering wheel tightly. "What happened to us," I said finally. "The way Dad hit us. It wasn't right."

"Huh?" she asked, caught off-guard.

"It was abuse, Joyce," I said. The words were heavy as they left my mouth.

There was a thick silence.

"That's a strong word," she replied. "Everyone got hit. You know how Asian parents are."

By *everyone*, she meant kids from other immigrant families— like Thao. It had been part of the culture: the violence and the silence surrounding it.

I told Joyce about the workshop. I left out the part about coughing up an imaginary hairball.

"You know they loved us in their own way," she said. "They never intended to hurt us."

"Maybe, but it's still not okay. And I don't think everyone got it as bad as we did."

"I'm sure they did," she insisted.

"Just ask your friends," I urged. "Talk to your therapist. Please, Joyce."

"Fine," she said with a sigh. "Look I've got to go. I'm late for a meeting."

We hung up and I focused on the road. Even if my father never meant to hurt us, he had. I'd thought because I survived the violence, the damage was over. I'd filed it away neatly, compartmentalized it, and built a life for myself. But now that my life had unraveled, it was clear: what happened wasn't over.

I was ready to heal, no matter how many imaginary hairballs I had to purge.

CHAPTER 23

THE ACT

I invited Jodi to meet me for dinner. She was part of a loose group of Bay Area folks who were at the intersection of technology, philanthropy, and spirituality. They were a Burning Man–adjacent crew—dabbling in psychedelics, inner-child work, and old-school self-help seminars. I called Jodi because she had done it all.

We met at a sushi bar in the Financial District. By the time the appetizers arrived, she was already prescribing me her off-label therapeutic regimen.

"There's Kambo," she said, loading her chopsticks with wasabi. "Frog poison. Intense. Changed my life. You've got to try it. Oh, and muscle testing—have you heard of that?" she asked, popping an edamame into her mouth. "Mixed results, but worth a shot. And Landmark. Have you been to Landmark?"

I shook my head. I had heard about Landmark, but it had a bit of a cultish reputation.

"Definitely worth it. And the time investment is low, given it's only a weekend."

That night, I looked up Landmark. Billed as a personal-growth training seminar to identify and address psychological blind spots, it promised "achievements that are extraordinary, outside of what's predictable." The website seemed a bit corporate and outdated, but many people I respected had done it. I signed up for a weekend seminar in San Francisco.

A few weeks later, I found myself in a sterile conference room sitting with a hundred other people. The space had the charm of a DMV office, with fluorescent lighting, mottled gray carpet, and the faint smell of industrial cleaning products. Our instructor, Jim, was a tall, elderly white man, with a snowy cap of hair, a square jaw, and the eerily smooth face of a ventriloquist's doll. After two days of canned air and workshops with names like "Always Already Listening," and "The Vicious Circle," I was restless. I hadn't spoken a word all weekend, strategically stationed at the back of the room to ensure an easy escape route.

Then Jim introduced a concept that piqued my curiosity. "The Act," he explained, in his slow Virginia drawl, "is a subconscious strategy you created to survive. It's the script you started writing after your first real experience of failure. And it's been running the show ever since."

He paused, scanning the room.

"To identify your Act, you must go back to your first moment of perceived failure. How did you respond? The Act protects you from feeling pain. It's a one-line command you've been screaming to yourself ever since—without even realizing it. You must locate it, then rewrite it."

I leaned back in my chair, mining my early memories. What was my first moment of failure? And what had I told myself to survive it?

After the session, I approached Jim. "I think I've found a memory that's connected to my Act," I told him hesitantly. "But I'm not sure."

"I can work through it with you in front of the group," he suggested. "Raise your hand tomorrow and make sure to sit up front so you have the best shot at getting called on."

The last thing I wanted to do was to speak in front of an audience of strangers. But I was on a mission. I was there to heal. I arrived early the next morning and recruited an Asian man from my group to sit with me in the front row for moral support. My nerves were all over the place. The chairs were packed so tightly I could feel body heat radiating from people on both sides. Jim stepped up to the podium to kick off the morning session. "Who has identified their Act?" he asked. My hand shot up. He waved me up to the podium like a lucky contestant on *The Price Is Right*.

Once onstage, Jim motioned for me to take the mic.

I took a breath. I had gotten up early to rehearse for this moment.

"My name is Jane," I began. "My father used to assign me extracurricular math on top of my regular math homework. One night, when I was seven, my cousins came over and I played with them instead of doing my homework. When my father saw the empty pages in the workbook, he called me into the hallway, forced me to kneel on the ground, took off his leather belt, and beat me."

My legs were shaking. I shifted my weight back and forth to make it less obvious.

"After he hit me," I pushed on, my voice cracking, "I had bruises and lash marks all over my body. When my mother put me to bed that night, she rubbed ointment on my wounds and bandaged them. Then, she said: 'Make sure no one sees this.' "

My heart was in overdrive, my palms slick with sweat. I

glanced at the audience. A few people shifted forward in their seats, eyes wide, leaning closer to hear what came next.

"The next day, even though it was warm out, my mother dressed me in a long-sleeved undershirt, a thick red sweater, and cotton pants. At recess, I played on the monkey bars and was extra careful to tuck my shirt in as I swung from bar to bar, to make sure no one would see my lash marks."

That was all I had rehearsed. I ended abruptly and stared at Jim.

"And what was the failure?" he asked. "Was the failure not doing your homework?"

"I don't think so," I said slowly. "I think . . . maybe . . . the failure was what my mother said?"

Jim nodded, a twinkle of validation in his eyes. "And what was the *one thing*—the most important thing that you told yourself in that moment?"

I paused. "Make sure no one sees."

"This is her Act," Jim proclaimed to the crowd.

His blue eyes bored into me. I was fighting back tears, trying desperately to maintain my composure. "And you're standing in your Act right now. There is so much sadness in those eyes." He paused. "How has this impacted you? Your life?"

"I haven't been vulnerable," I murmured, my voice trailing off.

"What else?" Jim pushed. "This has ruled your life, hasn't it? What happens when you make a mistake? You probably tell yourself *Make sure no one sees.*"

I thought about my public-speaking fear, about the beta-blockers I had taken in secret. About every time I'd plastered on a smile, even when I was barely keeping my head above water. *Everything is fine.*

All I could do was nod.

Jim led me off the stage to a different part of the room, as if to say *we're somewhere new now.*

"What's the new possibility you want to invent for yourself?" he asked. "Tell the group."

I stood straighter and cleared my throat. "I want to be more vulnerable and courageous," I said using my most polished CEO voice.

People in the room nodded politely. They weren't buying it.

"Try again," said Jim. "They will let you know when they believe it."

"I want to allow people into my life authentically," I declared, crisp and confident, looking directly into the crowd. Again, they nodded blankly. I shifted awkwardly.

"If before, you were making sure *no one sees*," asked Jim, "then what is it that you truly want?"

I hesitated for a moment. Then the words came tumbling out: "I want to be seen."

I didn't know exactly what I meant, but I knew it was true. I wanted to stop hiding. To stop performing. And with that realization, I started to cry. This time, I wasn't in the small, safe space of Christine's workshop—I was crying in front of a hundred strangers.

Yet instead of shame, I felt release. As if my whole body was exhaling the shakiness and replacing it with the steadiness of truth.

My truth.

It had a hum to it, a vibration. And it woke up the entire room. I locked eyes with a woman in the second row. Her body rocked ever so slightly, and I could see that she was crying too. Everyone in the room was looking at me. Not through me. They were seeing me. They clapped loudly, flashing me teary grins as I shuffled back to my seat.

Make sure no one sees had become my ghost mantra. One I didn't realize I'd adopted in almost every part of my life. I'd gotten so good at pretending that, over time, my smile had become more real than what it was covering.

The act was over.

I was ready to be seen.

CHAPTER 24

LUCKIEST MAN IN THE GALAXY

Determined to give myself all the time I needed, I took on a few consulting jobs to pay the bills but otherwise focused on surfing and healing. After Landmark, I asked around about other workshops and quickly found myself on the self-help circuit. No longer working like a maniac, I finally had time for myself. And, possibly, for a partner. I was turning forty in a few months and was the last of my friends to be single. While I wanted to keep working on myself for me, I also wanted to be ready when the right person came along.

I attended a weekend workshop led by authors Elizabeth Gilbert and Cheryl Strayed that involved writing letters to ourselves from concepts like Love and Courage. There, I met a corporate executive from Microsoft. She was also single. "If you don't already have a partner," she told me, "repeat this mantra for thirty days: 'The universe has already chosen the perfect person for me who will show up at the right time and the right place.' And it will happen. A friend told me she did this, and her partner just . . . showed up."

The next morning, I repeated the invocation.

And again, the one after that. And the one after that.

I added my own spin: *make him a surfer.*

When I wasn't busy manifesting my wave-riding soul mate,

I was spending more time with Joyce. She'd recently gotten divorced and moved into my apartment building. For the first time in over a decade, I had the emotional bandwidth to truly support my sister. Most nights, I cooked us dinner. On the weekends, we'd do simple things—hiking, shopping, trying new restaurants. After every outing we'd proclaim, "Best day ever!" It was like being kids again, but with credit cards. I'd run downstairs barefoot to see her, or she'd pop upstairs to my place. It felt free and easy to be together. We were both single and I was Embrace-less.

Something else had shifted too. After talking with her therapist and friends, Joyce had started to acknowledge that what we went through growing up was abuse. We were both beginning to face it—and to heal in our own ways.

One weekend, a swell hit Northern California, and some friends and I rented a house in Santa Cruz to surf. After traveling around the world, I realized some of the best waves were about two hours south of San Francisco. Santa Cruz was a laid-back surf/skate town, stretched along a rugged coastline, where long, glassy waves peeled for hundreds of yards. Tall, skinny palms lined the streets, and the air smelled of eucalyptus and sea salt.

Joyce was coming down with her friend Jordan that Saturday to join a barbecue we were throwing. She called early that afternoon.

"On your way?" I asked.

"Listen, I met someone," she said excitedly.

"Tell me everything."

"No, not for me. For you, Jane. A guy for you."

"What? Who? Where?"

"I want to bring him to the barbecue."

"Some random guy? I don't know . . ."

"Listen," Joyce said, "he flew up from San Diego just for this swell. And when I asked how long he's been surfing, get this, he goes: 'How long have I been doing it, or how long have I been *obsessed?*' You're the only psycho I know who talks like that."

My ears perked up. The more surfing became a core part of my life, the harder it was to imagine being with someone who didn't share my passion. I wanted someone who loved surfing as much as I did—but who also had ambition and preferably didn't live in a van. From what I'd seen on the waves, the guy I hoped for was a long shot. But Joyce was insistent.

"I could tell by the way this guy shook my hand that he was meant for you," she said.

Pacing the kitchen, my eyes fell to a small calendar on the wall. *Saturday, October 20.* I couldn't believe it. It was nearly thirty days since I'd started the mantra.

"Hello?" shouted Joyce. "You're killing me."

"Sure, bring him," I said. "Why the hell not?"

The day of the barbecue, I felt at ease for the first time in months. While dicing avocadoes for guacamole, I looked out the window at my friends laughing on the deck, sweaty beers in hand, making easy banter. I closed my eyes, replaying the waves I'd caught that morning—chest-high, perfectly peeling, with the sun twinkling across the water. I bent my knees, leaned into the dip, then sprang up, carving up the face of the wave. I could still hear the rush of water as I rode the wave to shore. I twirled around in a state of bliss, excited to ride more waves the next day.

"Are you Jane?" A deep voice broke through my daydream.

I spun around, my white cotton dress billowing around me as I came face-to-face with the softest blue eyes I'd ever seen. My heart skipped.

"Patrick," he said, extending a tanned, muscular hand. "Friend of Jimmy's."

Patrick had a short, scruffy beard and salt-and-pepper hair. His handshake was firm but easy. I smiled, unsure if he had seen me twirling around like a maniac.

"Can I help?" he asked, pointing at the cutting board.

"Sure," I said, handing him a bowl. "You can cut limes. I'm making guac." When his hand brushed lightly against mine, a spark shot through me.

That night, as everyone broke off into small groups, Patrick and I talked while sipping our beers. I felt bubbly, excited, and unusually open.

"So, what sort of work do you do?" I asked.

"Private equity," he said. "I worked in New York for years, but realized I wanted to be in California to surf." He was in his early forties and was confident, but in a very laid-back way. He wasn't like some of the power-hungry men I'd met in Silicon Valley—hungry for status, for money, for titles. He seemed grounded, but the spark in his eye was curious and playful.

"What about you?" he asked.

"Actually, I've been taking some time off. A sabbatical. I was just in Indonesia. Surfed the Mentawais."

"Okay, now I'm officially impressed," he said, grinning. "Those are serious waves."

I told Patrick a little about Embrace and my recent travels. I didn't mention that I'd almost had a nervous breakdown. He listened attentively, nodding and laughing as the music around us faded into the distance, and all the other voices became white noise.

Patrick was supposed to head back to San Diego the next day, so I was pleasantly surprised when I got a text from him in the morning asking if I wanted to surf. We met up that afternoon, put on our wetsuits, and walked in stride down a side road to the surf break. Being in the ocean with Patrick, everything felt amplified. Full-color. Easy. Aligned. The sets seemed to roll in more regularly, the water sparkled brighter.

It was Sunday, so the break was crowded with a mix of locals and out-of-towners. At one point, another surfer blatantly dropped in on my wave, cutting me off without so much as a glance. I rolled my eyes—standard behavior in the testosterone-drenched kingdom of surf. But Patrick wasn't having it. He stared the guy down, calm and steady. Finally, the surfer paddled over.

"Look," the guy muttered, "I'm sorry."

I blinked. Did that just happen? Guys in the water never apologized. They treated the ocean like it was their domain, and women as pests they had to put up with. Patrick, through the sheer power of his stare, had produced an apology. It wasn't just Patrick's protective instinct that impressed me—it was the way he handled it, no words or chest-thumping required.

Later that night, after Patrick had left to catch his flight back home, my friend Sandeep burst into the house clutching a pair of camo swim trunks.

"He left his shorts!" Sandeep cried. "Classsssic move. You've got to message him. I *really* like this guy. I think he likes you too."

I texted Patrick a picture of the shorts.

Shit, he replied. *We've got three options: 1) Mail them to me 2) Have dinner with me in Napa next week, or 3) Come down to San Diego and hang.*

Grateful he wasn't there to see me blush, I replied: *Napa.*

That Thursday, I put on a colorful sundress and drove to wine country. Patrick was there for a conference, and I met him in the lobby of his hotel. He looked handsome in a crisp navy suit. It was a warm evening, and he had made a reservation on the deck of a nearby restaurant.

"I have a confession to make," I told Patrick over appetizers. "I watch surf videos right before going to bed, in hopes that I will dream about surfing."

He laughed. "I do the same thing! I adore your style and your surf OCD."

"My ultimate surf dream is to get barreled—do you think that's possible?"

"Stick with me," he said, grinning, "and you'll get more tubes than you've ever dreamed."

The conversation flowed as easily as the wine. We talked about our families, our jobs, the places we loved to surf and the places we hoped to surf someday. We were both the last of our friends to be single, and both hoped to find our partners—in life and in surf. Maybe this was *it*, I thought, catching his eye in the candlelight. I wondered if he was thinking the same thing.

At the end of the night, Patrick walked me to my car. We stood there for a moment, the air between us charged. And then he leaned in to kiss me. I stopped him, pressing my hand gently against his chest. "Wait . . . I have to tell you something," I said. He froze, pulling back. I could see the flicker of confusion in his eyes. "I'm already having a love affair . . ." I paused, letting the words hang. "With the ocean."

His face softened with relief, his mouth curling into a grin.

"Then we have the same lover," he said, pulling me in and putting his soft lips on mine.

It was straight out of a cheesy rom-com, but we were cheesy together.

Patrick was supposed to fly back to San Diego the next morning, but ended up extending his stay through the weekend. That Saturday, we went longboarding in Bolinas, a sleepy coastal town about an hour north of San Francisco with gentle, rolling waves. The fog was so thick, we could barely see three feet in front of us. As we paddled out, the mist slowly parted and flares of sunlight sparkled on the waves, shimmering like crystals. It felt like we were inside a waking dream. Every cell in my body was tingling, throttled with adrenaline from the surf and the possibility of love.

Afterward, salt-soaked and muscles worked, we had brunch at a quirky café near the beach. As I dug into my eggs Benedict, Patrick put his hand on my thigh. Electricity shot up my spine. When I looked up, his eyes were glassy.

"I've been waiting to surf with you all my life," he said, choking on the words.

Me too, I thought, nodding tenderly as a lump formed in my throat.

Back at my place, Patrick drew us a bath. I got in the tub and leaned back against his chest, my body softening into the warm water and into him.

"I know exactly the board I want to buy you," he said. "Something special to help you get to the next stage of surfing."

I didn't care much for gifts, but the thought of a surfboard— our surfboard—felt symbolic. It represented our shared surf dreams and potential life together.

"Within a year, I see it," he went on.

"What's that?"

"Married and surfing around the world. And kids. I want to have kids with you."

My heart stopped. It was everything I wanted. And it was terrifying. We barely knew each other. How could he say all this within a few days of meeting? It all seemed too good to be true. As much as I wanted to believe him, a part of me recoiled in fear.

I told myself it was just old doubts. Part of healing was about letting good things come to me. To believe that I could find a love like this.

You manifested him, I reminded myself. *Try to trust. Allow this to happen.*

I shushed the noise in my head and pulled Patrick into a wet, warm embrace. This is it, I thought. My big surf love. My oceanic fairy tale. *I've found my person.* I closed my eyes and tried to soak in the moment.

This is what I deserved.

The next week, I left for La Paz, on the eastern cape of the Baja Peninsula in Mexico, still floating in a love daze. I had signed up months earlier for a free-diving course with Hanli Prinsloo, a record-breaking South African free-diver who could hold her breath for nearly six minutes. I'd heard her give a talk years earlier, and was transfixed as she explained the mammalian dive reflex, or the human ability to become like seals, calming our nervous system and holding our breath to dive deep undersea with no apparatus. Free-diving was supposed to increase physical endurance, boost mental clarity, and regulate breath. I figured it might also help me with surfing—especially with my fear of being held under by big waves.

When I arrived in my hotel room, there was a huge bouquet of flowers from Patrick. I was floored. He did everything right.

We spent the first day of the workshop doing practice dives near the shore. There were twelve of us in the group, and we were divided into teams of four. Hanli and her co-guide/life partner,

Peter, released a rope into the sea. One by one, we tied weights around our waists, slipped into the water, and pulled ourselves down the rope, hand over hand. The goal was to reach the end of the line.

To prepare, Hanli led us in the practice of "breathing up" to expand our lung capacity.

Breathe in, two, three, four.

Breathe out, two, three, four, five, six.

And again.

After the fifth cycle, hold your breath at the top and dive down, she said.

No problem, I thought. I've got this. Surfing almost every day, I held my breath underwater all the time. When it was my turn, I did my five breathe-ups and dove into the ocean. Gripping the rope, I started to make my way down, hand over hand, punctuating every few lengths with a flipper kick to keep me from floating back up. As I pushed deeper, the water around me grew denser and darker. I started to panic. At the midway point, my whole body contracted. I shot to the surface, kicking as fast as I could. When I finally broke through, I gasped for air.

Over the next few days, almost everyone else in my group eventually made it to the bottom of the line, surfacing triumphantly like deep-sea explorers. Meanwhile, I struggled. Again and again, I swam back up halfway down the rope. "You have to let your thoughts pass by like a cloud," Hanli said. "Every thought, every struggle, eats your oxygen." When you are closest to running out of breath, she explained, the key is to relax. Panic, as it turns out, is a real oxygen guzzler. But I couldn't beat back the fear that flared in my chest each time I went down. All my hours clocked at sea didn't seem to matter.

By the third day, I was frustrated. My usual approach to problems—brute force and sheer willpower—was failing me.

"How do I power through this?" I asked Hanli, my irritation bubbling to the surface.

"What if you tried asking yourself a different question," she suggested. "What if you ask: How do I *relax* into this?"

The notion of relaxing when there was a goal was completely counterintuitive. Back at the hotel, Peter, who had formerly been on the U.S. Olympic swim team before pivoting to underwater Zen mastery, helped me work on relaxation exercises in the pool. Supporting the small of my back, he held me as I floated like a tense starfish.

"Relax now," he said. "You can let go."

"I am," I insisted, trying to let my body hang loose.

"You're not," he said. "Your whole neck and jaw, it's all tense. I can see it."

Weird, I thought, trying to loosen parts of my body I didn't even realize were tense. It occurred to me that I might not actually know what true relaxation felt like. My body had been permanently set to *clench*. It felt unnatural to let go. My entire life, I'd learned to bear down and push through stress. Relaxing was its own challenge.

Peter patiently guided me through exercises to relax every part of my body, from my toes to my temples. After an hour of working with him, something softened. My body felt wobbly and loose, like a blissed-out jellyfish. He timed my breath hold again. It had doubled.

The next day, I joined the group for an open-water dive. This section of the Sea of Cortes was home to whale sharks, sea lions, and schools of jackfish that swirled in "fish tornadoes." The ocean was a deep navy color with occasional patches of turquoise that offered a window to a seafloor full of jagged volcanic rocks and coral. We anchored, pulled on our masks and fins, and got in line to disembark. When it was my turn, I dangled my legs over the side of the boat, breathed up, and slipped into the glassy sea.

As I kicked to descend, the water suddenly darkened. A cold stream pushed past, and a ten-foot wall of silvery jackfish swirled into view. A fish tornado! A figure floated up on my right and I turned to find a sea lion gliding beside me. I panicked but tried to regulate my breathing by relaxing. *Embrace your inner seal,* I heard Hanli saying. I looked to the sea lion, who hovered effortlessly. Together, we watched the jackfish circle around us, thousands of them moving as a single shimmering entity. I floated in awe, suspended in the blue; he waited for his moment to pounce. In a sudden burst, he shot forward, parting the curtain. Fish scattered in all directions, silver streaks darting past me like shooting stars. Following his lead, I kicked into the torrent as their slick bodies rushed by in a dazzling blur of light and motion. It was exhilarating.

Peter was taking underwater photographs of us. He'd been down below, shooting up, and captured the moment in an otherworldly photo that looked like a giant blue eye. The sun blazing through the water was a glowing yellow pupil; its rays, the striation of the iris; and the circle of fish swimming, its borders. At the very center of the eye was a silhouette of me, my body elongated, relaxed.

That evening, we camped on Espiritu Santo Island, where Hanli and her crew pitched cozy tents on the beach and cooked amazing food. The night sky was an endless canopy of stars, each one a pinprick of light piercing the darkness. The Milky Way stretched above us with such clarity and brilliance it looked as though someone had taken a paintbrush and swept it across the sky.

I wandered over to a piece of driftwood near the shore, soaking in the magic of the night. I felt so small compared to the vastness of the universe. Alone, I felt my body relax, my heart rate slow. I had spent years building armor; softness wasn't going to come overnight. All I had to do was remain present. To let life unfold. To be okay with not knowing or controlling. Less than a year ago, I'd been at the lowest point of my entire life. Now, Embrace had a shot at resurrection. I was facing big, painful things. I was letting life around me exhale. And I was falling in love.

Life happens for you, I reminded myself.

I am the luckiest man in the galaxy! Patrick texted me later. *I want to spend every possible future free minute, hour, month, year with you.* I smiled. This is what I'd always imagined being swept off your feet would feel like. I loved the way he loved me—with ferocity and certainty. But behind the flurry of infatuation, a small part of me was also whispering, *too fast.* I wanted to slow down, but was worried that if I asked Patrick to temper his grand proclamations, I might lose him altogether.

Patrick and I caught up over the phone on my last night in Mexico. I excitedly told him about everything I had learned about free-diving and all the wildlife I had seen in the ocean. I also told him about a book I was reading called *Tattoos on the Heart* by Gregory Boyle, a Jesuit priest who started a gang-intervention program in Los Angeles. Through his ministry, Boyle had created safe spaces and meaningful jobs for former gang members, reducing the death rate in their communities.

"You've got to read this book," I gushed. "It's really moving. I've cried every chapter." We'd been riding this wave of love, but my work—the kind that betters the world—was still core to who I was. I hoped the book would help him understand that part of me.

"I'll buy it by the time you come to San Diego," he said. "Promise. Can't wait to read!"

When I came home from Mexico, I had dinner with Joyce.

"Patrick said he yelled my name in the ocean today to ask all the sea creatures to watch my back in his absence," I told her, swirling my wine. "I can't think of anything more romantic."

Joyce laughed. "That *is* your definition of romance."

"This guy speaks my love language perfectly," I swooned.

"I know, it's amazing!"

"I think I'm going to marry him," I said.

"I think so too," she agreed, raising her glass with a smile.

A few days later, I headed to San Diego to visit Patrick. When I walked through his front door, I was stunned. He'd already cleared out an entire room in his house for my things. He showed me the gear he'd bought me: a new skateboard, swimming fins, and a paddle.

"For body surfing!" he said, grinning. "Oh, and wait, wait, check this out." He grabbed my hand and pulled me into the kitchen. "Ta-da!" he announced, pointing at a cast-iron stovetop griddle. "We can make those Japanese pancakes you love."

I couldn't believe he remembered. No one had ever done so much to make me feel at home. As if reading my mind, he said, "I just want you to feel comfortable. Like you could stay forever."

"Thank you so much!" I gushed. "Did you have a chance to get that book?"

"No." He shrugged. "I couldn't."

What did *I couldn't* mean? He didn't elaborate or offer a reason. He'd promised he would get the book. So why didn't he? I tried to shake it off. I didn't want to start a fight over nothing. I was here for the first time and Patrick had done so much to make me feel welcome. I should be grateful, not hung up on a silly book.

That afternoon, we went for a swim in his building pool. He had some scuba masks lying around and we put them on and cannonballed in. Underwater, I turned to find him staring at me, his face comically distorted by the mask. He crossed his eyes, and I stuck out my tongue. He started to laugh, which made me laugh, which made us both swallow pool water and erupt to the surface, laughing uncontrollably. We dove back down again and again, making goofy faces at each other, hollering as we came up for air, like kids who'd just discovered their new favorite game. From the diving in Mexico to this, I felt like something heavy had finally lifted off me. I was so glad I hadn't brought up the book.

In bed that night, I snuggled up next to him, lying my head on his chest.

"This feels so right," he whispered. "I love you more than I've ever loved anyone."

My heart melted. I wanted him to hold me like that and never let go.

It also scared the shit out of me. Being adored like this was intoxicating, almost too good to be true. *What if he changed his mind? What if his feelings faded?*

The next morning, we made Japanese pancakes. I mixed the batter as Patrick prepped the griddle. "I told my family I met the woman I'm going to marry," he said.

I felt a flutter of excitement. "Really? Have you ever been close before?"

"To marriage?" he asked.

"Yeah, or proposing," I said, trying to sound nonchalant.

He shrugged, thinking it over. "I dated my ex-girlfriend for three years," he said. "She had a little boy, and I fell in love with him. I never thought I would date someone who already had a child. But he was the only thing that made me want to cut my surf sessions short."

"What happened?" I asked.

"I think we just had different ideas of parenting," he said, his tone distant.

He paused for a moment, searching his memory bank. "Before that, I briefly hung out with a woman, but that was a flash. Rachel. Really nice girl, but nothing serious."

At her name, his face flickered with something—a wistful look that I immediately clocked.

"She passed away," he added quietly.

"What?" I gasped.

"Yes," he said. "It was a tragic accident."

"My God. I'm so sorry, babe."

"Really so tragic," he murmured. And there it was again— the wistful look.

That night, we curled up on the couch to watch a movie. Twenty minutes in, Patrick fell asleep, peacefully snoring on my lap. But I was restless, my mind racing. I started tracking back to something that had been bothering me. It seemed petty at the moment, but now it was like a splinter in my mind that I had to extract. The week before my visit, Patrick asked if I needed anything, and I asked him to pick me up a pair of surf booties. But when I arrived, there were no booties. And he hadn't bought the book he promised. He had gotten a bunch of other things I didn't ask for, like the skateboard, fins, and griddle. I was touched by his generosity, but he hadn't done any of the things I had requested.

Had he really been buying things for me—or for the idea of who he wanted me to be? I didn't even know how to body surf. And then there was Rachel. Was he still grieving her? Was I just filling a void she'd left behind? Maybe that look in his eyes was because she was the one he'd wanted to be with. Maybe he was just looking for someone to fill her spot. I knew I was spiraling, but I couldn't stop. I grabbed my phone and searched her name on Google.

Up popped photos of a skinny brunette, a socialite type who was a model. *Of course.* Heat crawled up my chest as I scrolled through images, comparing every feature of hers to mine. Straight button nose. Creamy golden skin. Flowing brown hair. Big green eyes.

My mind flooded with toxic thoughts. I had never been considered beautiful growing up. I had been Nerdy Birdy, the awkward girl who boys didn't pay attention to. *Why would Patrick—a handsome, athletic, successful man—choose me? He could be with anyone he wanted.* Maybe Patrick still carried a torch for Rachel. Maybe she was the woman he couldn't get over. Maybe he tried to sweep every woman off their feet, the way he was doing with me. By the time I finally fell asleep, I had convinced myself that I wasn't special to Patrick. That he didn't *really* love me. That he was bound to break my heart. It was only a matter of time.

At dinner the next night, I was totally silent. All day, I'd been agitated and unable to focus. Patrick kept trying to engage me in conversation, but I just sat there stoically. Halfway through our appetizers, Patrick banged his beer down on the table.

"All right. What the hell's going on?" he asked.

I looked up slowly. "What was it like when we first met?" I asked finally, narrowing my eyes.

"What?" He looked confused.

"What was going through your mind when you first saw me?" The question I was really asking, the one burbling up like a toxic spring was: *How could someone like you be truly in love with someone like me? How could I possibly be enough?*

Patrick sighed. "I told you. You were in the kitchen, twirling in that white dress, pretending to surf." He pulled up a text on his phone and slid it toward me. He'd sent it to me right after we met.

I met the love of my life on Oct 20. She was dancing in the kitchen, was so in love with surfing, and imagining waves.

Instead of reading the message as affirmation, I scrutinized each word, determined to locate clues of malintent, foreshadowings of manipulation. As he recounted, once again, the precise moment he'd fallen for me, I was listening for the moment he would inevitably decide to leave me.

"I was afraid that you were more attracted to her," I finally admitted.

"Who?" he asked, exasperation flashing across his face.

"Rachel," I said quietly. It felt ridiculous to say out loud.

"What?" His jaw slackened, underlit by the flickering candle on the table. He stared at me in disbelief.

"She's dead, Jane! Fuck. I mean, what do you want me to say? She's been dead for fifteen years. How can you discount my feelings for you like this?"

Patrick looked visibly hurt. But he softened and reached across the table to take my hands in his. "Sweetheart," he said, his voice gentle, almost pleading. "From the moment I sat with you on the deck in Santa Cruz, I've had a singular focus on you and nobody else. You are my woman. I want to have babies with you. Understand?"

But I didn't. For some reason, I couldn't. The wedding bells I'd dreamt up just weeks earlier had turned into alarm bells. I couldn't focus on Patrick's eyes, or the words he was saying, or the steady warmth of his hands. And I certainly couldn't remember all the things he'd done right. All I could think was that if this man could fall in love so fast, he could fall out of it just as quickly.

I should have told him what I was so afraid of. Instead, I felt myself retreat and harden. I angled my body away from him, my silence thick with all the things I was scared to say. Patrick let out a deflated sigh. He motioned for the waiter and asked for our untouched entrées to be boxed up. Neither of us spoke as we walked to the car. When he finally did, his voice was tight with frustration.

"You know?" he said. "You just took one of the most special moments of my life and made me never want to think about it again."

It was a knife to the chest.

But I knew it was true.

And I hated myself for it.

When we woke up the next morning, Patrick pulled me close and buried his face in my hair. His breath was hot and humid on my neck. "Just come down for Christmas, okay? My family is dying to meet you. And I'm going to get you a special gift. Let's put this behind us."

I agreed, desperate to let it all go. I was excited to celebrate the kind of Christmas together that I never got growing up. I made Patrick a scrapbook of our first few months together, carefully pasting in photos and writing captions in gold ink. I bought him a new wetsuit he'd mentioned needing. Patrick went all out decorating. He set up a huge Christmas tree and decked it out with blue lights and ocean ornaments—starfish, shells, a seahorse. I couldn't wait to see my present, imagining the perfect surfboard he had stashed away for the big moment.

Christmas Day arrived, and it was the four of us: Patrick, me, his mother, and his sister. His family embraced me immediately.

After dinner, we exchanged gifts. Then Patrick passed around three identical rectangular boxes. "Last gift!" he announced. "Open them together." I scanned the room, wondering where he'd hidden my surfboard. We all tore off the wrapping paper and reached through the tissue paper to pull out matching hoodies from a local surf shop.

"Awww," cried his sister, clearly touched.

Patrick looked pleased with himself. "We're going to be a family," he said, motioning for us to scoot closer and hold our hoodies up for a picture. In the photo, my smile is bright, my face beaming alongside his mother and sister. But behind my eyes, there is a steeliness, something suspicious and hard. For the rest of the day, I waited and waited, up all night and into the next morning, for Santa to deliver my surfboard. It never came.

After the ex-girlfriend spiral and the surfboard letdown, things went downhill quickly. I found myself constantly questioning Patrick's grand declarations of love, criticizing everything he did as a sign of his untrustworthiness. I think it was a fail-safe to make sure I wouldn't be blindsided when he eventually disappointed me. I was so used to anticipating violence and heartbreak on the other side of love that I couldn't stop scanning for danger.

We were stuck on an exhausting hamster wheel of emotion, where I pushed him until things exploded, then we'd make up. Most often, it was him apologizing. I knew it wasn't healthy, but I couldn't stop. Secretly, I think I relished the music of "I'm sorry" or "I still love you." Words that had never followed blowouts in my home. The cycle felt familiar, almost comforting, even as it slowly unraveled us.

After New Year's, Patrick planned a romantic surf trip. He had business meetings in Amsterdam, and I was going to tag along.

Afterward we would travel to Portugal's western coast to surf. It was our first international trip together and his first surf trip out of the country in years. Patrick wasn't a big planner, but he'd planned this trip meticulously and generously paid for all our travel expenses. I was excited. I hoped the trip would smooth things out and get us back into sync.

We flew to Ericeira, a picturesque surf village famous for its right-point breaks. It was idyllic—winding cobblestone streets lined with white stone buildings, blue accents, and quaint red-tile roofs. At the edge of town, rocky cliffs overlooked a pristine horseshoe-shaped cove. The water sparkled in shades of deep teal.

"This is going to be perfect," I squealed.

Our hotel had a slow-moving, beachy vibe—just what we needed. Surf. Ease. Hopefully this would be a reset. In the basement there was a game room with darts, and on the first night, we rushed downstairs like big kids to play. Afterward, we steamed in the cedar sauna before going to bed.

The next morning, I woke to sun streaming through the room. Wide-awake, I was giddy with excitement for the day. Patrick was still asleep, so I snuggled against his back and wrapped my arms around him. Groaning, he rolled away, pushing me and the blankets off. I felt the hot pang of rejection. This was the moment I'd been fearing. What happened to cuddling with me being "the best feeling in the world"?

I sprang out of bed, got dressed, and stormed off to breakfast alone. He came strolling in shortly after, oblivious.

"God, that room was baking," he said as he sat down. "Wasn't it hot in there?"

I shrugged and continued eating my eggs in silence. Still half-asleep, he didn't seem to notice that I was ignoring him. I looked out the window and tried to shake it off. *Jane, you're in this beauti-*

ful place. Stop whatever this is. Enjoy your day. Just fucking relax. But I couldn't. Patrick got a call and excused himself to take it outside. As I watched him pace the parking lot, phone pressed to his ear, I was sure he was complaining about me. Why couldn't he just take the call at the table? Clearly, he didn't want me to hear what he was saying.

By the time he came back, I was wound up and furious. This time, he noticed.

"Babe, what's up?" he asked.

I said nothing.

"Jane?"

I sipped my tea.

"Jane!"

I stared out the window.

"I'm so confused," he said. "We were having a great time. Playing darts last night. And then—you just turn on me?"

By then, I knew that silence triggered him. He'd told me about his dad, an alcoholic who would shut down and ignore everyone when he was upset. I'd never given any man the silent treatment. With past boyfriends, if I was pissed, they *heard* about it. But with Patrick, I shut down. I figured it would be better than yelling. For him, it was worse.

Even though I knew my behavior was childlike, I couldn't snap out of it.

"You pushed me away this morning," I said, my voice flat.

"I was hot!" he exploded, throwing his hands in the air.

Once I was in that headspace, his words were hollow. I didn't tell him how deep his rejection hit. How being pushed away, even just in bed, triggered every fear I had.

"Let's go," he said, sliding his chair out. "I'm not missing the surf."

We both dropped it for the moment and headed out.

Patrick might not have been detail-oriented, but when it came to scouting surf spots, he was obsessive. We drove around town, checking out every break. The waves were about head-high, glassy, and peeling. Perfection.

"Look," he said, holding my hand. "I love you. I'm sorry for whatever this is. Let's just get out in the water."

Patrick went into a rental shop to pick out boards. Meanwhile, I sulked in the car like a scorned teen, arms crossed, staring out the window. Eventually, I followed him in, only to start bitching about the board he'd picked out for me, saying that he didn't care, that he wasn't trying. In that moment, the surfboard became everything he hadn't done. It was the Christmas present he'd promised and never delivered. It was the book I'd asked him to read, and he never had. Finally, he charged out of the surf shop.

We ended up not surfing at all that day. It was the best surf day all week, on the first trip he'd taken in years, and we didn't surf because I was having a temper tantrum. Back in the hotel room, I melodramatically searched for plane tickets home. After the trip, we stayed together for a few more months. We even started to see a therapist. But the connection was severed. Patrick grew distant. "I've failed you," he told over the phone one night. "The more I do for you, the more you push me away." At some point, the therapist suggested we take a few days apart to reflect on our relationship. The day we were scheduled to reconnect and discuss our future, Patrick called.

"I'm sorry," he said. "But I can't be there for you the way you need."

I stared at the phone in disbelief.

We'd been together less than a year. Just the day before, he'd written me a florid note saying he would always love me and that we would get through this. I thought angrily of all his bombastic proclamations, the love-bombing, emoji-laden texts.

"Jane," he said, quietly before he hung up.

"What?" I asked, through my tears.

"I wish you could see yourself the way I see you."

And then he was gone.

Over the next few weeks, Patrick shipped all my things back, promising via text that we'd see each other at some point.

I never saw him again.

CHAPTER 25

BE BETTER

Losing Patrick crushed me. The relationship had been fast and furious, like a wave that carries you too far too quickly. One minute we were planning to move in together, the next, he was gone. He was the only man I'd ever seriously considered marrying and having kids with. Instead, my worst fear had come true: he'd left me.

I unraveled. I couldn't eat. I couldn't sleep. I replayed my mistakes over and over ad nauseam. Every time that I'd harangued him. Not trusted him. Gone on obsessive spirals. Subjected him to the silent treatment. Critiqued his attempts at love. I was always looking to confirm what I was already convinced of. That it was too good to be true. That I was not enough. Anything I thought I'd healed by coughing up hairballs, by speaking my truth at Landmark, by seeing the purpose of my childhood pain at Date with Destiny, didn't apply when it came to romantic love.

I read Marianne Williamson's *A Return to Love*, three times, cover to cover. It was the only thing that brought me solace. One passage hit me like a brick: "Our defenses reflect our wounds. But no person can heal those wounds. If you don't already love yourself, no one can love you." It sounded so simple. So obvious. And yet it gutted me. I could see how I had chosen fear over love with Patrick, over and over again. In trying to protect myself, I had created the very heartbreak I feared most.

Nancy and her kids were going on a trip to Taiwan with my mom, and I decided to tag along. I figured a change of scenery and being around my nephews might help me feel less depressed.

"Where's Patrick?" asked Joey, peering up at me with big, innocent eyes.

"We broke up, Joey," I told him.

He looked at me, puzzled. "Why?"

I opened my mouth, but how was I supposed to explain to a six-year-old what self-sabotage meant?

I just shrugged and muttered, "It didn't work out."

Nancy decided Joey should sleep with me at night to comfort me, like an emotional-support animal. Loving my nephews was the most uncomplicated, pure kind of love. One evening, my mom walked into my room, set a cup of hot tea in front of me, and said, "Try to be better. Maybe if you improve yourself, someone will love you. You can get yourself ready for your next relationship that way."

I stared at her, mouth agape. "Mom," I said, pushing the tea away. "I don't want to hear this right now."

But of course, I heard it. Loud and clear. I wanted to scream. What did she think I'd been doing? All I did was *try to be better*. My entire life had been an endless montage of self-improvement. As she spoke, I realized that her voice had become mine. *Improve. Fix yourself. Advance. Achieve.* No matter what I accomplished, the message was always to do more, to be more. I'd always believed that if I were someone else, I would have been more loved. Me, as I was, had never been enough.

Nancy wanted to show the kids around the island, so we decided to escape for the weekend to Kenting, a famous coastal town known for its white, sandy beaches and surf breaks. I'd never surfed in Taiwan and was dying to try. But the break was about an hour out from where we were staying, and my Mandarin wasn't good enough to navigate getting there on my own. At first, Mom scoffed at the idea. She'd never been a fan of my surfing obsession. She was afraid I'd get hurt and hated how dark the sun made me. Pale, porcelain skin was the standard of beauty in Taiwan, and in much of Asia.

"O se se!" she'd say. *You're so dark!*

But she knew how desperately I wanted to go, so she agreed to come along and help me navigate. She hired a cab to take us to the surf spot, and when we got there, she found a place I could rent a board. She even walked with me to the beach in the middle of the hot day, where she hollered at all the lifeguards to keep an eye on me. I was embarrassed, but touched.

The water was a beautiful, deep blue, and the waves were friendly and playful. I caught a series of easy rolling waves. And slowly, little by little, I felt my anguish wash away—something only being in the sea could do. For that afternoon, at least, my heartache was soothed.

On the cab ride back to the hotel, we passed by a scenic overlook of white-sand cliffs jutting out over the sea.

I wanted to go take a look. "Stop, please," I said to the cabbie in Mandarin.

"I'll wait here," Mom told me as the cabbie pulled to the side of the road. "I don't want more sun." Her eyes flashed on my darkened forearms.

"Give me twenty minutes," I said. I stepped out into the salty air, breathing deep as I took in the scenery. Rolling hills stretched out before me, the ocean glimmering endlessly. I wandered a little, then found a shady patch of grass and sat down to meditate.

I wanted to soak in all the beauty, to get perspective, and remind myself that life was more than this breakup.

When I opened my eyes ten minutes later, something inside me felt lighter. Calmer. It was time to let Patrick go. Maybe I could leave him here, at the edge of the sea, just where I'd found him. As I got up to walk back to the car, I heard a voice call, "Xiao Yu!" I looked up, surprised to see my mom standing there in her big blue bucket hat and checkered shirt, waving at me with a huge smile. She'd followed me, braving the sun to take in the view for herself. She looked so serene and beautiful framed by the picturesque hills. So free. So at home.

As I walked toward her, a thought flashed in my mind: if there were a heaven, it would look like this. One day, maybe this is how my mother would greet me, waving from a sunlit cliff over-looking the sea while I sat meditating under a tree, my surfboard alongside me.

Back in Kaohsiung, Mom and I went for lunch at one of our favorite outdoor food stalls. Mom got her favorite dish, *mi fen*, fried vermicelli noodles, and I ordered *wa guei*, a savory rice cake steamed in a bowl, topped with pork, salted duck egg, and a driz-zle of thick, sweet soy sauce. It was a local dish I loved, which I couldn't find anywhere else. I wanted to take in as much of the flavors of Taiwan as I could. Being here had been a salve. We car-ried our dishes to a small table and sat on the metal stools.

"Are you feeling better?" Mom asked in Taiwanese.

"A little," I responded, stirring the sauce into my rice cake. Then, without planning to, I added, "You know . . . I've been thinking a lot about things that happened when we were growing up. I've been talking about it in therapy—when Dad hit us."

Her chopsticks paused in midair. It was the kind of thing we didn't talk about, especially not here, with the bustling world around us. But after a week together, I felt an unexpected softness, the kind that made honesty feel possible.

"I realized I haven't really healed from those things," I continued slowly. "I think part of why I get so scared in relationships is that I'm so afraid the other person will hurt me."

Mom stayed quiet, her eyes fixed on her bowl, but she was nodding.

"Like Dad did," I said softly.

She set her chopsticks down and looked at me. "Everyone got hit, you know," she said. "That's what happens in Taiwanese homes."

I held her gaze.

"No," I said. "Not like this."

I took a deep breath.

"I was four the first time Dad beat me," I said.

I wanted to yell and scream and say that nobody got beaten as badly in other homes. My father didn't have an orderly penal system, one with rules and repercussions that we could keep straight. His violence was fast and ferocious; his rage was all the justification he needed.

I wanted to say all of this, but instead I just repeated softly, "Mom, I was four . . ."

My mother took her own deep and loud inhale. I was saying the secret things out loud, and there was no turning back.

"Everyone got hit," Mom repeated, like a mantra.

"Mom," I said firmly, "it wasn't okay. Do you understand that?"

Her shoulders dropped and she sighed. When she looked up, her eyes were heavy.

"You're right," she said quietly.

It was the first time she'd ever acknowledged that what my father did was wrong.

"I hope you can have a healing, Jane," she said as we finished our lunch. "I want you to be happy."

I wanted to say the same words back to her, but we had reached our limit on honesty for one lunch.

Being in Taiwan had grounded me, but for months after returning home, I continued obsessing over what happened with Patrick—every high and low, every conversation, every misstep. I'd lie in bed for hours, retracing the exact moment things fell apart. Yes, we had rushed into things. And yes, I was right to be cautious. But deep down, I knew that wasn't the real problem. I had been so scared that Patrick was going to hurt me—so certain love would end in pain—I had preemptively destroyed the relationship before it ever had a real chance. And I hated myself for it.

One afternoon, I met up with my friend Deepak. He and Jodi were good friends and ran in the same circles. By then, I had exhausted every other friend with my endless autopsy of the relationship.

"I'm so ashamed," I told him. "I did all of this because I was afraid. I ruined everything." Deepak listened, his expression soft and thoughtful. "Maybe the parts you're most ashamed of are the ones that need the most love right now," he said gently. He paused for a moment, thinking. "I have some people you can go to," he offered. He ran through a list of esoteric healers he had worked with over the years on his own journey. "You never know what's going to work," he said with a shrug, "but it's worth a shot."

I was desperate to do anything that would fix this void inside, this gnawing sense of not-enough-ness that had destroyed my relationship. Clearly, what I'd done so far hadn't worked. So I cranked up the intensity. I made a spreadsheet, meticulously mapping out every healer Deepak recommended. I approached my healing the same way I'd built my company—goal-oriented, obsessive, and all-in. If one modality didn't work, I quickly pivoted to the next. I was trying to heal using the same "do-do-do" mindset that nearly broke me in the first place.

I sat through an energy-clearing session with a woman over Zoom, who spent the entire thirty-minute call burping, claiming that it was energy moving through her body that needed to be released. I shrugged, letting loose a burp myself. I tried neuro-emotional technique (NET) with Dr. Cruz. It was a form of muscle testing to help you identify unprocessed feelings. Dr. Cruz would tell me to make statements about my life or my relationships and then push my arm down to test whether they were true. If my arm stayed up, it was true. If my muscles gave out and my arm fell down, it was false.

"I'm okay with my friend Uma," she instructed me to say. Uma had become one of my closest friends, someone I knew I could count on for anything. I repeated the phrase. Dr. Cruz pressed on my arm and it didn't budge. *True.*

"I'm okay with my parents," she prompted next. As I said the words, she pressed on my arm and it immediately flopped down. *False.*

It was fascinating to see the disconnect between what my mind believed and what my body was telling me. After that, I was supposed to curl up into the fetal position, notice any sensations in my body, and lie there until everything felt neutral. I always ended up feeling a huge knot in my stomach—like my body had been holding something in for years. I always felt lighter after the sessions.

I dragged Joyce to a weeklong Joe Dispenza retreat, or

Dr. Joe, as he insisted we call him. She bailed by the third day, after people started to scream and convulse during the meditations. "This is like a scary Halloween haunted house," Joyce said, bolting for the exit. I stayed the rest of the week and, by the end, was fully convinced that we have the power to heal our bodies completely with our minds.

I was even willing to try Kambo—something so extreme that Deepak hesitated to mention it at first. Jodi was hosting a retreat at her home in a few weeks, and she eagerly filled me in on the details.

"It did more to heal me than anything else," she said, her eyes sparkling with enthusiasm. "It's been used by Indigenous people forever. It strengthens the body's natural defenses."

An Amazonian healing ritual using venom from the giant monkey frog, Kambo is supposed to boost your immune system, improve your mental clarity, and enhance your spiritual well-being.

"So poison yourself to get stronger?" I asked, skeptical.

"Exactly!" Jodi exclaimed. "I have two shamans flying in from Costa Rica. This is the real deal."

Still dubious, I agreed to think about it. But then the universe decided to get involved. As we were walking out of the coffee shop, a frog hopped across our path. That night, I dreamt about a frog. Since things come in threes, I decided that if I saw one more frog, I'd do Kambo. Later that week, I went to pick up a new surfboard. The logo was *a frog*.

I called Jodi and told her to save me a spot.

A few weeks later, a small group of us met at her home for our amphibian-induced enlightenment. Jodi led us to the backyard, a small, private area enclosed by hedges and towering trees. Five chairs were placed in a circle, with a white plastic bucket under each one.

"For the vomit," she explained cheerfully.

I considered running. Instead, I took a deep breath and looked around for the nearest bathroom. We'd been instructed to drink a gallon of water right before the ritual, which would make puking easier. The shamans emerged from the far side of the deck, their expressions calm but intense. They had long, dark hair and wore colorful beads around their necks. One stood in the middle of the circle, playing a drum while chanting, "*Oh Kambo, Kambo!*" while the other moved methodically around the group, holding a small smoldering stick. One by one, he burned seven small holes into each person's leg, then sprinkled powdered frog venom into the wounds. I watched in horror as two people instantly retched into their buckets. What had I gotten myself into? I was second-guessing all the choices that had brought me to this moment.

Before I could back out, the shaman knelt in front of me and pressed the burning stick into my calf. I balled up my fists and squeezed my eyes shut. Within seconds, a ball of heat roiled in the pit of my stomach and shot up into my throat and face. My entire body lit up like a malfunctioning toaster on the verge of exploding. I heaved into my bucket. Once, twice, three times . . . four. Vomiting was a relief from the unbearable sensation of being on fire. It was the worst thing I'd ever felt in my life. Just when I thought it couldn't get any worse, I sprinted to the bathroom, where I discovered the purging wasn't limited to just one end.

When I finally emerged, someone led me to a dark room with a mattress on the floor. I lay down, breathing slowly, and a sense of calm came over me. This must be what Jodi had called the "euphoric" part. An overstatement, though I did feel lighter. After thirty minutes, I was well enough to rejoin the rest of the group in the living room. As I lounged on the couch, another shaman stopped in front of me and blew rapé, a type of tobacco, up my nose. I felt a sharp burn in my nostrils, and then nausea hit again. My head started to pound. I sank into the couch, catatonic. Six hours later, when I could finally move, I called Joyce and begged her to come pick me up.

"I told my coworkers I had to rescue my sister from frog poisoning," she said, helping me into the car. "What do you think all this is going to do for you?"

I was too nauseous to respond.

Kambo was supposed to be done in three rounds. Once you did it three times, the frog's spirit supposedly lived inside you.

Ribbit.

I decided not to keep going. I was good on frog energy. I wanted to heal as fast as possible, but why did healing have to be so painful?

CHAPTER 26

THE WAY I SEE YOU

I'd thrown myself into the trenches of healing, but maybe I needed to step outside my consciousness altogether. Everyone in San Francisco was talking about psychedelics. Michael Pollan had just published *How to Change Your Mind*, in which he examined the resurgence of medical interest in psychedelics, particularly for treating depression, anxiety, and PTSD. He highlighted groundbreaking research and the profound, often life-altering, experiences of participants in clinical trials. In his late fifties, Pollan even tried psychedelics for the first time while writing the book.

In one chapter, he described a conversation between two people—one freshly out of an LSD trip:

Love is everything.
Okay, but what else did you learn?
No—you must not have heard me; it's everything!

I wanted to feel that way. I wanted love to be everything.

While Pollan only briefly touched on MDMA, it was the substance that intrigued me the most. Nicknamed "the love molecule," MDMA is an entactogen—a synthetic drug that can heighten empathy, increase self-awareness, and induce feelings of euphoria and connection. It had once been administered by therapists to help facilitate couples counseling and emotional break-throughs, until it was classified as illegal in 1985. But in 2017, MDMA came back into the public conversation when the FDA granted it "breakthrough therapy" status for its potential to treat PTSD. The results from clinical trials were astonishing: participants with severe, chronic PTSD reported significant improvements after just three MDMA-assisted therapy sessions.

This wasn't about neon lights and bass drops; it was about introspection and healing. After attending the Wisdom 2.0 conference and hearing Pollan speak on a panel about psychedelics, I decided I wanted to do a journey myself. Therapeutic MDMA journeys required a trained facilitator. I called Deepak, my unofficial spirit guide. As expected, he had a recommendation. He connected me with his friend Heather, who guided journeys.

We set up a time to talk on the phone. "When it comes to these medicines," she explained, "it's important to think about set and setting. Set is your mindset, and setting is your physical environment. You want to feel safe in your setting, so that you're able to explore whatever might come up in your mindset. My job as the guide is to hold the space." Heather explained that she followed the same protocol used for clinical studies. After taking the medicine, I would be given an eye mask and headphones to help me focus on my inner world.

"I custom curate every playlist," she said. "It creates an emotional arc for the journey."

"Will I want to talk to you?" I asked.

"Maybe," she replied. "But everyone has a different experience. No two journeys are the same, so there should be no expectations. You have to just surrender to it."

There was that word again. *Surrender.*

"What is it you want to explore by doing this?" she asked me.

I told her about my childhood, how being with Patrick had made me doubt everything, how even after all the work I'd done, I still didn't feel like I was enough.

"Enough for what?" she asked gently.

In my career, I had feared I wasn't smart or competent enough be a "real" CEO. In my romantic life, I never felt pretty enough or worthy enough. This pervasive sense of not-enough-ness was always there, lurking just beneath the surface.

"Love, I guess," I said finally.

My words hung in the air.

"Before we go," Heather said, "a critical aspect of the journey is to set your intentions in advance. Really think about what you want out of this and write it down."

We set a date for the journey. Heather was coming to San Francisco for a conference in a few weeks. She didn't usually do house calls, but the timing worked out perfectly for her to guide the session in my apartment. In the meantime, she suggested I spend some time clarifying what I truly hoped to gain from the experience.

On the morning of the journey, I woke up anxious. I made myself a light breakfast and did yoga to prep my body for whatever was about to happen. Around nine A.M. Heather buzzed. I opened the door to find a petite woman with curly brown hair and ocean-blue eyes. She pulled a big bundle of sage from her bag, lit it, and waved the smoke toward the corners of the room. "To clear out any negative energy," she told me.

I drew a deep breath, taking in the sharp, earthy smoke.

Heather settled into my armchair, while I perched on the couch, my body buzzing with nerves.

"I'm scared," I told her, shifting uncomfortably.

"Of course," she replied gently. "That's totally normal."

"I invite you to read your intentions for the journey aloud," she said.

I cleared my throat, my hand trembling slightly as I held the piece of paper I'd written my intentions on. My voice was shaky.

> *Understand and forgive Mom and Dad.*
> *Have closure with Patrick.*
> <u>*Find self-love.*</u>

I paused, then added, "That last one is underlined."

Heather smiled and reached into her bag, pulling out a tiny crystal cup with a single white pill inside. I took it into my palm, then swallowed it with a big gulp of water. She said a prayer: "*Thank you for letting us work with this medicine. May it serve the highest benefit for Jane.*" She looked at me. "Would you like to add anything?"

I closed my eyes and set my hand on my heart. "I ask that this help me find the self-love and understanding that I am seeking," I whispered.

Heather set up her laptop to queue up the music, then handed me a set of large, cushy black headphones. She had another set for herself. "I'll be on the journey with you," she said. "I'll always know where you are." It was oddly comforting to know she'd be listening to the same music, like an invisible tether connecting us.

I put the headphones on, settled into the lotus position on the couch, and closed my eyes. Twenty minutes in, I felt nothing. At forty minutes, I wondered if I should have taken more. I got up to use the bathroom. While washing my hands, I caught my reflection in the mirror. My pupils looked huge, like saucers. Something was happening.

As soon as I sat back down on the couch, a rush of energy

swept through my body, rising from my core and vibrating through my fingertips. My heart started to race. A chill swept over me. The space around me seemed to go still, hushed. Time slowed, stretched, dissolved. I dropped into the music—a series of oceanic, instrumental beats that pulsed like the rhythm of the sea. Each note enveloped me, pulling me deeper into its resonance. I was surfing, riding the frequency of the sound, until I merged with it—becoming each note, each vibration. Until there was no separation between me and the music.

A vivid image started to form in my mind. I was in the ocean, my body submerged in the warm water. Rays of sunlight pierced the surface above, but I was descending. My hands were clasped around a rope. I was climbing downward, hand over hand, trying to get to the bottom. The deeper I went, the colder and darker it became. A wave of panic rose in my chest. It felt like the weight of the whole sea was closing in around me, suffocating me. I wanted to let go of the rope and swim to the surface. But something told me to keep going. *Relax into it,* I reminded myself. I kept moving farther down the rope, until I reached the ocean floor.

There, hovering in the stillness, was . . . me. Or a version of me. Her body was almost translucent, as if made from light. Her expression was soft and serene. She radiated a gentle, loving energy. She was smiling, as if she'd been expecting me. And somehow, I knew—this was the version of me free from pain, from the weight of the past. My truest essence. My Higher Self.

A thought flashed in my mind: *I want to understand what happened with Patrick.*

"Not yet," my Higher Self said gently, taking my hand in hers.

Scenes from my childhood slowly began to take shape. But this time, I wasn't alone. My Higher Self was there with me. She held four-year-old me after the first beating I remembered—punished for a harmless swat at a classmate's arm. I felt the sharp ache in the little girl's chest as her father struck her. I saw her scrambling to make sense of it, to understand what she'd done wrong. And when she couldn't, I felt a small part of her slip away.

I felt her tiny heart break.

She held seven-year-old me, beaten for not finishing her extra math homework. I felt the sting of the leather belt slashing her arm, every lash an explosion of pain as she shook and begged silently for it to stop.

She held twelve-year-old me, kneeling on the floor. I felt the slap of her father's hand across her face, the crack of her glasses against her nose. But worse than the pain was the realization that no one was coming to help her.

Help me.

A tsunami of sadness washed over me. As a child, I had never been witnessed in my pain—not by my mother or my sisters or my friends. But in the arms of my Higher Self, I felt the safety I needed to grieve. Healing wasn't about erasing the hurt, I realized. It was about allowing it to be seen and felt. About learning to meet it with compassion and tenderness.

Why? Why did my father hurt me? I longed to understand. If I could understand, maybe I could feel the compassion I needed to forgive him.

My Higher Self answered softly. "There is no need to understand the past. Just forgive."

In that moment, I saw my father. Not him exactly, but what I could only describe as his essence. We had hugged only once or twice in real life, but now, without hesitation, I stepped toward him and embraced him. My body flooded with waves of love as I felt the blockages between us fall away like crumbling bricks. I felt his love for me, and I knew he felt mine. I no longer needed to know the reasons *why*. They didn't matter. All that mattered was love.

Then in another flash, I saw Patrick. I could feel all of his pain too. In that instant, I understood that he hadn't left me because he didn't love me. He left because he believed he had failed me. I heard his last words to me: *I wish you could see yourself the way I see you.*

As his words echoed, a soft, white light appeared, illuminating everything around me with an ethereal glow. It expanded outward, spilling across the space until I was completely immersed— floating in it, letting it wash through me. I reached out and felt its subtle texture. It pulsed gently, as if breathing, and with each pulse, I could feel it infuse every cell of my body. A quiet warmth spread through me. I was enveloped by the light, held by something vast and eternal. It was breathtaking, unlike anything I had ever seen or felt.

And then, I understood.

I was the light.

Free from fear and doubt, I was a being of boundless love. This was the truth of who I was. The truth of who we all are.

You are complete. You are whole. You are enough.

The words resonated through me like the clang of a bell. It was the clearest, purest truth I'd ever known.

CHAPTER 27

UNLEARNING

After my journey, I was floating on a cloud—light, unburdened, at peace. *Love was everything!* That realization changed how I saw the world, and how I moved through it. In the weeks that followed, ordinary things felt luminous. At the coffee shop, I was struck by an overwhelming wave of love for the barista who handed me my drink. On a hike, every tree, every flower, seemed alive with divinity, as if I could see God in the intricate patterns of the bark and petals. The journey had shown me my Higher Self, and in doing so, had opened my eyes to that same potential in every living thing. I had discovered a hidden thread connecting us all—a thread woven from love and compassion. I felt peace. Joy.

I'm finally healed, I thought.

I did it.

A few months later, still feeling high on life, I headed to a surf camp in Costa Rica to celebrate Sandeep's birthday. A mix of his close friends came along, including a woman named Anjali. For years, mutual friends had been telling us we *had* to meet.

"It's going to be fireworks," Deepak had said to me.

We finally met at the welcome dinner at the resort, held in a chic open-air dining room with low-profile seating and bleached wood tables. Palm fronds and tropical flowers decorated the centerpiece. Sandeep sat at the head, laughing loudly as everyone chatted and filled their plates with salads and grilled fish from huge platters.

"Here!" Sandeep called out, gesturing to an empty chair next to a fresh-faced Indian woman with long curly black hair, wearing a sarong and a slouchy tank. "Next to Anjali. Finally."

"I'm Jane," I said as I sat down. "I hear we're destined for each other!"

"I've heard the same," she said, smiling. Her eyes were kind, and I immediately felt at ease.

We quickly fell into conversation, sharing stories about our lives and the many friends we had in common. I learned that she was a doctor and the youngest of three daughters. She was a "casual" surfer. "I do it for fun just a few times a year. To blow off steam," Anjali said.

"I'm a total addict," I replied, laughing. "I'm completely obsessed."

During our surf session the next morning, Anjali's board hit her lip. She had to get stitches at a nearby clinic. That night, when I went to warm up in the hot tub before dinner, Anjali was already in there, looking surprisingly relaxed.

"Mind if I join?" I asked.

"Of course," she said, nodding. Her lip was swollen and red, with a thin black thread stretched across it.

"I can't believe you had to get stitches," I said, shaking my head. "I'm so sorry."

She shrugged, unfazed. "When you've seen the things I have, a few stitches is nothing."

"Damn. I would be so dramatic, but here you are, cool as a cucumber."

"They told me to stay out of the water for three days. We'll see about that." Anjali raised an eyebrow, a mischievous glint in her eye.

"What sort of medicine do you practice?" I asked.

"Mostly intensive care," she replied. "But I've been getting into trauma work recently."

"Like in the ER?"

"Not exactly." She leaned back. "I'm exploring the therapeutic use of ketamine—for trauma."

I perked up. "No way. I just did a MDMA journey."

"Really? How was it?"

I told her about Patrick, and what had happened in the journey. "I met a version of me that was free of all the pain and doubt," I concluded. "The person I wish I could be."

"That's incredible," she said gently. "Patrick must have come into your life for this one reason. To help you see everything you already are."

I felt like Anjali understood me. Our connection was frenetic, like friends who'd been waiting their whole lives to meet and had to catch up as fast as they could on all they'd missed. The next day, we went into town for lunch and smoothies. As we relaxed in the open-air café, we took turns running through the details of our upbringings. She came from an immigrant family, too, and her parents had high expectations like mine did. I told her about my dad and the violence I experienced growing up.

"I didn't even call it abuse until recently," I told her.

She nodded. "It took me a long time to confront my own abuse too," she told me.

"I had to lock up my emotions for so long," I said, my voice cracking.

Anjali reached across the table and squeezed my hand. "Feeling wasn't safe for me either. I've done all the things—the outer trappings everyone was so eager for me to achieve. But feelings?" She laughed dryly. "They just got in the way."

"I'm only now starting to tap into how sad all of that was," I said. "The MDMA journey really helped me with that."

"There's a lot of unlearning to do," Anjali said.

"Wow," I said, sitting back. "Yeah, I hadn't thought of it like that."

Unlearning. I'd been doing the exact opposite. Courses, books, therapies, psychedelic journeys—I was always trying to *do* something to heal. But *unlearning?* That sounded softer, less confrontational, and way easier.

The next morning, the sky opened and dumped rain on us. The sea was churning, whitecaps bursting with each surge of the tide. The rain came down in thick, hazy sheets. A hurricane was moving in over the peninsula.

"We'll get out for a morning session before it hits," our surf coach announced.

We followed him to the beach and paddled out. It felt like swimming through cement. Every stroke was leaden. The wind whipped against our faces. The waves shot toward us in quick, chaotic sets. We bobbed up, down, and sideways like buoys, going nowhere

"This is pointless," I called out after ten minutes, and started paddling back to shore. Most of the others followed. When I reached the beach, I looked for Anjali. But she was already way out, beyond the break. Just as I spotted her in the ocean, a massive wave rolled through. When it cleared, I could no longer see her.

"Do you see Anjali?" I yelled to Sandeep, who was just down the beach. He shook his head, his face suddenly serious. A few minutes later, a white board floated to shore.

"Anjali's board," the coach cried. "She must have lost her leash!"

My stomach sank. The coach blew a whistle and started waving to the team on the shore to deploy the rescue squad. I squinted out at the horizon, scanning frantically. Nothing. We watched the rescue team swim out, their bodies becoming smaller and smaller, until they were black dots. A huge wave rose in the distance, and when it dipped, I saw something—or someone—in the trough.

"It's Anjali!" I screamed, pointing.

We sprinted toward the water as she came into view. She was backstroking through the churning waves, her arms cutting the water like soft butter, as if she didn't have a care in the world. She finally saw us and waved.

When she got to the shore, we all ran toward her.

"Anjali, are you okay?" I asked, breathless.

"My God," she said, her stitches stretching as she grinned. "What's the big deal? You afraid of a little storm?"

I finally understood why all our friends kept saying we had to meet. Anjali and I both knew how to weather storms. When you've grown up in chaos, the storm can feel familiar—even comforting. That's what we shared with the Sumba surfers, the thrill-seekers, the workaholics, the dreamers, the do-mores.

We weren't just survivors—we were builders and creators. We were proactive and productive. We launched businesses. We became doctors, CEOs, and leaders. We achieved to outrun our pain. It wasn't the hurricane we feared; it was the calm. We'd rather backstroke through a storm than face the terror that comes when everything is smooth sailing.

Like Anjali, I was great in a crisis.

And if there wasn't a crisis, I was really good at creating one.

CHAPTER 28

PLEASURE POINT

I'd started spending time in Santa Cruz whenever I could, renting a room at a local guesthouse in a beachside neighborhood called Pleasure Point. Surfboards leaned against weathered fences, and wetsuits hung over railings, drying in the afternoon sun. Everyone waved to each other as they rode beach cruisers or walked their dogs. The weather was almost always ten degrees warmer than San Francisco. Just seventy miles south, it felt like a different world—one synced to the rhythm of the water, where nothing needed to move faster than the next set rolling in.

At the guesthouse, my life was stripped down. I had a few outfits, flip-flops, a sunhat, my surf gear, a computer, and my journal. I planned my days around the surf, scheduling meetings only at high or low tide so I could catch the best waves at mid-tide. Every morning, after a breakfast of tea and toast, I'd grab my board and walk a few blocks to the beach. All roads in Pleasure Point ran to the sea, where a craggy bluff overlooked the Pacific. Just above the break sat a small park where neighbors milled about, catching up over morning coffee. Conversations were refreshingly light and down-to-earth—about the weather, surf conditions, or the latest burrito spot.

In Santa Cruz, no one cared what I did for work. No one cared that I had started a company that saved babies—or that it had shut down. And the more time I spent there, the less I cared myself. The more inner work I did, the less I could stomach the status-seeking achievement culture in Silicon Valley. I didn't feel the constant need to fix myself, to keep pushing, to achieve the next milestone. I was enjoying a slower pace of life, one wave at a time.

I was going for a walk on the beach one morning when Jonathan called. We'd been checking in occasionally since Date with Destiny.

"Morning," I said cheerfully. "How's your family?"

"Great!" he said. "I've got news."

My heart leapt into my throat.

"Tony and I have been talking about it. And we'd like to move forward with acquiring Embrace."

Oh. My. God.

"Jane?" he asked after a few seconds. "You there?"

"Wow. I don't . . . I don't even know what to say."

"Say yes!" he cried. "This is happening because *you* called it into your life."

"This is . . . this is the biggest gift from the universe," I said, my voice raw. "And from you. Thank you."

"Embrace is going to save a million babies," Jonathan declared. "A million and beyond!"

"This is incredible," I said. But even as the words left my mouth, anxiety was starting to creep in. "I need to be clear about something. I do not want to be the CEO. *I can't.*" My pulse shot up just thinking about it.

"No, no, we're fine with that," he reassured me. "We'll hire a new person for that role but would love to hire you as a consultant to get things up and running again."

Relief washed over me. If this deal went through, families around the world would continue to have access to our incubators—and I would no longer have to carry the weight of the operation on my shoulders.

Jonathan told me he'd start preparing the paperwork and be in touch soon. The acquisition offer would be small—just enough to pay off some of the company's debt—but it would give Embrace a future. I knew anything could happen before the deal was done, so I tried not to get my hopes up *too* much. After I hung up, I sat on the bench overlooking the bluff, awestruck, as the waves crashed and receded below. I thought about the prayer I had said less than a year earlier, asking for Embrace to be saved. This felt like a miracle. But for once, I wasn't attached to the outcome. Whether it worked out or not, my life would go on.

We completed the acquisition process a few months later. I was finally stepping out of what was *not yet known* into *what was next*. And what was next was a life of balanced work and play.

Then Covid-19 hit. The night the lockdown was announced I was having dinner with a friend, Lisa, and her husband, John. Lisa was a former dancer, and John was a retired lawyer; they had also moved to Santa Cruz for the surf life. Over grilled fish and wine, they offered to let me crash in their guest cottage for a few nights. I accepted gratefully, thinking it would be a short stay. A few nights became a few months. The three of us became a Covid pod, surfing and cooking all our meals together.

One night, they shared the story of how they had met on a dating app. It was a second marriage for both. The conversation turned to my love life—or lack thereof.

"You should be dating," Lisa declared, passing me the salad bowl. "Is there anyone we surf with you'd consider?"

I laughed. "It's a pandemic! Not exactly prime time for romance."

Lisa raised an eyebrow. "Come on, there's gotta be someone."

I shook my head. "Not really. It's great to meet all these surfers, but I think I need someone who also has career ambitions too."

"A great surfer who is handsome, ambitious, and financially secure? You may have to compromise on some of your criteria."

She had a point. Santa Cruz was worlds apart from the hyper-driven culture of Silicon Valley. My social circles had been dominated by type-A overachievers at the top of their fields. Between grad school and work, I'd spent the last decade in some of the most ambitious environments. My parents had raised me to believe that success was a duty. Achievement was woven into the fabric of my identity. While I aspired to traditional markers of success less and less, unraveling a lifetime of deeply rooted expectations wasn't going to happen overnight. Those influences still shaped my worldview—and, admittedly, my dating expectations.

Surfing in Santa Cruz had introduced me to a different kind of life. Many locals had grown up there and stayed to build lives centered around family and community. Most weren't climbing corporate ladders or plotting start-ups; they were catching waves and living in the moment. Despite what happened with Patrick, I still dreamt of being with a surfer. Someone who could flow on waves—and flow through life with me. Someone who was laidback but also understood the other world I inhabited.

A month into lockdown, I noticed Ryan for the first time. We were surfing at the break I'd been frequenting, and he was paddling for a wave. When he popped up to ride it, our eyes locked.

I felt a jolt of energy. Time slowed as I watched him, transfixed. His movements were minimal but powerful: a slight bend of the knee, a tiny flick of the board. For the most part, he let the wave lead, responding to its cues. Every motion was artful, skirting the edge between control and surrender. It was the most graceful surfing I'd ever seen. It wasn't just surfing—it was poetry.

Other surfers, mostly macho men, charged the waves aggressively. They muscled their boards forward, slicing through the water violently, all pumping legs and flailing arms, like they had something to prove. Not Ryan. He was relaxed. Confident. Powerful without being forceful. Ryan had *flow*. It was everything I was striving for, both in and out of the water.

The wave closed, and just before he disappeared from my sight, I caught a glimpse of a soft light emanating from him. It was similar to the light I had seen in my MDMA journey.

I paddled up to him. "That was beautiful!" I gushed.

He grinned. "Thanks."

Up close, he was strikingly handsome—sandy-blond hair, sea-colored eyes, square jaw, and a lean, muscular build.

"I'm Jane. It's inspiring to watch you."

"I'm Ryan," he said, his voice deeper than I expected. "I've seen you around."

After that, I found myself looking for Ryan whenever I surfed. Some days, he would wait patiently to ride a single perfect wave and then paddle in without a word. The more I watched him surf, the more drawn to him I was. Other surfers watched him, too. I could see in their eyes that he had something they didn't. Something you can't buy or teach.

One afternoon, we chatted between sets.

"How long have you been surfing?" I asked.

"Forever," he said. "Probably since I was ten. I still remember the feeling of catching my first wave."

"Is surfing the love of your life?" I teased. I figured a guy who surfed like that must be as obsessed as me. "It's mine."

He looked surprised at the question, then thought about it for a moment.

"No . . ." he answered with a wry smile. "I'm still hopeful."

I laughed.

"What sort of work do you do?" I asked.

"I'm in the trades," he answered.

"Like commodity trading?"

"No, agriculture," he responded curtly.

"Oh, where do you work?"

"Downtown."

Agriculture downtown? *Weird.*

He didn't offer anything else, and it seemed best not to press.

A week later, I had a vivid dream about Ryan. In the dream, we lived together in a stunning home with floor-to-ceiling windows overlooking the sea. He carried me up a wooden spiral staircase, looked into my eyes, and said, "I'm so happy you're the last woman I am ever going to kiss." When I woke up, I could still feel his arms around me.

Later that day, I saw him at the beach. He had just come out of the ocean.

"How is it out there?" I asked, trying to sound casual.

"Really fun," he said. "Bigger than I thought it was going to be. I'm going home to grab a different board." He ruffled his hair, flinging tiny drops of seawater. "What are you doing this weekend? I'm around if you want to borrow that board." He'd been encouraging me to try shortboards. It would help get my speed up, he said, and allow me to maneuver more easily.

"That would be great!"

Ryan got my phone number, which he memorized on the spot. When I got home after surfing, there was a text from him with his address. Two blocks away. After showering, I walked over. I followed a side path that led to a scruffy yard, where Ryan was reclined on a bench, smoking a cigar. A cloud of smoke lingered over his head.

"Hi," he said, looking up with a smile. I approached awkwardly, unsure how to interact with him out of the water. I'd never seen someone smoke a cigar so casually in the middle of the day.

"I know it's a nasty habit," he said, waving the cigar. "I thought about putting it out before you got here. But I needed it." He shrugged, his eyes falling to the ground. He didn't look like the relaxed, confident man I'd watched riding waves. He looked tired, withdrawn. Even his voice sounded different. He had a drawl I couldn't place. Almost a rural twang. Where before I'd seen a light, now there was something else—a shadow, an aura of sadness. He walked over to a shortboard lying on the grass.

"Here she is," he said. "Keep it for as long as you'd like. I tried to get the dirty wax off."

"Thanks!" I said. "So, this is where you live?" I gestured to the cottage behind him. It was marine-blue with weathered shutters. "It's sweet."

He shrugged. "It does the trick. You can check it out if you want." Ryan headed inside, walking with the slightest bow-legged swagger. I followed him into the small studio. In one corner was a coffee table with stacks of vinyl records and a glass fishbowl with two fish.

"Those are Othello and Iago," he said, pointing.

"From the Shakespeare play?" I asked, surprised.

He nodded and filled two glasses with water. I looked around. His bed was pushed into another corner and next to it was a towering stack of books. I wandered over and scanned the titles: *Crime and Punishment, Moby-Dick, Middlemarch.* All the classics.

Who was this guy?

"So, what is it you do, again?" I asked, even more curious now.

"I used to work at UCLA, after I graduated," he said.

"But what do you do now?" I pressed. Why was he being so secretive?

"I'm in cannabis," he said, his eyes darting to the side.

"What do you do in cannabis?"

"I guess you could say . . . I'm something of *a consultant.*"

The air crackled with tension. It was all so mysterious. The less he said, the more I wanted to know. I switched topics, steering us back to our common ground: surfing. A friend had filmed one of my waves from the shore, and I pulled it up and showed it to Ryan.

He watched, leaning closer to me just as the wave peaked.

"Nice," he said as the video came to an end. "Try bending your knees and opening your arms up more." He squatted low and lifted his arms out to his sides, his wingspan filling the space around us.

I grinned. *Very hot.*

"I have an idea," I blurted out. "How about you teach me everything you know about surfing, and I'll buy you a beer?"

Ryan raised an eyebrow. "You want me to teach you *everything* I know about surfing for *one* beer?"

I laughed. "That's the deal."

"Sure," he said, grinning.

As he walked me out, I scooped the board up from the lawn and waved goodbye without looking back, hoping he couldn't see the silly smile plastered across my face or the blush creeping up my cheeks.

A few days later, Ryan came over for a beer. It was a warm summer night. He knocked on the door, and I opened it to find him freshly shaven, in ripped jeans, flip-flops, and a blue flannel shirt that brought out his eyes. He held out a six-pack of IPA and I led him to the backyard, where I'd put out guacamole and tortilla chips. We opened our beers and plopped down on the lawn chairs. I tucked my hands under my legs to calm my jitters.

"So, what was it like growing up surfing here?" I asked.

"The skill level of the surfers was amazing," he said. "Back then, you had to prove yourself. As a kid, if I took off on the wrong wave, the older guys would throw my board into the kelp beds, and I'd have to go swimming after it." He laughed.

"Tell me about the regulars," I said. "How good are they?"

"Like, who?" he asked, his brow furrowing.

"Okay, let's see . . . Travis."

Travis seemed like a powerful surfer who was always in command.

"God," Ryan said, groaning. "I want to gouge my eyes out when I watch him."

I burst out laughing. "What? No way!"

One by one, I went through the "regulars"—surfers who were way more skilled than I was. Ryan delivered brutal and hilarious critiques, each more savage than the last. By the fourth or fifth name, he looked physically pained, but l was laughing so hard my stomach cramped.

"Don't make me do this," he pleaded, holding his head in his hands. "I really won't have anything good to say."

As the night cooled, I suggested making s'mores. By the time I came back with an armful of chocolate and graham crackers, Ryan had a fire roaring in the pit.

"Have you lived here your whole life?" I asked as we skewered marshmallows with metal sticks.

"No, I was born in Michigan and moved here as a kid," he said. "My parents split early. I barely talked to my dad growing up."

"I'm sorry," I said. "I don't have a great relationship with my dad either."

We sat quietly, the fire crackling between us.

"Golden brown?" he asked, holding up a perfectly toasted marshmallow.

"Sure," I answered. "How'd you wind up at UCLA, then?"

"I actually dropped out of high school," he said. "I struggled with drugs when I was a teenager. But I read everything I could get my hands on and got my GED. I sort of did better on my own, I guess. All the knowledge without any of the bullshit. Never liked rules."

A self-taught man. That was impressive.

He went on to tell me that he'd gone to community college for two years, then transferred to UCLA. His dream had been to become a lawyer or a writer. But he'd graduated around the financial crash, when getting a job had been almost impossible. He couldn't afford law school, so he'd begrudgingly come back to Santa Cruz, where cannabis was supposed to be a stopgap until he figured out what to do next. That was ten years ago.

Our marshmallows were ready. I gestured for Ryan to hand me his. I topped it with a square of salted dark chocolate, squeezed it between two graham crackers, and passed it back.

"Shit! This is gourmet," he said as he bit into it, chocolate oozing onto his lips.

I laughed and made one of my own. The firelight danced across his face in warm golds and reds. He looked illuminated again, like the man I'd first seen gliding across waves.

He relaxed back into his chair. "You haven't told me what you do," he said.

"I had a company for a long time. But things felt apart, and I set off on . . . a journey."

"Hero's journey?"

"You might call it that. A healing journey, you could say."

He listened intently as I told him the light version of Embrace and the last few years. "I've done all kinds of wild stuff. Even Kambo."

"What's that?"

"Frog poison. Wanna see the scars?" I pulled up the hem of my sundress and showed him the line of polka-dot burn holes on my calf. He raised his eyebrows, leaning closer.

"Wow, that looks pretty intense," he said. "Did it help you?"

"I'm not sure . . . but I've been open to trying all sorts of woo-woo things lately."

"My mom was into stuff like that," he said. "She was kind of a hippie when I was growing up."

"Wait here!" I said, jumping up. I ran inside and grabbed my deck of Rumi cards.

"Tarot?" Ryan asked.

"Tarot-esque," I said, showing him the cards with spiritual messages inspired by the poetry of the Sufi mystic. I'd been using them since I'd started vision-boarding.

"Shuffle, then choose one," I instructed.

He shuffled, pulled a card from the deck, and flipped it over. *Beyond Death, Life.*

" 'Footprints lead to the shore of the sea,' " he read aloud. " 'You are urged beyond what has been. The time has come.' " He gestured with his hands, his voice rising and falling like waves, pausing for effect in the perfect moments.

" 'Lay it to rest now.' " His voice dropped to almost a whisper as he read the final line. " 'What you have known is now too small for your soul.' "

Wow.

"What you have known is now too small for your soul," I repeated, more to myself than him. He caught my eye, nodding. I smiled, trying to stifle my surprise. Who was this man? An intellect and a soulful surfer. A high school dropout with a college degree. A man with a clandestine job—and now, a thespian.

It was almost midnight. We'd been talking for five hours. The stars were blazing, and the air hummed with the kind of connection you don't want to end.

"I should get going," Ryan said.

"Of course," I said sweetly, but couldn't help feeling disappointed. I could have hung out with him until the sun came up.

He stepped closer and hugged me good night. "You know," he said, flashing me a smile that lit up his face, "I think you're pretty all right."

I couldn't wait to see him again.

A few days later, we met up to surf. The sky was cloudless and brilliant blue. The break—usually packed—was miraculously empty that morning, as if the universe had orchestrated a perfect second date. We traded waves back and forth for hours.

"I want to surf like you," I told him.

"The most important thing is your breath," he said, which I was surprised to hear. Other surfers talked about the mechanics, but no one had ever talked to me about breathing. It was very Zen.

"Try exhaling when you pop up," he suggested. "It'll relax your whole body. That's the key to flow."

On my next wave, I gave it a shot, and he was right—my pop-up felt more easeful, more fluid. Ryan caught the one after.

"I really like watching you surf," I told him as he paddled back toward me.

"I like watching you too," he said, smiling. I blushed. It was a huge compliment, given his brutal reviews of other surfers.

I invited him over for dinner that night. We stood side by side in the backyard, grilling fresh halibut that my neighbor had dropped off. The smell of lime and spices filled the air. After dinner, we settled on the couch, and I told Ryan about the Conscious Leadership Forum, a group I'd joined that met once a month to explore topics of leadership, purpose, and how we show up in the world. A few weeks earlier, our facilitator, Diana Chapman, had posed a question:

What would you risk for your full aliveness?

I told Ryan how terrified I'd been during the last big swell. "I've had a couple bad wipeouts before . . ." I paused, remembering the monster wave that had held me under. "But then I thought about her question and realized that to catch the best wave of my life, I would one hundred percent risk a bad wipeout."

Ryan grinned. "And?"

"I ended up catching one of my most epic waves!"

He nodded. "Worth it."

"So . . . what would *you* risk to feel fully alive?" I asked.

He thought about it for a moment. "I'd be sitting halfway across the couch," he said. "Next to you."

His eyes locked with mine. Then he scooted closer and kissed me—unlocking a connection that would change us both.

After that, we were inseparable. I was doing consulting work for Embrace, which gave me flexibility in setting my own hours. Ryan started his day early at the cannabis farm and was often done by midafternoon.

"Wanna come play?" I'd text him after work.

Within minutes, he'd be on his bike, riding over to my house. We once counted that there were fewer than a hundred steps between our houses. It was comforting to live so close. We slotted easily into each other's lives, as if we were already living in our perfect little house by the sea. Because of Covid, we didn't go on typical dates—no dinners out, no movie nights. We became a pod of two with nowhere to go and nothing to do but immerse ourselves in each other. The connection deepened quickly. During those first few weeks, Ryan kept count of every day together. Each morning, he'd wake me with a count and a kiss. "Day Four! We've nearly made it through our first week." I think we were both surprised at how well we clicked, given we came from such different worlds. At bedtime, tangled in each other's arms, he'd look at me with childlike joy in his eyes. "I don't want this day to be over," he'd say. "It's too much fun with you."

One evening, I showed him a video about Embrace, sharing more about my time in India. As he watched, his eyes welled up. "That's really moving," he said softly. "The planet's better with you in it." Ryan was full of heart. I loved the way he looked at me. In the middle of a conversation, he would suddenly pause, his eyes locking on to mine with an intensity that made me feel like he was drinking me in.

We cooked all of our meals together. I had a sandwich maker, and we experimented with gourmet grilled cheese sandwiches, testing different flavor combinations. "Let's try raspberry jam with the Gruyère," Ryan suggested one day. "It hits all the notes on the savory/sweet axis." Before we started dating, he told me he'd subsisted on one meal: rice and beans. So I was surprised at how sophisticated his palate was. We made hors d'oeuvres of cantaloupe wrapped in basil. We mixed watermelon martinis and topped them with raw cacao shavings and shredded coconut. We combined flavors we'd tasted on our travels. Ryan had backpacked around the world a few years back—his first time abroad—and we fantasized about going back together to the places we'd loved most.

Ryan brought out a playful, goofy side of me. He knew I loved red pandas, so we'd watch videos of them standing on their hind legs to make themselves look bigger, then falling over instead. "It's you!" he teased. "Always trying to look tougher than you are." He nicknamed me Panda, and every morning he sent me a video of a panda doing something quirky.

I invited him to listen to one of my virtual talks about Embrace. Afterward, he did an impersonation. "Hi," he said, scanning an imaginary audience. "I'm a Panda! Have you ever thought about things like this? Or like this? *Empathize! Innovate! Iterate!* Okay, gotta go. Byeeee."

"Stop!" I said, laughing.

"I can't believe that's your job," he said, shaking his head and laughing with me.

Ryan started his days around four or five in the morning. His sleep was often erratic and restless. He tossed and turned, waking up many times in the night. I couldn't figure out how he was powering through the days with so little rest. Yet no matter how tired he was, on the nights we didn't stay together, he'd come by my house before work, slipping into bed to hold me for a few minutes before the sun came up. I cherished those moments, half-awake, held by the warmth of his body pressed against mine.

While Ryan worked, he listened to audiobooks. He loved Russian literature—the dark, depressed guys. His latest was *The Brothers Karamazov*. Ryan was a fascinating paradox: part sophisticated poet-intellect, part feral, undernourished animal. He inhabited two worlds. In one, he lived a life of the mind, immersed in literature and philosophy. In the other, he disappeared to an underworld, where he trimmed weed and was barely scraping by.

He mentioned that making rent some months was a challenge. But he always had whiskey and cigars on hand, so I assumed his finances couldn't be that bad. I wondered why he didn't just get a normal job, but it seemed like a sensitive subject. He didn't enjoy his work, and I knew he wanted more. I figured he just needed some encouragement.

Though it was hard to recognize at first, because everyone was in pandemic isolation, Ryan was sort of a hermit. I think, partially because of his work, he didn't interact with many people, even before lockdown. He wasn't on any form of social media. He didn't own a computer or a credit card. He was suspicious of everybody and always carried a pocketknife, just in case he needed to defend himself. If a car passed when we were walking at night, his body tensed. He eyed strangers on the street warily. I don't know if the threats were real or imagined, but I could relate to his hypervigilance.

As we got closer, Ryan and I shared our family histories. I told him about the physical violence growing up. He took my hand between his, nodding silently.

"I didn't spend much time with my father growing up," he said. "A week here or there. In my late twenties, I stopped talking to him for two years . . . and then he committed suicide."

"My God," I said, my heart sinking. "I'm so sorry."

"He'd been calling before that, trying to get in touch. But I didn't pick up. Then it was too late," he said, choking up.

Even a decade later, I could see that he was still wracked with guilt. I wondered if he'd been retreating from the world ever since. My heart ached for him.

On an emotional level, Ryan and I got each other. He didn't have his life together, but all practical considerations went out the window in the face of the passion I felt for him. There was a recognition between us—something unspoken and profound, beyond jobs or status or family history.

One afternoon, we sat facing each other on his bed. "I just want to look at you," he told me, gazing into my eyes. His eyes filled with tears, and mine immediately followed.

"Sometimes the gods smile upon you," he said.

A few weeks later, Ryan told me he loved me.

"I'm scared," he whispered as we lay in bed, nose to nose. "I haven't been into anyone like this in a long time. How do we make sure this works? I don't want to get hurt."

"I'm scared too," I said, pushing back his hair. "But I guess we just . . . breathe."

CHAPTER 29

A GUY LIKE ME

Ryan was turning forty and I was excited to celebrate a milestone birthday with him. But when the day came, he was somber.

"It's been ten years, and it doesn't get easier," he said quietly as we lay in bed, the room dimly lit by the soft glow of the bedside lamp. "What kind of son doesn't pick up his father's phone call for two years?"

I could hear the anguish in his voice.

"I don't know, babe," I said, thinking of my own father. "Probably a son who was deeply hurt and needed to draw a boundary."

Ryan sighed, his eyes distant. "You know, I never even fought with him," he said. "We didn't get close enough to fight."

Close enough to fight.

I'd never thought about fighting as closeness—as its own kind of intimacy.

"I'm just bummed my dad couldn't be around for this," Ryan said as he started to climb out of bed. I couldn't bear to see him in so much pain. I pulled him back to the mattress. I knew just what he needed. The Ho'oponopono. A Native Hawaiian ritual I'd learned about at Date with Destiny. A simple but powerful set of words that could soothe any scar.

I straddled him, sitting upright.

"Look at me," I said.

He stared into my eyes.

"Okay," I said, setting my hand tenderly on his heart. "Right now, I'm not speaking as me. I'm going to channel whoever it is you need to hear these words from."

I took a deep breath, closed my eyes, and grounded myself with an intention: *For healing.* When I opened my eyes, I locked my gaze with his and began, pausing after each phrase to let the words sink in.

I am sorry.

Immediately, Ryan's eyes welled up.

I love you.

His Adam's apple bobbed as he choked down a sob.

Please forgive me.

Tears began streaming down his face.

Thank you.

I took his hands in mine and pressed them to my chest. They were shaking.

I am sorry. I love you. Please forgive me. Thank you. The words he probably most needed to say to—and hear from—his father.

His whole body softened underneath mine. "What are you doing to me, woman?" he whispered, pulling a paisley handkerchief from his back pocket and wiping away his tears. In that moment, my heart opened to Ryan even more deeply. I saw the wounded animal beneath the tough casing. I wanted to fight for him with everything I had. To protect him. There was nothing I wouldn't do for this man. He just needed someone to help him heal, to guide him toward the life he deserved but couldn't yet see for himself. That person, I decided right then, was me. I had seen Ryan's light that first day we met in the water. It was my guiding light, drawing me in—the light in me magnetized to the light in him. Together, we could heal the wounds of the past and overcome any obstacles.

I plotted my course. I was now certain of the power of manifestation, of our power to create the life we dream. The facts of my life supported my bent toward magical thinking. I had manifested Date with Destiny, and a solution to save Embrace! At Joe Dispenza, we'd healed a man by vibrating collectively at the highest frequency of love. Surely this could work on Ryan too. All I had to do was tap into the vibrational field of universal love and extend it to him. *Easy.*

I committed myself to my new mission just as I had to the orphans in Henan, and to the mothers and infants in India. Ryan became my project, and I planned to pursue his betterment the way I had every passion in my life. Relentlessly. With ferocity.

Nothing was going to get in my way.

Not even him.

The next day I knocked on the door of his cottage, balancing a stack of books from my favorite spiritual teachers—Pema Chödrön, Eckhart Tolle, Marianne Williamson.

"Now, if you were in my complete care for the next three months," I said, walking past him as he opened the door, "you would be healed! I have the perfect program for you."

He raised an eyebrow as I dropped the books onto his bed.

"First," I said, "NET. A few of the Tony Robbins tools. And an MDMA journey!"

"Okay, Panda . . ." he said, looking both amused and wary. "What is all this?"

"Today, we begin!" I said, breathless. "And we begin with a mission statement. What do you *really* want in life?"

I handed Ryan a stack of colorful Post-its and a Sharpie, ready to get to work. He wanted to be a journalist, he said. That was his dream. I explained the design-thinking model we had used to create Embrace and together, Ryan and I brainstormed steps he could take toward his dream.

"Generate as many ideas as you can. Rapid-fire go!" I said enthusiastically. "There are no bad ideas!"

"Interview a homeless man in town and write a story," Ryan suggested, a little hesitant.

"Love it!" I said, scribbling the idea on a Post-it. "What else?"

"Maybe write an article for *Santa Cruz Waves*," he added, his confidence growing.

"Great, yes! Keep 'em coming."

We came up with several ideas and concrete next steps.

Then I pulled out my special vision-board supplies.

"It's vision-boarding time," I announced. "If you can visualize the life you want, you can make it a reality."

"I . . . I don't know," he stammered. "I don't really do arts and crafts."

"I once said the same," I said as I plopped down on the floor and started snipping images from magazines. I'd come ready for resistance. Leading by example worked best. At first, he watched with a smirk, flipping idly through a surf magazine I'd brought along to entice him. But soon enough, the ground was covered in a glossy confetti of paper scraps, and he was cutting happily alongside me.

Every day that week after he got off work, we worked on our vision boards. Ryan cut out his images meticulously, piling up more than his board could fit. The last night, we pared them down. Once we were done arranging and gluing, we shared our boards.

"Flip on three," I said, holding mine away from him. "One, two . . ."

Whatever I'd been dreaming of faded into the background

when I saw the images on Ryan's board. A happy older couple with a golden retriever. A stately wood-paneled library. A woman's hand with a wedding ring. And two penguins with jalapeños around them.

"Penguins mate for life," he explained. "But I want a little spice in there too."

I giggled. I was touched to see that what he really wanted was an ordinary domestic dream, with a splash of excitement.

"It's perfect," I said.

On my board, there were pictures of surfers in tropical locations, a house by the sea with a view of the ocean, and a little girl—a daughter I'd dreamt up a long time ago and named Miyo Tanabe, after my Japanese grandmother.

"Miyo Tanabe," Ryan said, a tender look in his eyes. "I love her already."

I saw our futures unfold in that moment. Ryan would become the writer he always wanted to be. We would live together in our dream house by the ocean. We would surf, have babies, and build a life together.

I hopped up to put on "On the Nature of Daylight" by Max Richter, one of my favorite vision-boarding songs. Because yes, now I had vision-boarding songs. "The key is to feel what it will feel like when these things actually happen," I said, repeating what my friend had told me years ago.

Ryan stared at his board for a long time, unblinking. Finally, eyes brimming with tears, he spoke softly. "I haven't let myself imagine what I want in so long."

I was fully convinced that if the two of us just believed enough, everything would fall into place, no matter the material realities we'd never discussed.

Over the next few months, I executed part two of my plan:

getting Ryan a better job. He had talent; he just needed the right opportunities and to believe in himself. I bought him a computer. I built him a website. I asked him to edit a proposal I was working on and tried to get him freelance editing jobs with my friends and contacts. At one point, I almost paid a friend to hire him and pretend the money came from her.

I assigned him a loose regimen of the therapies I'd done over the last few years. Every morning when he wasn't working, he'd meditate with me. He went to NET therapy, the muscle-testing modality. Dr. Cruz advised that Ryan journal for ten minutes a day, which he did for weeks. "She was wearing a lab coat," he joked. "So I figured I'd better trust her."

My love-high provided a two-month buffer of unconditional support. But as our honeymoon bubble burst and reality started to creep in, my self-help-guru glow faded. Ryan still hadn't taken any of the actions we'd brainstormed to get a stable job with a steady paycheck. Which is what he would need if he wanted the house and the jalapeño penguin love and the diamond ring and the golden retriever. His current job drained all his energy, leaving him broke and tired, with little left for me, or himself. He'd stopped meditating and journaling. Instead, he'd come home tired from long days at the farm, crack a beer, smoke a cigar, and lounge around. Not exactly the kind of verve I expected from someone who wanted to turn their life around. Not that he'd ever said that he wanted to turn his life around, exactly. But it was implied. *Clearly. Obviously. Right?*

Ryan's finances were getting worse. When he'd first come back to Santa Cruz, cannabis had been a decent gig with flexible hours and solid pay. But in recent years, it had been legalized;

as venture capitalists swooped in, the informal farms he worked for were shutting down. Ryan's work was increasingly sporadic. While it gave us more time together, the inconsistent schedule and paycheck made him moody and sullen. I knew he was financially strained, so I paid for more. But I started to resent putting all my extra energy and time and money into helping him. If he envisioned a life with me and really wanted it, he would clearly be making steps toward it. When I wanted something, I gave it every ounce of my body, mind, spirit. Maybe he just didn't want that dream life with me enough to fight for it.

Without realizing, I started to slip into a new story about Ryan. One in which his love for me equated to his willingness to fight for himself. I started to believe Ryan's inability to get a job or reciprocate my efforts were not emblematic of his shame or stuckness or self-doubt, but a reflection of his love for me. Whatever Ryan couldn't do for me was about me. And whatever he couldn't do for himself was increasingly about me too. Before I knew it, my fervor for Ryan's progress morphed into a familiar story. A timeless classic. *Why doesn't he love me enough?* If he just loved me more, he would change.

One weekend, after being strung along for weeks by a flaky boss, Ryan finally got paid and treated me to an expensive Italian dinner in San Francisco. It was a generous gesture, which probably cost half his paycheck. The next day, we walked around the city, stopping in Japantown. We shared our favorite snacks: rice balls, my childhood favorite, red-bean pancakes, and green tea. Wandering into a plant shop, I spotted a bonsai I'd been eyeing for weeks. Secretly, I was hoping Ryan would buy it for me. I pointed out two plants to him: the bonsai, and a smaller, cheaper houseplant. Without hesitating, Ryan chose the houseplant and headed to the register.

It wasn't an intentional test. At least, I didn't think so at the time. I didn't say anything, but inside, I was stewing.

We left the plant shop and went to a cigar store. While Ryan browsed cigars, I waited in the car, getting angrier by the minute. The bonsai suddenly became a symbol of everything Ryan hadn't done. He hadn't bought me any gifts and had rarely planned anything special for us. Sure, we had started dating during Covid, but it had taken him months to take me on a proper date. While he was probably doing the best he could, it still didn't feel like enough. I needed him to show me that I mattered, that he appreciated me.

When he got back in the car, grinning with his purchase, I peeled out of the parking lot, my emotions boiling over.

"How could you buy yourself nice cigars and not get me the bonsai I wanted?" I snapped.

Ryan stared at me, stunned. "Jesus," he muttered.

I jerked the car over to the side of the road and slammed on the brakes.

"I don't want to be around you anymore," I shouted. "Get out of my car."

Ryan opened the door to get out, looking shell-shocked.

"No, no, wait stay!" I demanded.

"I want to get out of here," Ryan snarled. His eyes flared. He looked pissed in a way I'd never seen. I drove to a park nearby. "I just need to calm down," I said as I stepped out of the car. I walked around slowly, taking long, deep breaths. Ryan stayed in the car, seething. We didn't say a word to each other the entire drive home.

Marianne Williamson, the famed spiritual author whose book had gotten me through my breakup with Patrick, was hosting a webinar. Desperate for guidance on my relationship with Ryan, I signed up. If anyone could help me choose love over fear, it was her.

When the Zoom started, I went into my closet. Ryan would be home from work any moment, and I didn't want him walking in on me talking to a screen full of strangers about our relationship. I logged on to the call and put my headphones in. Around two hundred people had joined. After thirty minutes of lecturing, Marianne asked the audience if we had any questions. My hand shot up, virtually. She called on me.

"I love my boyfriend," I said quietly, shifting on the laundry hamper. "But I don't know if the practical realities are getting in the way." I summarized Ryan's situation, my efforts to help him, and the increasing tension between us.

"What's your question?" asked Marianne.

"How can I act out of love?" I asked, thinking of Marianne's own saying: *What would love have me do?* I waited for her to remind me what unconditional love looks like. To tell me that I needed to accept him for who he was. That I was projecting my own fears and desires onto him. That in trying to see his potential, I was squashing the potential of our relationship.

Instead, Marianne leaned forward, squinting into the screen.

"How old are you?" she asked.

"Forty," I answered.

"Do you want children?"

"Maybe."

"You should leave," she said. "You don't have time to waste."

What happened to unconditional love? I started to ask, but she'd already moved on to another question.

A few weeks later, I woke in the middle of the night feeling sick. Ryan was sleeping soundly beside me. On my way to the bathroom, I saw his phone on the couch, an audiobook still playing. He was always super secretive about his phone, claiming it was because of work. That night, suspicion got the best of me. I decided to snoop.

What I discovered made my stomach drop. There was a string of messages from a woman he'd been involved with on and off since college. I recognized her name. Early in our relationship, when we first talked about our exes, he'd told me about her. They'd rekindled something just after Covid, months before we met, and he told me their last communication was just after we started dating. He'd claimed he told her that he was in a serious relationship, and they hadn't spoken since.

But there were months of texts, some from as recently as that week. And they texted regularly. I scrolled up, heart pounding, and was shocked to find that in over nine months of texts, there wasn't a single mention of me. Not only had he lied to me—he hadn't even acknowledged my existence. Even after all I had done for him. Shaking with rage, I stormed into the bedroom and ripped the blanket off him, reading aloud from her texts as he lay there wide-eyed in his underwear.

"Get the FUCK out!" I screamed.

Ryan scrambled to find his pants, tripping over himself as he shoved his clothes and books into a backpack. In the corner of the room was a huge plastic bin of weed he'd been trimming—it was the only time he'd ever brought his work to my house. For a split second, I considered dumping it all on the street. But then a shred of rationality kicked in. I wasn't about to become the crazy lady my neighbors whispered about. Instead, I stomped the top of the bin with my bare foot. The lid caved instantly, leaving a gaping hole.

Ryan was mortified. *"Jesus Christ,* Jane."

"How dare you lie to me!" I screamed. "I put ALL of my energy into helping you, and this is what you do to me??? OUT!!!!"

He grabbed the bin and ran for the door. Moments later, I heard his car squeal away.

I collapsed onto my bed, sobbing.

The next day, I called a friend in Hawaii and told him about what had happened. He had an extra bedroom and generously offered it to me. I packed my things as quickly as I could and booked the cheapest flight I could find.

The moment I stepped onto the island of Oahu, I felt a wave of relief. I surfed every morning, letting the saltwater wash away my anger and sadness. I threw myself into work. We were over a year into the pandemic, and Embrace was facing issues ranging from supply-chain shortages to difficulties recruiting a new CEO. At the same time, the need for our technology was growing. Hospitals around the world were overwhelmed. Newborn care units were under-resourced, especially in developing countries, and premature babies were more vulnerable than ever. We decided to put the for-profit arm of the company into hibernation and to reestablish our nonprofit, which would allow us to get our incubators free of cost to the people who needed them most. It was a relief to focus on the mission again, free from the pressure of chasing the bottom line.

Ryan sent flowers and handwritten love letters every week. He apologized profusely for lying to me, assuring me he had no romantic feelings for the woman he'd been texting. He ended their friendship altogether. He apologized for failing to court me properly, for taking me for granted. He started going to a men's self-help group. He read *Conscious Loving*, a relationship book recommended by Diana Chapman, sharing his insights with me over the phone. Every conversation we had became a mix of his tearful repentance and my TED Talk series, "How Not to Be a Terrible Boyfriend." I detailed his many failings point by point while insisting he take copious notes. He scribbled away like a man desperate to pass an exam he had already flunked. He even started looking for jobs.

Over the next two months, I started to believe that he had changed. He begged me to give him another chance.

"Please come home, Panda," he pleaded. "I miss you in my bones."

Eventually, I agreed—but with conditions.

"We're not back together until you get a stable job," I told him.

"Yes, of course," he promised. "I have a job interview in a few days."

When I got home, Ryan did seem like a different person in many ways. He tried to cater to my every need, planning his days around me. He took me on beach picnics and planned special dates. He bought me flowers, wrote me little cards, and showered me with love and attention. He did all the things I wished he had done during the first part of our relationship. But he still hadn't landed a job. In fact, it seemed like he stopped looking once I got back, while his finances continued to get worse. And he was still secretive about his work. Since trust had been broken, any hint of him being dishonest sent me into a rage.

One night, I asked if he wanted to use my car to get to work the next day, since his was on the verge of breaking down.

"I'm carpooling," he said.

"With whom?" I asked, casually.

His gaze dropped to the floor. He'd always been hush-hush about work, but this was just a car ride.

"Why won't you answer me?!" I shouted. "What's going on?"

The more I pushed, the more he retreated into silence. Until finally I was so lathered up that in a fit of fury, I grabbed his things and threw them out of my house, onto the street. "Get out!" I screamed, stomping on his groceries before throwing them out too.

It was midnight. Ryan had worked all day and had to get up at five A.M. to go back to the farm. He stood there for a moment, looking weary and defeated. Then, without saying a word, he gathered his things and left. When I finally calmed down, a wave of shame crashed over me. I was horrified by what I'd done.

This became a pattern. We'd break up and get back together over and over again. In a blaze of anger, I'd kick Ryan out. But as soon as he tried to leave, I'd do something drastic to hold him hostage. I'd take his keys. Lock the door. Sit on his suitcase. I wanted him to get the fuck out, but was terrified to see him go. I wanted to love him. I wanted to punish him. My rage became a fully formed creature—a being that rose up and took me over. I lost all control and rationality. I felt like an absolute lunatic.

After every explosion, I broke down, disgusted with myself. Why were my reactions so overblown? Why couldn't I control them? Or just leave Ryan for good? Where the fuck was my Higher Self when I was stomping on Ryan's groceries at midnight? A part of me wanted to make sure he would never hurt me again. Another part of me kept thinking I could fix him, our relationship, myself.

"I love you," Ryan said after a fight one evening, his shoulders slumped. "But I can't keep letting you treat me this way. When I allow this to happen, I'm disrespecting myself. Even a guy *like me.*"

Even a guy like me.

His words were a punch to the gut. The lack of confidence I'd wanted to nurture away had become the very weakness the rageful part of me was beating down even further. The more he didn't stand up for himself, the worse I became. His new nickname for me was *Jane-ghis Khan*.

When I was in Hawaii, Ryan had seen a therapist. "She told me that you're 'dating down,'" he said. "Maybe you're holding all of the power so that you can abuse me."

It was an awful thing to hear, but I wondered if there was truth to it. I punished him endlessly, feeling justified because of his lies. But maybe part of me lashed out because I knew he wouldn't leave? Because I was his best option?

Was the residue of my father's violence buried so deep that it took a *guy like Ryan* to bring it out? Having my heart broken had unlocked a rage I didn't know was inside me. I thought I had moved past the violence of my childhood, that I had risen above it. But as I sat with the weight of my actions, a chilling thought crept in: *I had become my father.*

The thought made me sick. I cringed remembering what it felt like to be on the receiving end of his anger—the fear, the helplessness. So many of his explosions never made sense. The littlest things seemed to set him off. I had spent my life vowing never to be angry like him. And yet, here I was.

I thought of my mother. She had never stood up to my father or held him accountable. Maybe I was doing what I wished she had. Fighting back. Fighting to protect myself. Was I becoming my father or the mother I wished had shielded us against him? Was I trying to hurt Ryan or ensure that I could never be hurt again?

One thing was clear: this wasn't just about Ryan or even our relationship. Desperate for help, I started seeing a new therapist and enrolled in an online anger-management class. As part of the class, we were given a worksheet to log the things that made us angry and then identify the thought that triggered the anger. As I tracked our fights, I saw a pattern: every time I believed that Ryan didn't love me, I'd rage.

Ryan not getting a job meant that he didn't love me.

Ryan not buying the bonsai meant he didn't love me.

Ryan not wanting to have sex meant he didn't love me.

I did not understand that Ryan simply didn't have the capacity to meet my needs. That we had fundamentally different lifestyles, goals, and expectations. I took every mismatch personally, as if it reflected my worth.

"You're re-creating a relationship of deprivation," my new therapist, Paul, said. "Because you were so used to being deprived in your childhood."

"What do you mean?" I asked.

"Well, you chose a man who couldn't take care of himself. Just like your father couldn't take care of himself emotionally," Paul said.

"The little girl in you wants to prove that she can change this man," he went on. "And win his love. But he's not going to change. You need to learn to give that love to yourself."

His words jolted me. "How do I do that?" I asked.

"You have to learn how to parent yourself," Paul explained. "To nurture the parts of you that feel unloved and unworthy. When you can give yourself what you needed back then, you'll stop looking for it from partners who can't give it to you."

The day we ended things for good, Ryan and I sat on the edge of my bed, facing each other.

I set my hand on his.

"I never want to stop looking at you," he said.

I held his gaze and watched the dream of the life we might have shared slip away. Both of us had sacrificed so much to be together. But it still wasn't enough. No matter how much we loved each other, this was never going to work. I'd been so focused on Ryan's potential, on the glimmer of hope, that I had refused to see the truth. To accept reality.

Neither of our vision boards pictured us in tears, saying goodbye.

I was done raging. And I was done trying to fix anyone who wasn't me.

CHAPTER 30

TRIGGERED

After the breakup, I was nearly catatonic. I flew home for the holidays and locked myself in my bedroom. I could *Not. Stop. Crying*. I was a cavern of grief, cracked open and spilling out. More heartbreaking than the end of the relationship was the crushing realization that after everything I'd done to heal and grow, I was in worse shape than ever. I loathed who I'd become. The idea that I was going to be the one to heal Ryan was laughable.

My family had no idea what to do with such big feelings. My sweet nephews, who were eight and ten, crawled into bed and petted my head tenderly. Mom and my sisters took turns coming to visit me, bringing food and water. When I finally told Joyce everything that had happened, she teared up.

"It's like you were both wanting connection so badly, but somehow couldn't reach each other," she said. It was perhaps the most generous interpretation of what had happened.

Nancy, the stoic, gave me a hug—something she almost never did.

"You're going to be okay," she said, but her eyes communicated something else. She knew that this was extreme. Even for me.

While everyone was out for dinner one night, I opened a book a friend had recommended: *The Body Keeps the Score*. The author was a Dutch therapist and researcher named Dr. Bessel van der Kolk, who had devoted his career to studying the science of trauma. I tore through the book, highlighting passage after passage.

Trauma almost always makes it difficult to engage in intimate relationships. How can you surrender to an intimate relationship after you have been brutally violated?

The words stopped me cold. I read on, thirsty for more.

If your heart is still broken because you were assaulted by someone you loved, you are likely to be preoccupied with not getting hurt again . . . In fact, you may unwittingly try to hurt them before they have a chance to hurt you.

Of course. My oldest trick. Strike first. In intimate relationships, I was so scared of getting hurt that I protected myself at all costs. I had done it with both Patrick and Ryan. And then came the words that hit me hardest:

Those who were brutalized as children carry a smoldering rage that will take a great deal of energy to contain.

I sat back, stunned. Suddenly, the chaos of my relationship with Ryan began to make sense: the rage, the self-loathing, the endless cycle of trying to both love and punish him. My eyes flooded with tears as I realized my anger went far deeper than anything that had happened between us.

Trauma, van der Kolk explained, especially childhood trauma, physically rewires the brain. It's not just a memory of the past—it is the imprint left by the experience, which shapes your *present* reactions. Trauma can create a hyperactive fear response, leading to disproportionate reactions to perceived threats—whether physical, emotional, or even imagined. Even many years later, survivors may feel chronically unsafe, switching quickly into fight-or-flight mode at the slightest trigger. A single word, a tone of voice, or even a fleeting expression can act as a portal to the past in which you're slammed back to the feelings of terror, rage, or helplessness. Your body reacts like the trauma is happening all over again.

Van der Kolk described the case of a Vietnam veteran he had treated early in his career. One night, the man woke up to a random noise outside. Before he even realized what was happening, he attacked his girlfriend, who was asleep in bed next to him. When he came to, he was horrified and consumed by shame. And it wasn't just him. There were countless cases of veterans and trauma survivors who hated themselves for their extreme reactions, convinced they'd become monsters. In reality, their brains and bodies were simply trapped in a survival loop.

As I read on, I learned about the three parts of the brain: the reptilian, the limbic, and the neocortex. The oldest part, in evolutionary years, is the *reptilian brain*, which is responsible for our most basic functions: eating, sleeping, waking, crying, pooping, and breathing. The stuff that keeps us alive. The *limbic brain* is responsible for emotions. It plays a crucial role in monitoring danger, judges what is pleasurable or scary, and decides what is important for survival. This is where the amygdala resides, which triggers our fight-or-flight response. This is also where trauma is stored—encoded not in language, but in emotion and sensation.

The newest part of the brain to evolve is *the neocortex*, which governs our capacity for thinking, reasoning, language, and abstract thought. It allows us to plan, reflect, and make sense of our experiences. It also helps us perceive time—to distinguish past from present.

When trauma hijacks the brain, van der Kolk explained, the limbic system takes over, drowning out the neocortex. Logic goes out the window. In survival mode, the brain cannot differentiate past from present. It reacts as if the old threat is happening all over again—right here, right now.

I put the book down, my pulse racing. Was that what had happened to me? Had my brain been reacting to Ryan as if he were my father? I began to track my reactions back through this new lens. After feeling continually disappointed by Ryan and then discovering his lies, I'd started to see him not just as untrustworthy, but as dangerous. My body registered him as a threat. In moments of rage, I was blacked out and totally out of control. Afterward, when I broke down sobbing, it wasn't just because I was ashamed, but because I was shocked. And scared.

I'd chastised myself for being overly dramatic. But now I realized that maybe it was an overactivated fear response. The lash marks had faded, but the imprint of my father's violence was still lodged in my body. I wasn't trying to excuse my behavior, but knowing *why* I'd felt so unhinged helped me feel a flicker of self-compassion.

All my life, I thought that being "traumatized" just meant having a dark childhood. That if you lived through it, it was over. *Why keep rehashing it?* I'd asked Dr. Theodore, my German therapist from ages ago. *What good was pointing a finger at my parents?* I'd asked Christine Price. If I couldn't overcome it, I'd always assumed I just wasn't working hard enough. And the rhetoric of much of the self-help world underscored that belief.

99% perspiration!

No pain, no gain!

Stay with the process!

My entire identity had been built on overcoming hardship. Pushing through. But now it was falling apart. And it wasn't because I wasn't trying hard enough or because I wasn't good enough. Part of what had kept me with Ryan was the shame around my behavior and my desperation to fix it. I was devastated that I couldn't control my emotions, especially after all the inner work I had done. I'd gone to Tony Robbins seminars. I'd meditated in silence. I'd done Landmark and Joe Dispenza and been counseled by the channeling-burping lady. I'd lain in flotation tanks, read countless spiritual and self-help books, made vision boards. I'd joined the Conscious Leadership Group and the Wellbeing Project. I'd seen my Higher Self. At one point, I was seeing three therapists at the same time.

And the thing is, everything had helped. For a moment a week, a month, even a year. Everything I had learned had given me tools to shift my perspective, open my heart, and reframe my thinking. But when my deepest fears were triggered, those tools didn't mean shit. Joe Dispenza had taught us to exude love until we morphed into quivering atoms of bliss. But he left out the part about what to do when that love turns you into a raging bitch.

Changing my mindset, it turned out, was not treating trauma.

Trauma wasn't just a bad memory or a negative thought pattern to be undone with enough affirmations. It was more like a hidden disability. When you break a bone, everyone can see it. There's an injury and it needs care. If a child is dyslexic, you don't tell them to just *try harder*—you teach them using different tools. But trauma doesn't always come with visible proof. It hides in the nervous system, rewiring the brain, dictating reactions before you even have time to think. From the outside, you might look completely fine. But inside, it's like being trapped in a malfunctioning alarm system, constantly firing off danger signals even when you're safe.

Reading van der Kolk's book was like looking into a mirror and realizing the very image I had of myself was fundamentally distorted. Understanding that my brain may have been altered as a result of the violence I'd experienced was a total paradigm shift. I wasn't a monster. I wasn't broken beyond repair. My reactions were survival instincts—remnants of a past that had wired me to expect danger. This didn't absolve me, but it gave me hope.

Maybe I wasn't beyond saving.

Maybe there was a way out.

Anjali had recently done a clinical ketamine training with Dr. van der Kolk. I called her immediately.

"This book is incredible," I gushed. "Everything suddenly makes sense. I have to work with Bessel. He might be my only hope." Anjali agreed to reach out and, incredibly, helped me land a coveted one-time Zoom consultation with *the* Dr. Bessel van der Kolk. I was elated. The appointment was four weeks away. In the meantime, I listened to every podcast I could find that featured him. The more I listened, the more respect I had—not just for his expertise, but for his approach. He was data-driven but open-minded to exploring new, even fringe, approaches to treating trauma. He welcomed having his ideas challenged and openly acknowledged how little we still know about the science of trauma.

A few weeks later, I sat in my kitchen in Santa Cruz, buzzing with anticipation as I signed on to the Zoom call. The window opened, and there he was: Bessel van der Kolk, in the flesh—or at least on my laptop screen. With a full head of white hair, a matching mustache and beard, and square rimless glasses, he had the elegance and whimsy of a great snowy owl. Though he was in his eighties, he looked closer to seventy. He was instantly warm and open. Grandfatherly almost.

"Why are we here?" he asked in a thick Dutch accent.

"I have an anger problem," I said. I launched into the bullet points of my backstory: the violence in my childhood, the explosive anger with Ryan, the heinous fights, the out-of-control behavior. "I'd throw all of his stuff out of the house," I said. "I couldn't even just set it outside. I had to hurl it out the door." I told him how I'd alternated between kicking Ryan out and holding him hostage, and how I felt like a hostage too—trapped by my own reactions, by the part of me I couldn't seem to control.

As I spoke, Bessel leaned closer, like he was really connecting to what I was saying. After I finished, he nodded slowly. "I'm not surprised at any of this," he said calmly. "Your brain is wired for danger, you see. You're going to have extreme reactions to protect yourself."

I felt a rush of relief. He didn't think I was a lunatic.

"Another therapist I'd been seeing said that I was re-creating a cycle of deprivation with my father? That I was trying to get from Ryan what I hadn't gotten from my dad."

Bessel furrowed his brow. "I think that may be a bit oversimplified. It's deeper than that. Trauma reshapes the brain and body. Your anger is being manifested as bodily sensations that may not even be consciously associated with memories of the past."

"So how do I fix it?" I sighed, falling back in my chair. "I'm exhausted. I've done everything, and I still feel like a horrible person."

Bessel nodded, his empathy translating through the screen. I trusted him instantly and implicitly, in a way I had never trusted a therapist before.

"Talking about the past usually isn't enough. You have to learn to tolerate the uncomfortable sensations and emotions in your body, like anger and fear," he said. "The body must learn to feel safe. Only then can you integrate memories—by safely returning to and processing them. Otherwise, they will continue to be stuck in your body and get triggered unconsciously."

He cupped his hands together into what looked like a tiny nest. "To survive the abuse, you see, you encapsulated a younger part of yourself. That's the part of you who is so pure and loving. You must get back to *her*."

I imagined my younger self, sparkly and bright, tucking herself into a capsule, a place where she could be warm and safe. Long before I'd created an incubator to help keep babies alive, I'd unknowingly built one for myself. I burst into tears.

"How do I do that?" I asked, sniffling. "I'm exhausted. I've tried everything."

"What you need is a steady guide," he said. "One person you can work with."

You, I thought. *You're my only hope.*

"Will you be the guide?" I asked, squeezing my eyes shut and praying. *Say yes, say yes.*

"No," he said. "It's not possible. I'm not taking new clients. And my travel schedule is very intense. It would be unfair to the type of work you need." He paused, leaning in toward the screen. "How do you know you want to work with me anyhow?"

"Well," I declared, pasting on my brightest smile. "You're the best!"

His raised an eyebrow. Clearly, flattery wasn't going to work.

"I love your lifelong quest to learn," I added.

He smiled, looking more satisfied. "Still," he said. "The answer is no."

I slumped back in my chair, trying to hide my disappointment.

"Maybe you can come to my retreat at Esalen in March," he offered as we were about to sign off. The legendary Esalen retreat center was perched on the cliffs of Big Sur, just a few hours away from Santa Cruz.

"Oh, great!" I said.

"Actually, no wait," he said, his tone apologetic. "I'm sorry. It's been sold out for a while."

"I understand," I said. "Thank you again for your time. Truly, it means the world."

He smiled and waved as we signed off.

As soon as the meeting window closed, I called Esalen. The receptionist confirmed that yes, the retreat was full, and yes, there was a waiting list, and yes, I could be put on it, but it was already several hundred people long. I left my name anyway and started brainstorming who could get me into the retreat. My years in India had taught me an important lesson: *No* really just meant *maybe*. I had built an extensive network through my work at Embrace. I reached out to someone I knew who was connected to Esalen and begged for his help getting into the retreat. A few days later, when I got bumped off the waitlist and into the retreat, I took it as a sign from the universe that I was on the right path.

Bessel van der Kolk felt like my last and only hope. I was going to do whatever it took to get him to work with me—including deploying my elite-level stalking skills.

CHAPTER 31

ARE YOU MY FATHER?

There are few places in California as dramatic as the Big Sur coastline, which made Esalen the perfect place for a trauma retreat. Jagged cliffs plunged into a wild-looking sea, where frothy waves crashed against craggy rock formations. Driving through a tunnel of towering redwoods—the oldest of which had been there for thousands of years—I had the distinct sense of entering a place out of time. It felt ancient and primal.

Bessel was co-hosting the retreat with his wife, Licia Sky, a somatic therapist of Black and Japanese heritage who had helped create the Trauma Research Foundation. She specialized in incorporating movement, music, and touch to help people reconnect with themselves and each other. Our group was about thirty people. During introductions, I learned that about half of them were therapists. The rest were a mix of people curious about Bessel's work and a few who just wanted an excuse to come to Esalen.

In the first session, Licia paired us up at random and directed us to stand on opposite sides of the room. "People with trauma often disassociate from their bodies," she explained as she circled the space. She was soft-spoken, her energy warm and grounding. "Before we can really address the trauma, we have to get back into our bodies."

I was paired with a white guy in his early forties, wearing a hoodie and sneakers. Probably a tech bro who didn't really care about being here, I figured. Next to me, a middle-aged blond lady with a stiff posture was paired with a white-bearded man who wore wire-rimmed glasses and had a Santa Claus belly. The blonde seemed jittery and checked-out.

"Advance towards each other slowly, using only body language to express *stop* or *come closer*," Licia instructed. "If you get close enough, you can indicate nonverbally whether touch is okay." Tech bro and I approached each other stoically, one step at a time. When we were close enough to touch, we stared blankly at each other. Neither of us gestured to go further.

Out of the corner of my eye, I saw that the blonde and Santa Claus were fully engaged. Step by step, they moved closer to each other. Then he motioned to her, and she nodded. He stepped forward, they embraced, and she broke down crying in his arms. I felt a pang of jealousy. I wished Santa had been my partner.

After lunch, Bessel lectured in the Aldous Huxley Room, a bright, airy space with big honey-wood beams and strips of skylight cut into the ceiling. Floor-to-ceiling windows looked out onto the Pacific Ocean. I'd reintroduced myself to Bessel at lunch, but he had so many groupies swarming him that he didn't have much time to chat. Now he sat up front next to a screen, and we all gathered on floor cushions in a semicircle at his feet.

"Trauma is the largest hidden cost to our society," Bessel began as sunlight dappled the room. "One that we are still failing to address systemically." Childhood trauma, he explained, was more difficult to treat than adult trauma because it happens when your brain is most malleable. And the effects could be incredibly long-lasting, not only for individuals but for entire families, communities, and future generations.

Bessel shared findings from a landmark study on Adverse

Childhood Experiences (ACEs), which surveyed over 17,000 adults about their exposure to ten categories of childhood adversity, including abuse, neglect, and household dysfunction. The participants were primarily middle-class, middle-aged, college-educated, and white.

The results were staggering. Nearly two-thirds of participants reported experiencing at least one ACE. Higher ACE scores were strongly associated with an increased risk of heart disease, diabetes, cancer, depression, anxiety, substance use disorders, and suicide. Without protective factors—such as safe, nurturing relationships—ACEs can lead to toxic stress, which can disrupt brain development and wreak havoc on the body, contributing to chronic inflammation and a weakened immune system.

"Childhood trauma is the biggest predictor of a person's health outcomes," Bessel noted. "But I do believe that all trauma, even childhood trauma, can ultimately be healed."

That was all I needed to hear. I was ready to do anything he suggested.

Bessel showed us slides on his research findings. He explained cognitive behavioral therapy, or talk therapy in general, often fell short when it came to treating trauma. Not because it wasn't useful, but because trauma wasn't stored in the thinking brain. If you weren't going to the place where the trauma was located, you were always working around it, instead of addressing it directly. "Trauma has nothing whatsoever to do with cognition," Bessel said. "It lives in the body and imprints on the limbic system— the emotional brain." Talking about trauma without engaging the body could keep a person stuck in the same physiological and emotional loops, endlessly reliving the past rather than truly healing from it.

Bessel emphasized that before logic and reasoning could be

applied, the body first had to feel safe. Through his research, he'd found that practices like yoga and breathwork were often more effective than talk therapy or antidepressants because they could help people safely reconnect with their bodies. He went on to share some of the latest research on psychedelics; he was involved in the largest study on the use of MDMA to treat PTSD, and the results were remarkable.

Then he introduced something called a psychodrama.

"I've seen decades of therapy done in a single session," he said, leaning forward in his chair.

Decades of therapy? I perked right up. Fast-tracking results was my love language. I was ready to hack decades of therapy, be cured for good, and maybe hop into the famous Esalen hot tubs and get a massage. Bessel explained psychodrama, a guided group role-play therapy technique. One person, "the protagonist," chooses people from the group to play the roles of both their real parents and their ideal parents. With their real parents, they reenact traumatic scenes from the past. Then, with the ideal parents, the same scenes are acted out again—this time with the love, tenderness, and care they had longed for. The goal of psychodrama was to allow a person to physically and emotionally experience a loving alternative to a traumatic event. This can create a new imprint of feeling safe and nurtured, which can be profoundly healing.

"At the end of the week," Bessel said, as we stood to break for the day, "I'll choose one person from the group to do a psychodrama."

The rest of the week, we started each morning with somatic group exercises led by Licia, followed by Bessel's lectures in the afternoons. The morning when Bessel was scheduled to do the psychodrama, I rushed to the meeting room immediately after breakfast and grabbed a seat closest to where he'd been lecturing, hoping he'd call on me. But when he arrived, he switched things up and asked us to form a circle. *Dammit.* Now I was farther from his line of sight.

"Volunteers?" he asked.

My hand shot up, along with three others.

"Choose a number between one and ten."

I picked my lucky number: 8.

"The number is four," Bessel announced.

A woman in her fifties with long dark brown hair broke into a pleased smile. With Bessel's prompting, she told us a bit of her backstory. Her sibling had passed away in a tragic accident as a child. Overcome with grief, her family had shut down and she was left to fend for herself emotionally.

"Come to the center of the circle," Bessel instructed. "Take your time and look around at the group. Choose who you would like to play the roles of your real parents and your ideal parents. I will play the role of the 'witness' and will give lines to each participant."

The woman stepped forward, scanning the faces in the room. After a moment, she chose two people to represent her real parents.

"Place them wherever it feels right," Bessel said.

She positioned her "real parents" at the far end of the room, reflecting the emotional distance she had felt growing up. Then she chose two people to play her "ideal parents," directing them to sit beside her, holding her hands. She chose Santa as her ideal father. Bessel gave Santa lines to repeat.

"Tell her, 'I would have paid attention to your needs.' "

"I would have paid attention to your needs," said Santa, looking into her eyes with earnest concern.

"I would have remembered that I had a daughter who was alive, not just a son who died," Bessel continued.

Santa repeated the words tenderly. We all held our breath.

The woman's eyes welled up, and her hands started to tremble. "That's it," she whimpered through tears. "That's exactly what I needed to hear. What I never heard."

She and Santa embraced, and the room broke into applause.

Everyone was crying. Bessel was beaming. I wiped away my tears, feeling equal parts awed and envious. Just hearing those words had seemed to instantaneously fill some void in her. It seemed too simple to be true. Miraculous, even. Maybe psychodrama was the missing puzzle piece. Maybe hearing some loving words from my "ideal father" would finally free me from the past. I was already plotting how to sign up for another one of Bessel's workshops.

That evening, after a break, we reconvened in the lecture room. Licia made a surprise announcement: Bessel would conduct one more psychodrama.

"Any volunteers?" she asked.

My arm shot up so quickly I nearly dislocated my shoulder. I stared at Licia with laser focus, willing her to pick me. She conferred briefly with her assistants, then looked back in my direction. "All right," she said. "You." I couldn't believe it. I'd just won the healing lottery.

Bessel turned to me. "Step forward."

My heart was racing as I stepped into the circle.

"My father was physically abusive," I said nervously, offering a snippet of my backstory. "My mother never stopped him, but I don't have many memories of her from my childhood for some reason."

Bessel directed me to choose someone to play the role of my

real father, and to position him where it felt appropriate. I chose a man in his forties with brown hair—quiet, unreadable—and asked him to stand about six feet away from me.

"What happens when you see your father?" Bessel asked.

I searched my body but felt nothing. Just a strange sense of distance, like I was watching someone else's scene from the outside.

"What would you like to say to him?" Bessel asked.

"Mmm . . . I guess I'd want to ask, 'Why did you do it?'"

"Do you feel angry toward him?"

"Yes, I guess so . . ." But even as I said it, I wasn't sure. I knew I *should* feel angry. But I didn't feel much of anything at all.

I hesitated. "Maybe I can pretend to punch him?"

Bessel handed my "real father" a pillow to hold over his chest.

The man fidgeted, holding up the pillow. I stared at him blankly, feeling stiff and awkward. But I went for it, punching the pillow as hard as I could.

"Fuck you!" I screamed.

It felt hollow. I hit the pillow again, harder this time.

"FUCK YOU!" I screamed.

I still didn't feel anything. I was going through the *motions*—saying the words, making the movements—but the *emotion* wasn't there.

"Let's move on," Bessel said. "Carefully look around the room and choose your ideal mother and father." I didn't need to look—I already knew who I wanted to play my ideal father. *Santa Claus!* I'd been thinking about it all week, preparing myself for this moment. He was the opposite of my father in every way. I wanted to break down and cry in his big, jolly arms like the other woman had. For my mother, I chose Linda, Bessel's assistant. She was a Vietnamese therapist with a soft voice and nurturing energy.

My ideal parents sat next to me in the middle of the circle, each holding one of my hands. Linda placed her other hand over my heart. Bessel turned to Santa.

"Tell her: 'If I were your ideal father, you would be the apple of my eye.' "

Santa stared at me. Up close, I could see his jolly old eyes were rimmed in red.

"If I was your ideal father," he repeated clunkily, devoid of emotion. "You would be . . . the uh, the er, apple of my eye?"

Apple of my eye? My father would never say that.

Bessel looked at me expectantly. "What do you feel?"

I closed my eyes and scanned my body.

"I don't feel anything," I told him, shrugging.

Bessel pushed forward, turning again to Santa.

"Tell her: 'I would cherish you and would be proud you were my daughter. I would protect you.' "

"I would cherish you . . . and . . . ummmm . . ." It was late in the evening, and poor Santa couldn't remember the sentences. He kept stumbling over the words.

"Can you simplify the language?" I asked Bessel, imagining what my father might say in his broken English.

Bessel adjusted the lines. Santa tried again but faltered.

"Try to get into character!" Bessel barked at Santa. "How would you feel if you were *truly* her father?"

Santa slumped over, looking dejected. "I never even said 'I love you' to my own father until his deathbed."

Fuckity-fuck. Of course, the man I'd chosen to play my ideal father had unresolved issues with his own father. Every man in my life had the same story. Patrick. Ryan. Even my new fake dad.

"I would cherish you . . ." Santa tried again.

Bessel looked at me. "What do you feel?" he asked again.

I glanced around. People were shifting in their seats. The room was stuffy. It'd been a long day. Everyone was waiting for me to have a breakthrough so we could go to bed. I wanted to feel something. But I didn't, and I couldn't lie. Between Santa's performance and the fact that I couldn't imagine my father saying one word of this speech, especially in English, this wasn't working.

"I feel nothing," I admitted.

Bessel's brow furrowed. He turned to Linda, my ideal mother, and gave her a few lines to say. She repeated them with warmth and tenderness: "If I were your ideal mother, I would have loved and protected you. I would have shown you what it is like to stand up to a man."

She was a lot more convincing than Mr. Claus. But I still felt nothing. And then I felt bad for feeling nothing. Bessel sat back in his chair and grimaced. "I think this is as far as we can take it tonight," he said finally, to the collective relief of the group.

I was crushed.

Even the world's best trauma expert couldn't help me.

CHAPTER 32

ACCIDENTAL PSYCHODRAMA

Surfing, particularly in Santa Cruz, is dominated by white men. At the break I surfed regularly, there was one female for every ten male surfers. There were even fewer women who dared to shortboard. After I switched to shortboarding, I understood why. The shorter your board, the more you had to fight for your waves, competing with ultra-aggressive men who didn't understand the concept of taking turns. I loved the waves in Santa Cruz, but it was the most toxic surf culture of any place I had ever surfed. And if you were a woman, it was ten times worse.

Two months after the workshop at Esalen, a south swell hit. I paddled out, eager to catch waves. The lineup was crowded—at least thirty surfers out, jostling for position as they waited for the sets to roll in. I hung back, feeling intimidated.

I heard a voice from behind me. "Jane!"

I turned to see my friend John, one of the best surfers at the break, paddling toward me.

"Follow me," he said. "We're getting you a wave."

I swallowed my nerves and paddled after him toward the peak. We looked to the horizon and saw a bump forming. The glassy face of the wave shimmered, its wall thickening quickly. A handful of more seasoned surfers shifted into position.

"You're going," John insisted firmly. "Paddle!"

I hesitated for half a second, then started paddling, ignoring the chaos around me. As I glanced to my left, I saw a man already on the wave. He was built like a truck driver, with a long gray mustache and a board twice the size of mine. Tim.

"There's someone on the wave already!" I yelled at John.

"He just caught one. It's your turn. Go!" he shouted back.

The wave's lip began to curl as I paddled with everything I had. I popped up to my feet, flying down the smooth, glassy face. As I carved back up the wave, I glanced back and saw Tim behind me. I could hear him screaming over the rumble of the wave.

"Get off my wave!"

Adrenaline shot through my body. No way was I giving this wave up.

"Get off my wave, you DUMB FUCK!" he hollered, louder this time.

The wave closed out and I popped out the back, breath ragged, heart pounding. I'd never had a grown man swear at me like that. Shaken, I paddled in, grabbed my bike, and pedaled home as fast as I could. As soon as I got in, I called George, a local old-timer who'd surfed the break for decades. I recounted the entire scene, my voice shaking as I repeated Tim's words: *you dumb fuck.*

And then it hit me.

I *had* been yelled at like that before.

"Dumb fuck" was basically the equivalent of my father's go-to insult in Taiwanese.

Gong ga be xi. You're so stupid, you should die.

It wasn't the first time I had heard those words.

It was just the first time I'd heard them in English.

The next day, George called me around lunchtime. "I ran

into Tim at the top of the stairs," he said casually. "We had some *words*. Let's just say he won't be fucking with you anymore."

"What'd you say?" I asked.

"Oh, I told him that he cursed at the wrong woman. That you help save babies. I mean, what the hell has he done with his life? I told him he's not allowed to surf there anymore. I was ready to throw down."

"Wait . . . what?" I stammered, shocked.

As George recounted the confrontation, I felt something shift inside me. My shoulders dropped. My jaw softened. The knot in my stomach began to loosen. I didn't realize how much tension I'd been holding since the day before. After we got off the phone, I sat in silence, letting myself *feel* what it was like to have someone stand up for me. Feeling that in my body, it suddenly seemed possible that someone could have stood up for me when I was little. Someone could have shielded me from my father's rage and simply said *No*. Or *enough*.

I wondered what it would have felt like to have a father who protected me. Or a mother who defended me. Protection is supposed to be written into the role of parent—it seems instinctual, even primal. But growing up, I'd felt so alone in protecting myself. Even as I went out into the world on a crusade to defend others, I never stopped to consider that I needed protection too.

I didn't see Tim again that year, and I never got an apology. But it didn't matter. When George stood up for me, something clicked, opening my body to a new possibility. Maybe healing didn't always look like a breakthrough in a circle of strangers. Maybe sometimes it was just someone having your back when you needed it most.

~~~~~~~~~~

I hadn't given up on Bessel. After reaching out a few times, he finally agreed to another online session.

"Hello, Jane," he greeted me warmly. His accent was thicker than I remembered. He was wearing a blue-and-white Hawaiian shirt, loosely buttoned. Scholarly and relaxed—very professor-on-vacation. After some catching up, I told him about the confrontation in the water and how George standing up for me had allowed me to *feel* what it was like to be protected.

"I think I might be able to receive some of those messages from the psychodrama now," I said. "Can we try again? And . . . could you play my ideal father?"

"Sure," Bessel responded. He took a deep breath. Then, looking steadily into the camera, he said, "If I were your ideal father, I would love and cherish you. I would protect you, not hurt you. I would be proud of you. You would be the apple of my eye."

Apple of my eye again, I thought, cringing a little. But I closed my eyes and tried to take the words in. Slowly, warmth began to bloom in my chest, radiating outward. I sat with it for a moment, then exhaled.

"Wow, okay, I felt something this time!"

Bessel looked pleased, his face lighting up.

"So," he said at the end of our session, "when do we meet again?"

I tried to contain my excitement. He'd only agreed to the one session, which I was lucky to get.

"Whenever you're free?" I responded, trying not to sound too eager.

"Reach out to my assistant."

I did. We set up a meeting for two weeks later. And at the

end of *that* session, he told me to schedule again. That's how it went, every other week, until eventually his assistant just put me on the calendar for the rest of the year. And that is how one of the world's foremost trauma researchers accidentally-on-purpose became my therapist.

CHAPTER 33

LIKE AN EXHALE

"And then, he hit me," I said. "Again."

I recalled my father's belt landing on my body, the terror that flooded my system as I braced myself against his rage. On the other side of the screen, Bessel winced, like he'd taken the blow himself. His shoulders caved slightly as he leaned forward, collapsing the digital space between us.

"Mmmhmm," Bessel hummed. His face was pruned with concern, his eyes soft and watery. Instead of speaking, he inhaled deeply, then exhaled slowly, letting the air out in a long, steady *whoosh*. I followed his lead, taking a breath, then another. I noticed the rise and fall of my chest, the nervous tingle of my toes and fingers, the buzzing sensation at the crown of my head. And somewhere in the space between speaking and breathing, crushing sadness bubbled up in my throat.

Bessel and I had been meeting for months. When I recounted stories of the past, he left long, deliberate pauses. Instead of plowing ahead or flipping on my intellect like a light switch, I was forced to slow down and linger quietly on what I'd just said. To truly feel what was buried beneath the words. After I spoke, he always asked: "What does it feel like in your body?" I'd search for the answer. Some days, I couldn't feel anything. Other days, it was an anvil pressing against my chest. As Bessel listened, he leaned in—both physically and energetically. His reactions mirrored the emotions I'd never been given the space to feel.

My first therapist at Stanford, Dr. Theodore, had probably been trying to do the same thing when he cried during one of our sessions. But back then, I wasn't ready. I had to lose more first—Embrace, Patrick, Ryan, and eventually myself—to arrive here.

All the things I'd tried before working with Bessel, from the earnest to the wacky, had been valuable in their own way. Each experience had opened the aperture another millimeter and let slivers of light in that brought me closer to seeing the whole picture. But Bessel was right about needing one steady guide.

"Everyone who warms up to you, you seem to dismiss," he said to me one day. "But not me. I'm struck that you seem to trust me, and your heart is open to me, probably more than to most people."

"Yes," I agreed. "I feel like you're really honest with me."

"It's nice to see that little window of you," he said with a soft smile.

I think part of what made me trust Bessel was the fact that he'd said no to working with me several times. I knew he was going out of his way to see me, which meant that I was not just another client. In our sessions, I felt seen and valued—a feeling I'd never realized was so important in the therapist-client relationship. With other therapists, even if we clicked at first, I quickly grew skeptical, scanning for flaws in their methodology or on high alert for ways they might fail me. Vulnerability had always felt dangerous, and my instinct was to stay on the offense. But Bessel demonstrated a warm, genuine care that disarmed me. I looked forward to my sessions with him the way I might look forward to time with a beloved family member.

Still, I was impatient for results.

"So," I'd ask at the end of every session, "do you think I'm ever going to be healed?"

"Yes," he'd say calmly, his voice reassuring. "I do believe that."

"But when?" I'd push, like an impatient CEO whose quarterly healing report was overdue. "And how?"

"The key," Bessel said, "is to really confront these painful experiences, to allow yourself to know what you wish you didn't know—or else they have a life of their own. Over time, you develop a different relationship with a traumatic memory. You realize you have agency, that you are no longer stuck. You can eventually put the past in the past. You can say *that happened then*—*this is now.*"

With infinite patience, Bessel guided me back to the same painful moments again and again. Growing up, I'd done the only thing I could to survive—harden. Turn to stone. Freeze. I had to disconnect from my body, from all its sensations and messages, good or bad. But slowly, I was starting to thaw. And in the puddle left behind was pain—perfectly preserved, as if it had been waiting through the decades for me to move through it.

It felt as though I was constantly uncovering new layers of grief. Incrementally, I let myself feel the feelings I had repressed for so long—without immediately dismissing, justifying, or rationalizing. Feelings that had once been too much to bear. The deeper we went, the more the pain started to soften into something more tender. I could see how small and scared I had been.

I was just a kid. Just a little kid.

Healing, I was coming to learn, had no quick fixes. Its timeline was not linear but elliptical. I couldn't bulldoze my way through or bend it to my will. The work was painful and excruciatingly slow. I'd feel better for a while, then worse again. Even after months of excavating my worst memories, my progress was so subtle it often felt imperceptible. Over time, I began to understand that healing was an accumulation of small, almost invisible, shifts—a two-degree adjustment here, a moment of clarity there. Each time I revisited a memory, I could see and feel it differently, as my system became ready to process more.

When I talked to Anjali about it, she compared the process to exploring a new town or city. "When you're a tourist going to a new place for the first time," she said, "you take in the sights, but only at a surface level. You stick to the main attractions, the places everyone tells you to visit." Revisiting an old memory for the first time is like that: you only see it in broad strokes. But as you return to that place—or that memory—again and again, you start to notice the details. You explore the side streets, the hidden gems, the local cafés.

Healing felt just like that—like stepping into an internal landscape I had to navigate over and over again. Every visit to those painful experiences revealed a forgotten detail, an emotion I hadn't fully processed. Every time I returned, I felt and understood a little more.

"Do you know what emotion is missing when you talk about these memories?" Bessel asked me one day in a session. "Do you remember what you first came to me about? After your breakup with Ryan?"

I paused. "Anger?"

His brows knitted together. "Yes," he said. "You told me you had an anger problem. Yet, I've never once heard you express anger towards your father."

I was taken aback. Bessel was right. I could conjure rage at Ryan for the smallest things, but when I talked about my father's beatings, the anger was . . . absent. There was plenty of sadness. But anger, which should have been the most natural reaction, was completely missing.

I closed my eyes and tried to connect with the feeling. I imagined myself at seven years old. A carousel of fuzzy images flashed by. Me chasing my cousins. My sisters and I roller-skating in the driveway, my hair slapping my face as I spun, laughing. Then the memory darkened. My cousins were gone. The house was quiet except for the sound of the belt against my skin, as my father struck me for not doing my extra math homework. As I described it to Bessel, my whole body tensed.

"It hurts," I told Bessel, my eyes filling with tears. "And it's not just pain but something else. Shock? Yes. It's shocking to the system to be hit like that. It feels like a violation."

A rush of sensation flooded my chest. I paused, letting the feelings rise without pushing them away.

"I feel so sorry for that little girl," I said. "She didn't deserve that. I felt so rejected. It's no wonder I never felt like I was enough."

"Yes," Bessel said, his voice a calming salve. "And why didn't you fight back?"

"How could I? I was so little. I had no choice . . ."

My voice trailed off. Bessel leaned in, his face filling the screen.

"Maybe say that to the seven-year-old child? Tell her that you know she couldn't defend herself. I think that's really important."

Closing my eyes again, I tried to enter the scene, telepathically talking to seven-year-old me. *I'm so sorry this happened to you. You couldn't defend yourself.*

A stabbing pain shot up my right arm.

"My arm hurts!" I cried out.

"Listen to it," Bessel said. "Send some energy to that arm. Let that arm know *you understand*."

I grimaced, but followed along, placing my hand gently on my forearm.

"That feeling," I whispered, my voice wobbly. "Of rejection? It's so deep, you know? So ingrained in my body. I don't know how to get rid of it."

Bessel nodded.

"Every time I get intimate with someone, I feel it again. No matter what they do. No one can get it right with me."

"My hunch," Bessel said, "is that it has something to do with you rejecting yourself. The most critical thing is to get to know this little girl better. I think that's the missing piece. For *you* to see her for who she is. To allow her to feel what it's like to be treasured. And I don't think you're quite there yet."

He paused. "Can you imagine how you might rescue this little girl and take her somewhere safe?"

In our past sessions, I'd tried to save her before—to get her out of danger, to give her the comfort and love she hadn't received. In the moment, I would feel relief. But afterward, as I returned to my life outside of therapy, I would fall into the same patterns of self-doubt and criticism.

"Can I imagine an ideal father coming into the scene?" I asked Bessel. "To rescue her."

"Sure," Bessel said, shrugging. "But I'd prefer it was you."

"It's just . . . I've done it before, and something never clicks fully. She still feels rejected. Can you tell me what *you* would do for her?"

"Oh sure. I would celebrate that kid and point out what was lovable about her." He grinned. "I would take you surfing!" I chuckled at the thought of this grandfatherly Dutch academic in board shorts, getting crushed by the waves.

"I'd help you stand up on your board," he continued. "And sit out there, waiting for the next wave to come. I would put some ointment on your legs after you scraped yourself on the reef. I would challenge you, and we would stand up together. Maybe I'd tow you in at the end of the long day. Then take you out for soda and ice cream at the end."

"That sounds perfect," I whispered.

For a moment, we sat quietly. I felt enveloped by his words, by the ease with which he conjured the scene. In his story, I wasn't hard to please or love. I wasn't a burden or a problem to contend with. Caring for me was the most natural thing in the world.

"What are you feeling?" Bessel asked.

"I feel . . . longing," I said. "I wish I'd had a father like that. When I imagine it, it feels like . . . like, an exhale."

"Yes," Bessel said, letting out a soft breath. "Precisely. Like an exhale. I feel sorry for your father—he missed out on the opportunity to really know you. Anyone who knows you can see what a special person you are."

I tried to let the words in. I wanted to believe them.

"The main way to rescue this little girl is really for *you* to get to know her," he continued, setting his hand on his heart. "And for *you* to know how precious she is. Can you see her?"

I closed my eyes again and turned inward. I pictured the crop of her hair, the mischievous flicker in her eyes.

"Yes," I whispered. "I can see her."

"Can you imagine how *you* could have rescued this little girl?" Bessel asked again.

I took a deep breath.

"I would hug her and hold her. I would let her cry, and make sure she knows it's okay to feel sad. I would soothe her," I said softly. I couldn't remember anyone ever soothing me.

"I would protect her. I would fight anyone who tried to hurt her. I would let her know she's safe now."

Bessel leaned closer to the screen. "Is *she* hearing it?"

Could she hear it? Could she hear me standing up for her? All those years I spent fighting for other children, I'd never spoken directly to her.

"Is that little girl hearing it?" he asked again. He closed his eyes and waited.

I turned my focus to the little girl, feeling her heartbeat, her small, strong body, her fear, her sadness. *Are you hearing me?* I asked silently. Slowly, her eyes lifted to meet mine. And I knew she had heard. She wanted to believe me. She wanted to trust me.

"Yes," I said finally, looking to the ceiling to hold back tears. "She's hearing it. She's still scared, but she's beginning to hear me."

CHAPTER 34

NO BAD PARTS

I bolted upright in bed, my T-shirt soaked in sweat. It had been nearly a year since Ryan and I broke up, but I kept having the same recurring nightmare. In it, Ryan was always leaving me— not because things between us were broken, but because he'd found someone better. Someone he loved more. I'd wake in the middle of the night, heart pounding, breath shallow. Then I'd lie there, tossing and turning, wondering.

Did he ever really love me?

The rational part of me knew it didn't make sense. He couldn't get his life together. I had ended things. But logic didn't matter. The self-doubt lived in my body. It was old and familiar—the sense that I wasn't good enough, pretty enough, lovable enough. I could fake confidence, lead teams, even give keynotes on resilience. But in the quiet of night, that deep, cellular belief that I wasn't enough surfaced like a phantom limb—unseen but aching.

I knew this went deeper than Ryan. And I was terrified that if I didn't get to the root of this belief, it would spread like a cancer inside me, poisoning my chance at ever having a healthy intimate relationship. Deep down, that's what I really wanted. Not the accomplishments, not the accolades. Just someone I could love— and be loved by.

"I don't understand," I grumbled during a session with Bessel. "I've done so much work. But something still isn't clicking."

"Maybe you should also do some IFS therapy?" Bessel suggested. IFS, or internal family systems, was a therapy model created by Dick Schwartz. I'd been reading his book *No Bad Parts*, and Bessel and I had already been using a version of his methodology in our sessions.

The premise of the IFS model is that we all have multiple sub-personalities, or a family of "parts." There are three types of parts: Exiles, Managers, and Firefighters. At the center of these parts is the Self. Exiles are the wounded parts of us. They carry our deepest pain, fear, and vulnerability, often stemming from childhood. These parts often feel alone, ashamed, or abandoned. Because these emotions can be overwhelming, we push these parts away—we exile them. One of my Exiles was the scared little girl I'd been talking to in the sessions with Bessel.

Managers protect Exiles, doing everything they can to keep pain from surfacing, often by controlling our behavior, emotions, or environment. These parts can manifest as overachievers, cynics, and control freaks. One of my managers was the hypervigilant part, always suspicious and scanning for potential fallout—the one who distrusted therapists, boyfriends, and anyone else who tried to get too close.

Firefighters step in to handle emergencies. When an Exile's pain breaks through and threatens to flood the system, they jump in with distraction or destruction. Anything to numb the pain. One of my chief firefighters was Jane-ghis Khan—furious, impulsive, and destructive. She tried to protect me from heartbreak by unleashing anger and chaos. *Ryan is trying to hurt you! Kick him out! Throw everything out now!!!*

Finally, there's the Self: the calm, compassionate core of who we are. The Self is courageous, connected, and confident. It's our true loving nature. The Self knows innately how to heal and cannot be broken, though it can be hidden behind our parts. I'd glimpsed my Self during my MDMA journey—she could let go, and didn't need to understand in order to forgive. She was joyful and free, surfing life's waves with ease and grace.

Like members of a family, each part has its own perspective, interests, and ways of coping. The ultimate goal of the IFS model is not to judge, shame, or banish these parts but to understand and accept them. To develop a trusting relationship with each one, the way a stable, nurturing parent would with their children. Over time, as the parts begin to trust the Self, they start to soften. They stop taking the driver's seat and allow the Self to lead.

Bessel introduced me to Dick via email. By the time of our online appointment, I'd dog-eared my copy of his book and tried some of the exercises on my own. Logging on, I felt the same excitement I'd experienced when I first met with Bessel. I couldn't believe I'd gained access to the inner sanctum of trauma-healing royalty. Surely *this* was it. The Holy Grail of healing was just one Zoom session away.

Dick appeared on the screen, a middle-aged white man in a polo shirt. He had a neatly trimmed beard and short gray mustache. My skeptical Manager perked up immediately, scanning him for flaws. I reminded myself he was an expert. And if Bessel trusted him, then surely I should too.

We introduced ourselves and I shared a succinct summary of my childhood. "I'm constantly second-guessing myself," I told Dick. "With partners, I don't feel safe. And then I feel the need to protect. I get *really* angry. In my last relationship, I felt like I was becoming my father at times. It scared the shit out of me."

Dick leaned back in his chair, nodding slowly. "No doubt there's a part of you that absorbed a lot of your father's energy," he said matter-of-factly.

"I think my angry part is my Firefighter," I said. "And it's protecting the Exile who doesn't believe she's worthy of love."

"That could be," he said. "Which part should we work with today? Should we start by working with your angry part or the insecure part?"

"Maybe the insecure part?"

"All right," he said. "But let's check with the angry one first because it might be protecting the insecure one. They often work together. Go ahead and try to find it in your body. Where is it, the angry one?"

I closed my eyes and took a deep breath. Immediately, I felt a dense, tarlike sensation in the pit of my stomach.

"In my gut," I said. "I feel it in my gut."

"As you notice it, how do you feel towards it?" Dick asked.

I let my attention settle on the sensation.

"Curious," I replied.

"Good. Follow your curiosity," Dick instructed. "Ask what it wants you to know about its anger. Don't think of the answer in your mind. Just see what comes to you. From your gut."

I took another breath.

"Why?" I asked. "Why are you so angry?"

It didn't answer but started to morph into something else—a suit of armor standing behind a thick brass shield.

"Holy shit," I said, narrating to Dick what was happening.

Next to the suit of armor, a silver sword came into focus. It was suspended in midair like something from a fantasy novel.

"Why are you so angry?" I asked again.

A response came—not in words, but more like a transmission.

Because this is heavy.

I repeated the message to Dick.

"Let it know you get that," he said. "It feels like it has to have all this heavy protection to keep you safe."

Without words, I told the armor.

Suddenly, I was hit with a wave of exhaustion. I could barely sit up.

"I'm tired," I cried, my voice raspy. "So tired."

"Of course you are," Dick said. "Keeping you safe has been a heavy job for a long time. Tell the angry part you understand."

"I understand you have a big job," I said to the angry part. "And you're probably on guard all the time. So, of course you're tired."

We moved back and forth like that for a while, me sitting with my eyes closed, navigating my surreal inner space, and Dick guiding me like a therapist Wizard of Oz. With his help, I ventured deeper and deeper into myself, inching closer to what the armor was protecting: the scared little girl.

Finally, I saw her. She was curled up alone in the dark, knees pulled tight to her chest. Her shiny black hair was cropped at her chin, a thick fringe of bangs brushing her forehead. But her energy wasn't carefree and joyful like a child's should be. Fear pulsed from her in great, undulating waves. My heart ached as I took her in. I knew this girl. She was the one who'd learned how to swallow her pain. The one who kept quiet about what happened at home to keep her family safe.

"I want to hug her," I told Dick, grief piercing through me.

"Can you do that?" I heard him ask, his voice steady. "Try to do that and tell me what she says."

I approached her slowly.

She eyed me warily. "Stop," she said suddenly, her voice soft but firm.

"She's telling me to stop," I relayed to Dick.

"We go at her pace," he replied.

I didn't move closer. Instead, I settled where I was and waited.

"Why don't you trust me?" I asked her gently.

"Everyone gets mean," she murmured. Her voice was low, muffled. "I like it better by myself."

I nodded, trying to show her I understood. I tried to tell her without words that she was safe with me. I tried to transmit love, to let her *feel* it in her body. To tell her I wasn't here to hurt her or take more than had already been taken. I just wanted to get to know her. To sit beside her, if she'd let me.

Slowly, she began to relax. Her small body unfolded, and she scooted back against a wall.

"I'm scared something bad is gonna happen," she whispered.

"I know," I said softly. "You have good reasons to feel that way. Trust me. I know."

She pushed her bangs out of her eyes and gave a slight nod, signaling that I could come closer. I moved toward her, inch by inch. When I reached her, I sat down slowly, leaning back against an invisible wall. Our arms touched, heat humming between us. Her breath was shallow, her heartbeat wild.

I reached out and tried to touch her hand. She flinched.

I drew back, listening to the patter of her breath.

"You're safe here," I said in my most soothing voice. "You're safe now."

After a while, I reached out again. This time, she didn't pull away. She softened and stretched her limbs out, lying her head in my lap.

"I'm here for you," I said gently, stroking her hair. "You don't have to be alone anymore. I'm so sorry I didn't get to you sooner."

I felt her heart begin to slow. The space around us softened, enveloping us in a warm cocoon. After what felt like hours, Dick's voice floated in. "Let her know that when she's ready, she can tell you where her fear came from."

I set my hand gently on her back.

"Will you show me?" I asked. "Where did your fear come from?"

She turned to face me and blinked. Once, twice, three times, and then I was moving with her, sucked through time and space. I landed in her body, my child body, seeing through her eyes as I was struck, again and again, by my father. My body stiffened with each blow as I tried to absorb the shock without bracing or flinching. It was horrifying.

But I felt nothing.

"I'm feeling stuck here," I cried out to Dick. "I can't feel anything."

"That's okay," he said calmly. "You're not stuck. There's a part that's blocking feelings to protect you. Talk to that part. Ask it how old it thinks you are."

I wasn't sure where to direct my question. Out of the darkness, another figure appeared—a shapeless, solid mass.

"How old do you think I am?" I asked.

Eight.

"It thinks I'm eight," I told Dick.

"Ah," he said. "It would have been too much to feel these things back then. It had to block the feelings. It did its job. Let it know how old you are now. And see how it reacts."

"I'm forty-three now," I said to the mass. "I can handle a lot more. I'm ready to feel it. I'm ready to feel it all."

The mass pulsed and expanded. It didn't speak, but I understood its message. It would let its guard down but stand by in case things got too overwhelming. As it retreated, I was suddenly throttled with sensation. The girl started to tremble in my lap, her body convulsing with fear. I could feel her terror—the terror she had been forced to suppress. It coursed from her body into mine, seizing my limbs, my face, the top of my skull. We were shaking together.

We were being beaten.

I was being beaten.

By someone who was supposed to love and protect me.

I was so stupid I should die.

"You're doing great," Dick said, his voice steady. "She really needs you to understand how terrifying it was. As soon as she feels like you get it, we're coming in to get her out. We're coming in to help her."

"I'm here," I whispered to her through the shaking. "I know how scared you are."

"Where's my mom?" she cried out suddenly.

My stomach dropped.

"She wants her mom," I called to Dick. "She wishes her mom could have helped."

"Mom, where are you?" she pleaded, this time louder and more urgent.

"You can be with me now," I said to her. "We can go somewhere safe." I wanted to run her out of there, to never look back.

I stood and tried to pull her up. But she didn't budge. She stiffened, her body rigid.

I knelt to meet her eyes. "What is it?" I asked.

"It's my fault," she said, her voice shaky.

"It wasn't your fault," I said firmly. *It wasn't your fault.* The words I'd blurted out over a decade ago in a session with Dr. Theodore, not knowing what they meant. Now it was so clear. It wasn't my fault. But as a child, I'd had to believe it was—because it was easier than believing my father would intentionally hurt me, and my mother would stand by in silence.

"Are you ready to leave with me now?" I asked her. "I'm going to take you to a safe place."

She hesitated, her wide eyes darting past me. "You need to say it to him," she whispered.

I froze. Of course.

Of course, I had to say it to him.

As I turned, my father came into view. Anger rose in me like a tidal wave, curdling in the pit of my stomach. I scooped the little girl into my arms and stepped forward, closer and closer, until I was face-to-face with him. I could feel the warmth of his breath. I took in the lines around his mouth, the droop of his eyes, and for a brief flash I felt sorry for him. But then I locked eyes with him, and the pity was replaced by something far more powerful.

"Don't you EVER FUCKING touch her again!" I screamed, my voice thundering through the air.

The little girl clapped her hands over her ears.

"You hear me? Don't you ever fucking touch her again," I repeated, quieter, my whole body shaking as I held her away from him. "If you hurt her again, I will kill you."

And with that, a wail escaped my throat. The little girl and I clung to each other. I had finally stood up to my father. But what came after wasn't catharsis or relief. It was a profound, crushing sadness. Safe in my arms, she was no longer scared of being hurt, but of losing him. Of being disconnected. Of losing what love she did have.

We are free, I wanted to tell her. *We are finally free.*

And it was devastating.

CHAPTER 35

BOUND AND CONSTRAINED

I was in the middle of my workday when Joyce called. It'd been a few weeks since the session with Dick.

"Jane," she said, her voice strained. "I have something to tell you."

I imagined the worst. Nancy. My nephews. My parents. "What? What is it?"

She paused, taking a breath. "Grace's brother died. They found him in his apartment a few days ago."

"My God."

"They think he may have killed himself."

I gasped. "That's crazy . . . how is Grace?"

"A wreck. She hasn't told her mom yet."

Grace, a friend of Joyce's growing up, was also a first-generation Taiwanese American. Her brother Matt had been a year ahead of me in high school. I didn't know him well, but I knew he had been a star student and track athlete, the kind of kid everyone expected to succeed. Through Joyce, I'd heard stories about violence in their home. I didn't think much of it then, assuming all kids in Asian families got beaten.

After Joyce hung up, I stared at my phone, numb with disbelief. I wondered what Matt had gone through and how bad it must have been for him to take his own life. And then a thought gripped me: *It could have been us.* Me or my sisters.

The tears came in waves and over the next few weeks, they kept coming. I had terrible dreams, bolting awake in the middle of the night, imagining what Matt must have gone through. My speculation on his life started to merge with memories of my own—moments from childhood when I'd wanted to die. Something I'd only ever told Joyce about.

The first time, I was ten. My sister and I were watching TV one night. I started goofing around, dancing and laughing, stepping in front of the screen to block her view.

"Stop, dork!" she cried. "You're so annoying!"

But I kept at it, gunning for attention. At some point, she snapped and shoved me out of the way. My father exploded. He pulled her into the other room and beat her. I ran to my bedroom and closed the door, heart pounding as I hunched over my desk. I heard Mom in the other room trying to intervene, which she'd never done before. Dad must have tried to push her out of the way, because I heard my sister scream, "Don't touch her!"

A few minutes later, Mom flung open my door. Her eyes were red.

"Look what you did," she said, wiping away tears.

My stomach dropped. I'd just been kidding around.

"I didn't mean it," I whispered. "I didn't mean it . . ."

She walked away. My whole body went numb.

The guilt was unbearable. My eyes landed on a half-sharpened yellow no. 2 pencil on my desk. I grabbed it and stabbed the back of my hand, again and again, leaving blotchy gray marks. *You're so stupid you should die.* I was the one who deserved to be punished, not my sister. I pressed harder, grinding the dull graphite into my skin, willing it to pierce through. This would all be easier if I were just dead.

By junior high, I assumed suicidal thoughts were a normal part of growing up. But in seventh grade, when a boy in our class hanged himself, the shock that reverberated through the school made me realize that they weren't normal. Not for a twelve-year-old. I decided to stash my darkness away entirely. I swung in the opposite direction, becoming bright and bubbly—easy to like, but hard to read. I learned to put a smile on my face, no matter what happened at home. I tried not to ruffle feathers, going along with everything. I never expressed my true desires, or fears, or anger. Being the "nice" girl became my refuge.

But the darkness still lived inside me. It emerged when I got angry at Joyce, or during explosive outbursts with boyfriends. It surfaced only with a handful of people I was close enough to feel vulnerable around. The ones who saw beyond the smile.

I wondered now how many of my peers had suffered in silence too. How many of us had been on the edge while clocking straight A's and overloading ourselves with extracurriculars that looked good on college applications? How many had crashed when the scaffolding of success fell apart?

With Embrace, I'd found a purpose. A reason to keep going, to fight for a better world. I'd been incredibly lucky to have financial stability, a world-class education, and connections to some of the best therapists and healers. I basically had the Avengers of trauma support. I knew most people didn't have the kind of access I did, nor the borderline-obsessive drive to heal. And even with *all* that, the darkness still loomed. What about those who didn't have resources? The ones who were struggling in silence, without support? I'd been deep in my own healing, but Matt's death woke me up. The pain I was feeling wasn't just mine—it was part of something much bigger. This was about the health of my community.

As immigrants, many of our families had endured war and violence, survived oppressive governments, fled persecution. Our parents had come to America in search of something better. They arrived with hope and started from scratch, swallowing their pride while facing an endless stream of discrimination. They navigated their new world in half-formed sentences, unable to fully communicate their ambitions or their hearts. And they had been the lucky ones.

As children, we knew we were carrying something heavy. Something laden. Something that was not ours. We became our parents' channels for this new world. We were everything they left behind and everything they hoped to become. We carried both the pain from the past and the pressures of the future. Everything they couldn't say aloud was transmitted through our bones.

I started researching domestic-violence statistics and found study after study linking it to PTSD, depression, and suicide. Those with high Adverse Childhood Experience (ACE) scores— particularly those exposed to physical or emotional abuse—were up to twelve times more likely to attempt suicide. The pattern was undeniable. The cycle kept repeating, in silence, behind closed doors. I realized . . . my silence was complicity. What happened to Matt could happen to any of us if we kept telling ourselves, "That's just the way it is."

I thought about a recent conversation I'd had with Diana Chapman. "This trauma won't be over until you confront your parents," she'd said.

"That will never happen!" I'd responded. "Anyway, what's that going to change?"

"This isn't about changing them," she'd said. "It's about taking the hand of that little girl, going up to your parents, and telling them the truth, so that she can really hear you standing up for her."

Talking to my parents seemed unfathomable. Not only was I terrified, but we had no shared language for deep, vulnerable conversations. How could I communicate the impact of what had happened? Therapy had helped me work through the darkness of my past, but I didn't know how to translate any of that into Taiwanese. And my parents' English wasn't strong enough to understand what I wanted to say. Without language as a bridge, it was hard to imagine getting through to them. But even beyond that, there was a deeper fear. If I unbottled my grief, what if I couldn't contain it again? What if it poured out endlessly, drowning me in an ocean of pain? Besides, I had already tried—with Mom, at least. That was enough, I had told myself.

But after Matt's death, I couldn't ignore the weight of what had been left unsaid. Maybe it wasn't enough to confront my parents in dream-space therapy sessions. Maybe Diana was right. I had to do it in real life. Over the last few years, I had started talking about the abuse more openly with my sisters. Nancy wanted nothing to do with it. She had her own family. Her life was stable and secure, and she didn't want to risk disturbing it. Joyce, on the other hand, was on her own journey to come to terms with what had happened. On a recent trip home, she had told Mom how the violence had shaped us, and how we carried it still. She even told her about how I had tried to hurt myself.

"She cried the entire time," Joyce told me.

Hearing that cracked something open. I realized I didn't need to explain PTSD, or inner-child work, or the love molecule, or any of the self-help modalities that my parents certainly wouldn't understand. All those things had helped me get to the core of what mattered. The pain. The heartbreak. That was all I needed to express. I didn't need to say it perfectly. Things would be lost in translation no matter what. I just needed to speak my truth.

It was time to stop talking about my parents and speak directly to them.

The words would come.

In the end, beyond all the therapy and retreats, it was just about what happened.

My father beat me.

My mother didn't protect me.

I wanted to die.

Sometimes I still wanted to die.

I decided to talk to Mom first. It felt less daunting. I had started talking to her about the abuse in Taiwan, but had never truly opened up about how deeply it affected me even all these years later. I had never talked to her about the ways her actions—and inactions—had hurt me.

I wasn't ready to face her in person. So I decided to call instead. I spent weeks preparing, culling moments from my childhood, sobbing as I wrote down every painful memory. Processing the past with a therapist had been safe and contained, but preparing to say these things to my mother somehow made the pain more real.

I tried to recall moments of love and tenderness too. I remembered Mom taking to me to violin lessons every week and sitting patiently through them. How she coached me to perform the Noah's Ark poem, her beaming face when I won—my success had been hers too. I appreciated how she always took us girls to try new things: ice skating, singing, ballet, art. She wanted us to have the opportunities that she didn't. I thought of her generosity. After I graduated from college, I was dying to travel around

Europe. Dad was adamantly opposed to it, but Mom gifted me the funds to go. If there was anything I desired, Mom wanted me to have it.

She showed her love in gestures, in quiet acts of care. Every time I came home to visit, she made my favorite meals and stocked the pantry with my favorite snacks. She always had a tray of freshly cut fruits waiting for me on the kitchen table. We'd go shopping together, eat hotpot, laugh. Before I left, she'd wake up early to make sushi rolls for my trip back and slip me some cash, saying, "Go buy yourself something nice." But what I admired most about my mother was her unwavering ability to see the goodness in others. No matter how my father treated her, she chose to see the best in him. She rarely let his anger bring her down. In some ways, she was the strongest person I knew.

And yet, even as I mapped out these moments and the things I appreciated, it struck me how few intimate memories I had with my mother from childhood. I couldn't recall a single time she had soothed me after my father's beatings. I couldn't remember hugging her or curling up in her arms. As I worked over the years to untangle the relationship with my father, my mother had remained in the background, a shadowy figure obscured by his image. She was always there, in the frame, but when I tried to recall her presence, her touch, her voice, it was like trying to bottle air.

I stared at my notes. At the top of the page, I scrawled in big, block letters: MOM, WHERE WERE YOU???

For weeks, I procrastinated. Finally, I gave myself a hard deadline. The morning I planned to call, I meditated on the beach to clear my head, then walked back to my cottage, where I sat at the kitchen table. I held my breath and dialed.

Mom picked up on the first ring.

"Hello?"

"Mom, it's Xiao Yu. I need to talk to you."

"Sure," she said. She sounded ready. Joyce had given her a heads-up weeks ago that I'd be calling.

"I want to talk to you about some things that happened when I was little," I said, my voice wobbly. "Things that still really hurt me today."

"Mhmm," she said softly, waiting.

Grateful for my notes, I began reading through the memories without stopping to second-guess.

"In the fourth grade, I was made fun of at school for being Chinese," I said. "I came home in tears, which I never did. Do you know what you told me when you saw me? You told me to shut up. You didn't even try to make me feel better."

I continued, my voice trembling more with each memory. "And when I was ten, you told me it was my fault that Dad hit my sister. How could you blame a ten-year-old? I wanted to die that day."

She was silent, but I could hear the soft lilt of her breath. The space between us felt vast.

"You *never* stepped in when Dad was beating us up, and you never comforted me afterwards," I said. "You never said anything, except to tell me to make sure no one could see the marks he left." I burst into tears, a full-bodied sob. I'd rarely cried in front of my mother. She sat quietly, holding space.

When I finally quieted, she spoke. Her voice was somber.

"I am sorry, Jane," she said. "I was so engrossed in my own pain and struggles. Once we came to America, I was struggling with fitting into this country. And then I faced health issues. I was trying to keep the family together, and I didn't do a good job."

Her words were heavy with regret. All that she'd said was true. The racist neighbors. The isolation she felt in a new country.

A dental procedure that went horribly wrong, which led to pain in her jaw for decades. An early hysterectomy I hadn't known the details of until later in my life, which required a second, emergency operation. I remembered the faraway look in her eyes for months after the procedure. I was in high school then, and didn't register it as depression, but now I wondered if she had been depressed the whole time.

"My father hit me growing up," she continued quietly. "There is a Chinese saying: *Dǎ shì téng, mà shì ài.* It means 'to hit is to care, to scold is to love.' It was such a part of our culture that I never stopped to think it was wrong." There was a long pause.

"I want you to have a healing," she said, repeating the words she'd said to me in Taiwan. "I want to spend my life making this up to you."

I softened. "Thank you, Mom."

After we got off the phone, I sat in silence. I was grateful for my mother's openness and receptivity. I knew she loved me. And yet, there was a void between us. A void I'd never named because I'd never tried to close it. Her words were sincere. Yet it felt like she was reading from a script too—like she had prepared for this conversation as carefully as I had. I wished I'd spoken to her in person, so I could see in her eyes that she really meant it. So that I could register her words with my body. So that with a warm touch of her hand, she might make up for what had been lost. Having the conversation over the phone had been another level of protection that didn't allow for true vulnerability. What I needed was the soft quiver of a moment between two people baring their souls. Instead, we both said the things we'd meticulously planned to say, but we were still unable to fully touch each other. To reach each other.

After the workshop at Esalen, I'd kept in touch with Bessel's assistant, Linda. As a Vietnamese immigrant, she understood the nuances of the first-generation experience. I'd done several sessions with her, and she helped to piece together a cultural element that was missing in the work I had done with other therapists. She helped me see the expectations I'd internalized from American culture, as well as norms from my own heritage that I'd taken for granted.

In one session, I complained about my parents' rarely celebrating my birthday as a kid. I'd taken it to mean I didn't matter. Linda offered a different lens, pointing out that birthdays hadn't really been celebrated in Asia when my parents were growing up. In traditional Japanese culture, everyone turned a year older together on the new year. Personal birthdays weren't celebrated until after World War II, when Western customs were adopted. Linda's reframing immediately helped me see things differently.

After the call with my mom, I called Linda to process the conversation.

"It felt somehow incomplete," I told her, after recounting the exchange.

Linda listened thoughtfully. "I think it went as well as it could," she said. "Look—it wasn't going to all get resolved after one conversation. But the key thing is you stood for yourself by expressing your truth."

The goal, she reminded me, was not to seam-rip and suture every childhood wound but to *relate* to them differently. I realized part of me had been holding out for a cinematic catharsis, but I understood what Linda meant. Nothing my mother said could change what had happened in the past. But expressing to her how it made me feel was important to regain trust with myself. That was the real healing.

"Have you ever asked yourself what *she* was missing?" Linda asked.

"Meaning?"

"What do you think your mother would have needed from her ideal parents?"

It was a surprising question. One that I had never considered. My mind turned to stories I'd heard of Mom's childhood—things she'd told me over the years, or snippets I'd gathered from family during trips back to Taiwan.

My mother was born in 1949, a year that marked a huge political shift for Taiwan. The communists had taken over China, and the KMT had retreated to Taiwan and declared martial law. The country was engulfed in fear and uncertainty, still reeling from war and fifty years of Japanese rule. Mom was born into this world—to the disappointment of her own mother, who was in distress upon discovering that she was a girl.

At her birth, her paternal grandfather, Lan Wei, said, "She's no better than something I could find in the trash." At the time, being born a girl in Taiwan was considered a misfortune, especially if a boy hadn't come first. Girls didn't carry on the family name and legacy. Boys did. Girls didn't take care of their parents financially in old age. Boys did. As the second girl in a row, my mother was an even bigger disappointment. Lan Wei threatened to find another wife for his son if my grandmother didn't birth a boy next.

When a local psychic proclaimed that my mother's arrival harkened the birth of a son, Lan Wei was thrilled. The prophecy came true—two years later, a boy was born, and Mom's existence was redeemed. Lan Wei threw a grand celebration. When my grandmother strolled around the neighborhood holding her new baby boy, the neighbors whispered: *He saved that woman.* With the arrival of a boy, Lan Wei treated my grandmother and mother with more tenderness. But the message had been imprinted—she would always be secondary to men. Her role was to serve.

Lan Wei owned a successful brick company and had a large home in Kaohsiung. Back then, houses were given names. Theirs was the only home in the neighborhood with three stories, so they called it Three-Level Home. As a little girl, my mom loved to dance. She wanted lessons, but her grandfather didn't believe women should dance. She played songs on the record player in her room when nobody was around and danced in the mirror. My mother was raised with love and material comfort and was given a good education. But the culture instilled the belief that the best thing that could happen to her was to secure a good husband—a man who could provide for her financially.

She grew up with a Confucian saying, Sān Cóng, which translates to the "Three Obediences":

Before marriage, obey your father.
After marriage, obey your husband.
After the husband's death, obey your son.

After Lan Wei passed away, Mom slept in the same room with her grandmother, who had bound feet. It was a tradition from the Qing dynasty that had been practiced for over a thousand years and was considered a status symbol and a mark of beauty. The custom required breaking and tightly binding the feet of young girls, resulting in permanently deformed, tiny feet—referred to as *lotus feet*. The process was excruciating. Toes were splintered and tucked beneath the sole, the arch forced into an unnatural curve. The goal was a foot no bigger than the *three-inch golden lotus*. More than just appearance, foot binding served as a form of control, limiting a woman's mobility and ensuring her life would be centered within the home. In some regions, it was impossible for a woman to marry well without bound feet. Refinement was measured by suffering, status etched into bones.

Walking was extremely painful for my great-grandmother. But she loved the theater and there was one at the end of their street. Whenever a new show opened, Mom would take her arm and they would stroll slowly, carefully, down the street to watch. Mom never saw her grandmother walk beyond the road she lived on.

As a child, Mom often cleaned her grandmother's feet. Every few days, she carefully washed them with warm water and a soft cloth, dusted them with powder, then rewrapped them.

I asked her once what they were like.

"Tiny and so white," she said. "Like a baby's foot."

I shivered. It sounded so archaic. It was wild to imagine someone in my direct family living with bound feet. It collapsed time between ancient and modern, me and my ancestors, East and West. Imagining Mom as a child, bound in her own ways, I understood that maybe her way forward had been silence. Maybe her need to survive and keep the family together left no room for standing up for us. Instead of fighting, she endured, like all the women before her. Because of her sacrifices, I was able to do all the things she never could.

My entire adult life had been driven by the belief that things could be better—*should* be better. I didn't realize how many generations I was tending to, unconsciously. My great-grandmother, who'd never walked beyond the road she lived on. My grandmother, shunned for having a daughter. My mother, accepting it all, agreeing to marry a man she'd met twice, and following him halfway around the world, where her three daughters would accomplish more than she'd ever imagined possible.

I imagined my mother traveling back to Three-Level Home, standing before her parents and her grandparents, and asking them to see her as *more*. More than a wife. More than someone destined to serve. I imagined her dancing—free and unburdened—moving through the world on her own terms.

My pain wasn't just mine alone—it was the pain of my mother and grandmother and great-grandmother. Generations of women silently screaming with bowed heads.

Their rage, like their feet, bound and constrained.

CHAPTER 36

LOST IN TRANSLATION

Talking to my mom had been nerve-racking, but the idea of confronting my dad felt insurmountable, like staring down an enormous wave that might swallow me whole. It was more daunting than any professional challenge I'd faced, or any ocean I'd ever paddled into.

But I knew I had to do it. This time, I would do it in person. I asked Joyce to come with me, and thankfully, she agreed. It was a warm weekend in April. Dad picked us up at the airport, like he always did. No matter what time our flights arrived or departed, he insisted on picking us up and dropping us off. It was one of his ways of showing love.

We made small talk in the car about the flight, the weather—anything to fill the silence. Once we got home, I puttered around the house, stalling. Did I really want to do this? Dad was an old man at this point. His health had been deteriorating. He'd had diabetes for years and gave himself daily insulin shots. Every morning, he logged his blood pressure and sugar levels on a piece of paper. Now his kidneys were starting to fail. What was really going to change if I talked to him? I mean, what if it *killed* him? I didn't want to hurt him. Despite everything, I loved my father. I even hoped that one day, we could have real closeness, like we had in those brief flashes snuggling on weekend mornings or getting ice cream after violin competitions. I was still that little girl waiting for his approval and affection.

I cornered Joyce in the kitchen. "Maybe it's better to just leave it," I whispered. Out the window, I could see Mom tending to her plants in the yard. One was a plant I had bought in college and nearly killed. She had lovingly nursed it back to life, and nearly twenty years later it was still thriving. Mom had always nurtured in the quiet ways she knew how.

"Not a chance," Joyce said firmly. "You got me on a plane. This is *happening*."

The next day, we sat together for lunch. Mom made her signature chicken broth, with shiitake mushrooms, ginger, and Chinese herbs. She set a baked miso-glazed sea bass on the table, along with stir-fried spinach and rice. We ate quietly, appreciating her cooking. As we finished eating, Mom spoke up. "The kids want to talk to you," she said to my father in Taiwanese as she cleared the plates. I knew she was trying to take a stand for us in her own way.

I gathered my nerves. This was the first serious sit-down conversation we'd ever had with Dad. Joyce sat directly in front of him and I was at the seat to his right. My heart jackhammered against my chest. I didn't know where to begin.

Dad tapped his hand on the table.

Joyce spoke first. "Dad, we've been working with therapists," she began, her voice calm and measured, "and we think it's important to talk about what happened in our childhood."

His eyes shifted to me, like he knew this was my doing. My gaze was fixed on Joyce. "In my last marriage," she continued, "I was constantly afraid my husband was going to explode over tiny things."

There was a pause.

"The fear was there because you hit us, Dad," she said.

"What happened was in the past!" he snapped defensively, his voice pinched. He shoved away a plate of sliced fruit that Mom had left on the table before leaving the room. "I was trying to help you to be better so you could succeed. And anyway," he went on, his voice rising quickly, "I don't treat you like that anymore, so what do you want from me? And what are you going to apologize to me for?"

"Apologize to *you*?" I asked, incredulous.

He didn't respond.

"Dad," I said, as evenly as I could manage, "we just want you to listen. We're not saying you're a bad person. We also appreciate everything you've done for us."

"Yes!" Joyce chimed in. "I really appreciate you paying for my wedding. We know you tried to be a good father."

"I'm grateful you always pick us up from the airport," I added. "And that if we ever need help financially, you are there for us."

He warmed at our appreciation, his shoulders relaxing. But just as quickly, his body contracted and his expression darkened.

"You know, I was treated horribly as a child," he said, his voice quieter now. "My older brother would punch me in the head and tell me how stupid I was anytime I asked him for help with my English homework. 'Gong ga be xi!' he'd say."

Looking at Dad, it was suddenly clear how much pain he still carried from his own childhood. But I wasn't going to let that stop me from sharing my truth. Joyce had been doing most of the talking. I couldn't hide behind her anymore.

"Dad, for most of my life, I thought there was something wrong with me because of the way you treated me," I told him, my heart pounding outside of my chest. "When I was seven, you hit me so hard that I had lash marks all over me. When I was twelve, you beat me up because I was reading a history book out on the lawn." I pointed at the kitchen floor. "Right there, do you remember?"

He shifted uncomfortably in his chair but didn't say anything.

I kept going, recounting every violent moment that had haunted me for years, moments I'd dissected and replayed in therapy over and over. Everything I said had to be simple. I didn't have the language to tell him how profoundly his actions had affected me. As I spoke, tears came, and I let them flow. I hadn't cried in front of my father since I was a little girl. Tears said everything I couldn't say with words.

Dad sat silently, his shoulders slumping under the weight of my words. He wasn't deflecting anymore. He was listening.

When I finished, he sighed. "I'm sorry," he said, his voice heavy. "I was beaten growing up, and it was all I knew. But I should not have treated my daughters in this way." He looked at me, his eyes weary. "What do you want me to do?"

I hadn't expected that question. But the answer came to me immediately—something I'd been asking of him for years.

"I want you to treat Mom nicely," I said. "I can forgive what happened in the past, but when it happens now—when you put her down and insult her, I get really triggered. Please speak to her with respect. Stop telling her she is stupid."

I'd asked him this before, on the motorbike in Taiwan, and many times since. Nothing had changed. Initially, I thought I was speaking up for Mom. But I was speaking for myself, too. The more inner work I did, the less I could stand Dad's abusive behavior in any form. Projecting his anger at my mother instead of

323

at me and my sisters didn't make it any better. Every time I heard him belittle her, I was right back in that house as a child, terrified and small.

Dad gave a slight nod. "I'm an old man." He shrugged. "It's hard for me change. But I'll try. You might have to remind me at times."

It seemed like a fair request, and I was surprised he was receptive. We stood from the table, and I leaned in to hug him. We never hugged when I was a kid. But over the last few years, I'd started giving him a hug and saying "I love you" whenever he dropped me off at the airport. He always stiffened awkwardly, never fully embracing me. This time, he stepped an inch closer and held me for a second longer than usual.

As he shuffled out of the room, I let out a sigh of relief. I felt buoyant, even hopeful. I hadn't said everything, but I was glad I'd done it at all. And in a strange way, I was proud of my father. He'd shown up the best he could. He'd even apologized. Joyce must have read my mind.

"Remember, this isn't just one conversation," she said. "This was just the start. It's a journey. This stuff takes time."

"How'd you get so wise?" I asked, cracking a smile.

She grinned.

"Tea?" I asked.

Joyce nodded and munched on a piece of fruit from the platter on the table as I boiled water and brewed two cups. A quiet filled the room, the kind that comes after a storm settles.

A few minutes later, as we were sipping our tea, I heard my dad yelling upstairs. Joyce and I looked at each other, our eyes wide. *It couldn't be.* As I strained to listen, I could hear my father screaming at my mother with the same words I'd heard a thousand times before. Words I was shocked to hear him saying again, right now, after all of this.

"Gong ga be xi!" *You're so stupid, you should die.*

My heart sank. Joyce and I sat frozen, silent.

In that moment, there was nothing left to say.

CHAPTER 37

THE WAY HOME

When I was in high school, Dad discovered a baby sparrow lying in our front yard, its tiny wing bent at an unnatural angle. He brought the injured bird inside and made it a soft nest out of an old shoebox and some scraps of fabric. We all crowded around and *oohed* and *ahhed*. The bird was no bigger than the palm of my hand. Every day, Dad fed it with baby food he'd bought at the store, carefully putting the paste on the end of a toothpick. I'd stand and watch, quietly. "Here, then," he'd say in Taiwanese, gently holding it above the bird's mouth and moving slowly when it opened its beak. I was struck by the tenderness Dad showed. It was a warmth and patience I'd rarely seen in him. Over the next few weeks, the bird began to heal. Its missing feathers grew back. When it was strong enough to fly, Dad bought a small cage and a feeder, hanging them in the backyard. Every morning, the bird flew off into the wide, open sky. And every night, it came back to eat and rest.

Then one day, it flew off and never returned.

Mom said it must have found its way home.

I don't think my father ever found a true sense of home. He once told me a story about his father—one of the only things that he ever shared about his childhood. He was seven years old, a thin boy with a slight frame. In photographs from the time, he had a smooth baby face and a thick head of jet-black hair. One day, my grandfather brought home noodles from a local street vendor. My grandmother made all the family meals at home, so outside food was a rare treat. Dad's eyes lit up at the sight of boxes on the kitchen table. He opened one and peeked inside, excited to find steaming rice noodles—his favorite food.

Just then, his father stormed into the room.

"What do you think you're doing?" he shouted. "Don't be so rude! Those are for my guests and nurses!"

Dad shrunk back, mumbling an apology. I think, in his mind, other people mattered more to his father than he did. The way my father told the story, I came to believe those noodles represented all the love he never received.

My grandfather died before I was born. Most everything I knew of him was from my aunt A-go. On sticky afternoons during summer trips to Kaohsiung, I'd sit on her couch, captivated, as she told me about him. My grandfather had lost both of his parents at a young age and was raised by relatives. Despite the hardship, he studied diligently and excelled in school, eventually becoming a doctor. In the community, he was known for his generosity and revered for his medical brilliance. But at home, he could be volatile and violent. The same hands that healed strangers were capable of inflicting harm on his own family.

A-go told me a particularly heartbreaking story that always stayed with me. After martial law was declared, people were being beaten, jailed, and executed without cause. "The KMT saw us Taiwanese people as slaves back then," she told me. The air was thick with fear. One morning, after a long shift at the hospital, my grandfather came home in a rage. My grandmother was sleeping on a straw tatami mat, her body curled around Dad's brother, Xiong, who was just a little boy. My grandfather began kicking the blanket, thinking he was lashing out at his wife. But his foot landed in his son's belly. Xiong leapt out from under the blanket and ran to the other room. The other children huddled behind the door, eyes wide, as they watched my grandfather kick my grandmother over and over. A-go didn't say if my grandmother screamed or cried. Only that for days afterward, she urinated blood.

I imagined the world Dad was born into. A world at war, a country gripped by upheaval and uncertainty, an environment steeped in terror and oppression. I imagined the alienation of being half-Japanese, half-Taiwanese, never wholly accepted by either. The inborn conflict of being colonizer and colonized, of yearning for autonomy and wanting to belong. I pictured my father as a little boy, never knowing when his father's fury would erupt. I imagined the macabre landscape of destruction he grew up in. He once told me that he and his friends swam in the craters left behind by World War II missiles. When it rained, the blown-out holes filled up with water, turning them into murky pools laced with pieces of shrapnel. The kids dunked and splashed, turning the remnants of war into their playground. It was a haunting image.

I imagined moments of joy and innocence that my father must have clung to. I felt his heartbreak, his longing for the love he never received. I could feel the depth of his pain because it was mine too. I imagined the words he must have needed to hear from his father. Simple expressions of love.

Do you need help with your homework, son?

Come, sit here next to me. I'll help as best as I can.

You're so smart.

Eat all the noodles you want. We can get more. There's always more.

For the longest time, my father loomed over me. I couldn't imagine anything more terrifying than confronting him. But I'd done it. And in doing so, I did something he couldn't have done with his own father. I had expressed my truth, letting it fly free, uncaged, like that little bird he'd nursed back to health. The truth was now alive between us.

Maybe that was enough.

Maybe I'd said enough for both of us.

CHAPTER 38

EMBRACED

If life were a movie, confronting my father would have been the epic final scene. The dramatic showdown where I, the protagonist, faced my greatest fear. The culmination of my hero's journey.

And we all lived happily ever after.

In the cinematic version of our conversation, my words would have sparked his transformation—a breakthrough moment where everything shifted. But in real life, there was no great catharsis, no sweeping music, no flood of relief. Just the familiar sound of my father's voice berating my mother moments after our talk. While I felt compassion for the wounded parts of him, it was painfully clear: he didn't have the capacity to heal me, or even to hear me. I was left with the ache of everything my father could never give me. And I couldn't help but wonder: What if growing up, I had felt love consistently, not just in fleeting moments? What if I had always felt safe? Who would I love? Who would love me?

I decided that if life wasn't going to give me a movie ending, I would have to write my own.

"What about combining psychodrama *with* MDMA?!" I asked Anjali over the phone. She was in New York; I was in my apartment in San Francisco looking at the Golden Gate Bridge shimmering in the distance. "Since I confronted my real father, maybe *now* I can receive an ideal father's love? With some help from the love drug!"

I'd come to rely on Anjali as a guide with one foot in the medical world and the other in the metaphysical realm. She was the rare kind of doctor who didn't blink at words like *ideal father* or *love drug.*

"It's possible," she said thoughtfully. "The medicine might help break down the walls that block you from receiving love. It could create an opening."

"Yes!" I shouted. "Exactly."

Anjali agreed to come to San Francisco to guide a drug-assisted psychodrama journey for me. Now I just needed the perfect person to play the ideal father. Who the hell do you call when you need a temporary, drug-enhanced father? I sat down and made a list of my male friends, cycling through the retreats and workshops I'd done over the years. One by one, I crossed off those who didn't quite fit. *Not touchy-feely enough. Too touchy-feely.*

Phil! We'd met at Landmark and had kept in touch since. Phil was a big, gentle guy who was grounded, yet open to spiritual exploration. He was one of the few men I knew who took inner work as seriously as I did. He had even done a version of psychodrama, so I knew he wouldn't be weirded out.

He agreed without hesitation.

Next, I scripted out exactly what my ideal father would say:

I adore you.
I see your inner goodness. I see your inner light.
I will protect you, not criticize or hurt you.
I love you. There's nothing you can do that would make me not love you.

I'd come so far since the retreat at Esalen. I was ready to hear the words I'd yearned for all my life.

The day before the journey I had a session with Bessel.

"No matter all the horrible things that happened, I still long to be loved by my father," I told him.

"Do you remember feeling loved by him as a child?" he asked.

"I do," I said slowly. "When I was seven, I would climb into bed with him on the weekends and we would practice times tables. That was the only physical touch we ever really had."

"What happens when you talk about that?" Bessel asked.

"I feel teary," I said, my voice cracking. "I guess I didn't realize how rare it would be to have that kind of interaction. How limited or time-bound it would be . . ."

"Is it okay for you to just feel that?" he asked. He put his hand over his heart and exhaled. "Just feel it for a bit."

I closed my eyes and recalled the warmth of my dad's embrace.

"It feels lovely," I said as tears fell down my cheeks. "I felt safe. I felt loved. I felt cherished. I treasured those moments. I think that's what every child wants."

"It's what every child deserves," Bessel said. "But your hope never died."

"You're right," I admitted. "Those moments make it hard for me to let go. I hold on to breadcrumbs and collect them like they're treasures." I looked up at the ceiling. "I can't let go of hope. It's my best quality . . . and my Achilles' heel."

Bessel nodded tenderly.

"It's why I'm really hoping I can receive my ideal father's love this time," I continued. "I scripted out exactly what I want him to say. It's bound to work."

"I hope it does," Bessel said. He paused, rubbing his fingers over his chin. "But I really think what is most important is for *you* to spend more time with that little girl. Really get to know her. How scared she was. How brave she was. How much love she had. How she never let that love go. See this child and appreciate her. Adore her."

I understood his point. But I was convinced that receiving an ideal father's love was the missing piece. The key to finally believing I was worthy of love—and to my ultimate healing.

On the morning of the journey, Anjali and I went for a walk near the Golden Gate Bridge, taking in the sunshine and crisp air. Waves lapped gently at our feet as we walked barefoot along the shore.

"I'm so proud of the work you're doing," she said. "It's not easy to confront all of this."

"Sometimes it feels like going in circles," I admitted. "Like I'm obsessed with some endpoint I'm never going to reach."

"You can't see it clearly because you're so deep in it," she said. "But I can. You're much more open. More compassionate with yourself. Healing isn't a straight line—it's a long arc."

Just then, I spotted something ahead. A jellyfish had washed up on the beach.

"Let me guess," Anjali teased. "It's a sign!"

I immediately googled the spiritual significance of jellyfish and read aloud: "As they gracefully float in the ocean's currents, they make their beauty look effortless. They are symbols of beauty and remind us that true beauty is a radiant glow that shines from within."

For most of my life, I hadn't known what my Chinese name meant. I'd only recently learned that it translated into "knowing beauty." What would it feel like to know I was beautiful? Maybe if I heard it from an ideal father, I would finally believe it.

We headed back to my apartment to prepare. Sunlight streamed through the windows as I buzzed about, arranging my favorite crystals and setting up three framed photos on the coffee table: one of me in kindergarten, with round cheeks and a bright smile; another of my sweet nephews; and one of my aunt A-go. Next to them, I laid out two pieces of clothing: a shirt with a blue swirly pattern from my paternal grandmother, Miyo Tanabe, and a black sweater from my maternal grandmother. They had come to see us off the day we left for America. Now, almost four decades later, I was summoning their spirits for love and guidance in my San Francisco living room.

At eleven on the dot, Phil knocked on the door. "Thank you for being here," I said, giving him a hug. Dressed in a flannel, khakis, and tennis shoes, with a backpack slung over one shoulder, he looked like a dad chaperoning his kid's field trip. He'd even packed snacks and water.

Anjali eyed him warily. "Can I sage you?" she asked brusquely, already lighting the bundle of herbs. Before he could answer, she swirled the smoke around his head. Phil coughed but waited patiently. Anjali gave a satisfied nod and let him pass.

I settled on the couch and Phil sat in the armchair beside me. His foot tapped against the floor as he dabbed sweat from the back of his neck. He was clearly nervous, but it didn't faze me. With him on one side and Anjali on the other, I felt blessed to be sandwiched between two friends who cared enough to go on this voyage with me.

I handed Phil the script I had written.

As he scanned the lines, he pressed his hand to his heart.

"This is so simple," he said quietly. "Every kid should hear these things."

I nodded, already fighting tears.

"I would be honored to say this to you."

Anjali passed me the Rumi deck. It had become our ritual. I shuffled the cards, fanned them across the couch, and closed my eyes. Hovering a hand over them, I waited until one pulled me in like a magnet and handed it to her.

She turned it over and read aloud:

This oracle comes to you with a special message. Just as the sun breaks through darkness with its own light, so too does your inner sun, your soul . . . An issue too difficult for you to understand, no matter how hard you have been working on it, is about to be resolved.

She paused, locking eyes with me, then continued:

You have no need to become more worthy of the resolution . . . your job is to allow it to happen, to simply bear witness.

I felt a tingle up my spine, as if we'd crossed an invisible threshold. I read the intentions I'd written for the journey:

I want to heal my inner child
who doesn't feel worthy or beautiful.
I want to receive my ideal father's love.
I want to find my way home.

Anjali gave me the pill. I swallowed, pulled a mask over my eyes, and lay down. She started the music—a symphonic wave that moved through the room, its lilts and crescendos lifting and carrying me. After about twenty minutes, my heart began to race. I was hot one minute, cold the next. I took slow, deliberate breaths, trying to stay present as waves of sensation moved through me.

An image started to form. The little girl. *Me.* She was surrounded by a dense, impenetrable fog. An invisible barrier was between us, keeping her just out of reach. I could feel her presence, but she couldn't feel mine.

"Anjali," I murmured anxiously, my eyes closed behind the mask. "She's there. But she can't see me. Why can't she see me?"

"Can you reach your arm out to her?" Anjali suggested.

I extended my arm. But the space between us was cold and empty.

We'd made contact before. I'd held her in my arms, protecting her from my dad. I hadn't considered that she might still retreat, that I hadn't earned her trust for good. I kept reaching my arm toward her. Slowly, the fog began to lift. I could see her more clearly now. She was curled up in a dark corner.

I sat up on the couch and pulled off my mask, squinting back the daylight.

I turned to Phil.

"It's time," I said.

He sat next to me and took my hand in his. In his other hand, he held my script.

"I adore you," he said, looking into my eyes. "I see you. I *cherish* you."

He paused, letting the words settle.

"I see your inner goodness."

I tried to transmit his words to the little girl, imagining them wrapping around her like a soft cloak, cradling her.

"I will never hurt you intentionally," he said. "I will protect you."

I took a breath and waited for the heart connection to click, for the catharsis to come pouring through.

Instead, I felt . . . nothing.

Maybe Phil wasn't delivering the lines right?

"Can we try without words?" I asked. "I'd like to just look into your eyes and take in your loving energy."

"Of course," he said. He inched closer, sitting face-to-face with me. His eyes were watery and blue, tender with care. I imagined my heart as a cabinet and flung open the doors, ready to let love rush in.

Still, I felt nothing. All I could see was Phil, my buddy from Landmark who was trying so hard to be my ideal father.

Why wasn't this working?! I'd handpicked my ideal father. I'd written every line. I was high on the love drug! Exasperated, I lay down again and put my eye mask back on, retreating into the music. Bit by bit, the little girl came back into focus. She was in the same dark corner, watching me warily.

That's when it hit me. Swooping in to save her wasn't what she needed. She needed consistency. She needed to know that I would be there for her over and over again. She needed to know that she mattered—not only when she was hurting, but in everyday moments.

"I'm so sorry I haven't always been here for you," I said gently. "But I'm here now. And I'm not going anywhere. No matter what happens."

Her eyes flickered. I felt her presence soften.

"I see you," I whispered. "I see you now."

I saw the depth of her loneliness, her fear. I saw the tenderness behind her strength, the fragility she had fought so hard to hide.

"I see you," I said, louder this time. "And I adore you."

The corners of her lips turned up in the slightest smile. A warm stream of bliss trickled through my body. She took a big breath, and I mirrored her. We exhaled in unison.

It was working.

Bessel was right. She didn't need an ideal father.

She needed *me*.

I sat up and grabbed the script from Phil. I picked up the photo of five-year-old me and looked into her big, brown eyes.

"I cherish you just as you are," I said, reading to her the lines I had written.

I saw flashes of her—onstage, reciting the Noah's Ark poem, pantomiming *two by two*. In the kitchen, humming as she stirred flour and sugar together.

My skin tingled.

"I see your inner goodness," I went on. "I see your inner light and it shines brightly." A warmth ballooned in my chest and spread outward.

"I am here for you. You matter. *You matter. You matter.*"

With each line, she opened up to me more and more. She wasn't just hearing me—she was *receiving* me. Every word I breathed out, she breathed in. I spoke, she felt. She felt, I felt.

"I love you," I said.

In that moment, everything faded away. There was no more past—no hurt, no abandonment, no striving to fix. There was only the present, only me and her. There was no agenda, except to love her.

"There's nothing you could do that would make me not love you," I went on, saying everything I'd always longed to hear. "You are beautiful. You are special. You are perfect just as you are. I choose you."

A soft light started to glow around us. We'd met in the dark, but now it was bright, as if the sun had finally broken through. Without realizing it, I'd been the one banishing her to the dark all these years—so I could keep going, so I wouldn't have to feel her heartbreak. For so long, I'd been focused on what *to do* to heal myself. I thought about all the healers and gurus, the endless therapy sessions, the search for affirmation and love from my father, from other men, and even the pursuit of purpose and justice. None of it was what she needed. What she needed was for me to sit with her feelings, however painful, instead of fleeing or fixing. For me to welcome her into my arms. For me to let her be a part of me, all the time.

I clutched the photo of her to my chest, projecting waves of unconditional love from my heart into hers until it felt like an ocean, and she was floating in it, weightless and free. For once, I didn't ask for her to change or be better. I didn't shame or criticize her. I embraced her exactly for who she was.

Her heartbeat slowed to a steady rhythm. She no longer had to fight, to brace for an attack, or do anything to earn love. She knew she mattered. That she was cherished. That she belonged.

Decades of tension melted from my body. A warm, soothing energy slowly filled the fractures left by old wounds, all the places where a bomb had gone off and left a crater in its wake. It moved from my chest outward, radiating into my limbs, up into my throat, and out the top of my head, restoring parts I'd lost or banished along the way. I felt a fullness I'd never experienced.

"Loving her. That's what this is all about . . ." I mumbled as the music reached a crescendo of sparkly bells. It was so simple, but I had to go around the world and back, and to the edges of my own psyche, to finally get it.

I turned the photo of five-year-old me toward Anjali and Phil.

"Who wouldn't love this little girl?" I asked. "She's the cutest!"

They chuckled hearing me realize what they had known all along.

I looked around the room at the people who loved me: A-go, who embraced and cherished me, sharing stories of my lineage, believing I could grow up to do anything. Joey and Kyle, who loved me with abandon, as only children can. Anjali, holding my hand and crying with me. Phil, who cared enough to try this crazy experiment with me. I thought about all the others who had loved me into being: my parents, my sisters, Uma, Thao, Bessel, Tony, Jonathan, Diana, Christine, Rahul, Linus, Patrick, Ryan. The list stretched on, endless and overflowing. I was surrounded by so much love. I never had to feel alone again.

Most important, I saw that little girl for who she truly was. Long ago, I'd exiled the most tender part of myself to keep her safe. I'd pushed her into the shadows, tucked her away where no one could reach her—not even me. I'd encapsulated her, incubated her. Little did I know I would grow up to help incubate other children, giving them a chance to survive, to thrive. And yet, young me had been left behind, frozen in time, waiting for the day I would come back for her.

Now that day had come.

In that moment, we were no longer separate or alone. I could feel her heart beating inside mine. I felt her embrace me, or maybe I embraced her. In that moment it didn't matter. It was all the same.

There was nothing left to heal, change, or fix.

In that moment, we were perfect.

Epilogue

February 28, 2025
和平念日/Peace Memorial Day
Kaohsiung, Taiwan

I have returned to the place where my story began, standing at the mouth of Kaohsiung Harbor. For the first time in years, I am back in Taiwan with my parents. The city around me is almost unrecognizable from the one I knew as a child. Skyscrapers now pierce the skyline. The harbor hums with the movement of ships, each one tracing a path forward, as if leaving the past behind.

History, culture, and unspoken wounds have shaped my parents—just as they have shaped me. But families evolve, just as individuals do. My conversations with my mother have shifted. After years of attributing violence to culture, she is beginning to understand my pain—and, for the first time, to reckon with her own. For a while, I stopped speaking to my father. But something in me has softened. The compassion I am learning to have for myself, I can now extend to him.

Nations evolve too. Seventy-eight years ago today, these streets ran red. Thousands of innocent people were slaughtered, imprisoned, silenced as they fought for their right to exist. I understand now that war doesn't end with the last shot fired. It seeps into the streets, into the homes, into the bloodlines of those who live through it. Fear is absorbed and carried forward, folded into the fabric of families, passed from parent to child.

And yet, something is changing. Taiwan is taking a bold step forward. Legislation is now being introduced to ban corporal punishment in homes—a shift that would have been unthinkable years ago. The data is undeniable: the scars of physical and emotional violence linger far beyond childhood, no matter how deeply rooted in culture. Progress requires reckoning. To build a society guided by love rather than fear, we must break free from the past.

Looking out at the harbor, I picture my father fishing as a boy, grinning when he catches something. Beneath his laughter, his tender heart breaks, longing for a love from his own father that always feels out of reach. I think of my mother as a young girl, walking along this very harbor, imagining an unbound future beyond these shores. One day, they will leave, crossing an ocean to begin again. Just as I would, years later. None of us realizing we were searching for the same thing.

I think of my own journey—into the depths of myself. I close my eyes and dive down, descending into the coldest, darkest part of the sea. The water closes in around me. And then—I see her. She glows softly, radiating light and love. Little by little, she guides me home to myself. I float weightlessly, untethered from the past. I am held by the water, by the sky, by something greater than myself.

I am free.

True healing happens when we release the past. Not by forgetting, but by allowing our hearts to break wide open. By confronting our pain, instead of running from it. When we tend to the wounds we've inherited, we don't just mend ourselves—we mend the generations that came before us and rewrite the possibilities for those who come after.

It is easy to believe that we are defined by our circumstances, by the wounds of our past, by family, by fate. But circumstances, however powerful, are just the waves—rising, crashing, ever-changing. Beneath their churning lies something steady. Infinite. No matter what we have endured, no matter where we've come from, our essence remains. And that essence is love—unconditional and limitless. We are not the waves but the sea itself.

The waves will always come. They will rise, they will crash, and at times they will pull me under. There will always be forces beyond my control, moments that threaten to swallow me whole. But now I know the way back. Back to the surface. Back to myself. When I wipe out, I know I will rise again—even when my lungs burn, even when my skin is scraped raw from the ocean floor. The voice that once taunted, *You're so stupid, you should die* has been replaced by something softer, and stronger. *You got this. You are enough.*

I journeyed to the corners of the world, seeking the love I thought I was missing. I sought it in conference rooms and straw huts, in silent meditation retreats and crowded seminars, in therapy, in medicine. I searched for it in the rhythm of waves, in the fire of rituals, in the stillness and the storm. Only to discover it was always already within me. Love is not a distant shore; it's the current that courses through us.

Healing is not about fixing ourselves. It's about embracing who we are—the mess, the chaos, the grief, the fear, the heartbreak. It's not about erasing our pain, but finding the courage to hold ourselves through it.

Like a wave, we break.

Like an ocean, we can never be broken.

Acknowledgments

To my agent, Lara Love—thank you from the bottom of my heart for believing in me and in this book. Your friendship, brilliance, and endless support have meant the world. I love that we bonded over frog poisoning. Thanks to the whole team at True Literary—Miles Michelle, Janelle Julian, and Elizabeth Wachtel. And a heartfelt thank-you to Dave Evans for your guidance and for introducing me to Lara.

To Nina St. Pierre, my collaborative writer—this book wouldn't exist without you. Thank you for your talent, your time, and your willingness to sit through so many horrifying therapy videos. You now know more about me than anyone else in the world. It's been a wild ride, and I am so deeply grateful.

To the team at Harmony, especially my editor Michele Eniclerico, and to Matthew Benjamin, Lulu Martinez, Jessalyn Foggy, Andy Lefkowitz, Allison Fox, Sandra Sjursen, Rachelle Mandik, Rachel Tockstein, Hannah Dirgins, and Kelly Doyle—thank you for helping to bring this book to the world with such commitment and heart.

To Shannon Welch and Diana Baroni—thank you for believing in this story and for your essential role in bringing it to life.

To my parents—thank you for loving me and for encouraging me to share a story that became a critical part of my healing, even when parts of it were hard to hear. So many of the leaps I've taken in life were possible because I knew you'd catch me if I fell. To my mother—thank you for your quiet strength, boundless generosity, and infinite patience. To my father—thank you for your irreverence, generosity, and the fire you passed on to me. Thank you for showing me love and care in all the ways you knew how. To my sister Joyce—my lifelong partner in crime, my companion in healing. Thank you for being my anchor, my best friend, and for standing beside me through the hardest conversations. To my sister Nancy—thank you for being the trailblazer and caretaker in our family. I've slept on your couch more times than I can count, and I wouldn't be where I am without you. To my nephews: thank you for showing me what unconditional love feels like.

To the healers and teachers who have walked this journey with me: Bessel van der Kolk (thank you for being my steady guide), Linda Thai, Licia Sky, Dick Schwartz, Christine Price, Paul Dunion, Zoe Gerlach, Vicky Cruz, Erica, Stephanie Snyder, Deb Katz, and so many others—thank you for your wisdom and guidance. Diana Chapman, thank you for pushing me to my edges and encouraging me to feel my heartbreak. You were always a phone call away in my moments of crisis. Jim Dethmer, thank you showing me what living in integrity looks like.

Ram Dass—thank you for showing me what it feels like to be loved for simply being.

To Tony Robbins and Jonathan Cohen—thank you for your love and generosity, and for showing up in my darkest hour. You were living proof that my prayers were being heard.

To Jason Watt, Mark Hinchliffe, and Meg Brunette at Fishbird—thank you for helping me find the freedom I was seeking, and for your support in moving into my next chapter.

ACKNOWLEDGMENTS

To my chosen family on this healing journey—Uma Jayaku-mar, Thao Nguyen, Geeta Arora. You have held me through it all. Thank you for your unconditional love and presence. I've never felt alone because of your friendship. Thank you to Aarti Shahani—for your wit, your sage advice, and your countless reads of drafts. To Yumi Adachi for reading so many versions of this manuscript in the final hours and being my Honolulu sister.

To Julia Scheeres—for your guidance in my first attempt to write this book. To Joseph Papa and Annie O'Dell for your help with PR and marketing, and for believing in my story enough to stand by me, even in my *very* anxious moments.

To Aaron Pereira—thank you for starting the Wellbeing Project, a source of light and healing for so many of us social entrepreneurs.

To the Embrace team—my co-founders Rahul Panicker and Linus Liang, and Jim Patell for teaching the class that started it all. To Alanna Shaikh, Melody Westen, Leslie Rohrbacker, and Julie Wang—thank you for keeping the mission alive and giving me the freedom to move into the next chapter. To Embrace's supporters over the years—Brad Freeman, John Hennessy, Robert Joss, Marc Benioff, the Bezos Family Foundation, the Tony Robbins Foundation, the Barrett Family, Vinod Khosla, Lata Krishnan. Your generosity and belief made the work possible.

To the Dow family—JB, Charlene, Rachel, Hannah, Ian, and especially Nathan. Thank you for being my source of strength and inspiration.

To Adam Grant—thank you for believing in my story from the start and helping open so many doors.

To all those who gave feedback on early drafts and helped me shape the launch of this book—Justine Espiritu, Scott Douchon,

ACKNOWLEDGMENTS

Mark Krassner, Aaron Horowitz, Julie Wang, Marika Strauss, Lisa Okuhn, Ferose V.R., Steve Hicks, Charles Duhigg, Greg McKeown, Steve Chen, Cindy Kan, Robert Perkinson, Alt Kagesa, Jenny Barchas, Andrea Kates, Nilfoer Merchant, Eden Xenakis, Goh Kuan Tan, Veronica Rocha.

To Janet Lau—thank you for your stunning artwork and for lending your soul to this cover.

To the many friends who have been there for me in moments of struggle and have joined me on my healing adventures, especially Sonia Yu, Phil Cartwright, and Tabreez Verjee.

Thank you to all those who played a role in my surfing journey and love affair with the ocean: John, Rory Cleary, Alex and Ane Epsir, Tommy Potterton, Gregg Petereson, Sandeep Sood, Ashley Lloyd, Lisa Okuhn, Ed Fernandez, and the crew at Concessions—especially Brandon Itagaki, Rick Higa, and Kevin Kawai.

To the ocean—my mother, father, sister, teacher, healer. Thank you for holding me through it all, and for teaching me what it means to surrender, to trust, to begin again.

To my ancestors—A-go, my grandmothers, my grandfathers, Aunt Tina, Uncle Xiong, and all my extended family. I wouldn't be here without the lineages that shaped me. May this book break the chains of intergenerational pain and honor all that came before me.